MY SMART
PUPPY

MY SMART PUPPY

Fun, Effective, and Easy Puppy Training

BRIAN KILCOMMONS
and SARAH WILSON

WARNER BOOKS

NEW YORK   BOSTON

Warner Books
Hachette Book Group USA
1271 Avenue of the Americas
New York, NY 10020

Visit our Web site at www. HachetteBookGroupUSA.com.

Printed in the United States of America

First Edition: October 2006
10 9 8 7 6 5 4 3 2 1

Warner Books and the "W" logo are trademarks of Time Warner Inc. or
an affiliated company. Used under license by Hachette Book Group USA,
which is not affiliated with Time Warner Inc.

Library of Congress Cataloging-in-Publication Data

Kilcommons, Brian.
   My smart puppy : fun, effective, and easy puppy training / Brian Kilcommons and
Sarah Wilson. — 1st ed.
      p. cm.
   Includes index.
   Summary: "The definitive guide to raising a happy, obedient puppy using new
training techniques that work fast for any puppy and any lifestyle."—Provided by the
publisher.
   ISBN-13: 978-0-446-57886-8
   ISBN-10: 0-446-57886-X
  1. Puppies—Training. 2. Puppies—Behavior.   I. Wilson, Sarah, 1960–   II. Title.
   SF431.K55 2006
   636.7'0887—dc22
                                                                    2006015023

Book design and text composition by L&G McRee

To all the shelters, rescue, and
humane society personnel who work tirelessly
to help one more homeless puppy
find a loving, forever home

CONTENTS

CHAPTER **1** · **THIS IS YOUR PUPPY!**

TEN KEYS TO UNDERSTANDING YOUR PUPPY　2

DOG-TO-HUMAN PICTIONARY　7

MYTHUNDERSTANDINGS ABOUT DOG BODY LANGUAGE　9

THIS IS YOU! HOW PEOPLE IMPACT PUPPIES　10

PUPPY PERSONALITY PROFILES　16

　Assertive/Pushy　**16**

　Independent/Aloof　**18**

　Appropriate/Social　**19**

　Reactive/Energetic　**20**

　Sensitive/Shy　**21**

　Avoidant/Fearful　**22**

PUPPY AGES AND STAGES 23

How "Old" Is My Puppy? **24**

Birth to Three Months: The Age of Attraction **24**

Sensitive/Fear Period **26**

Special Circumstances **27**

Singleton Puppy **27**

Sick Puppy **28**

Older Puppy from Limited Environment **28**

Special Needs Puppy **29**

Separated Too Early or Orphaned Puppy **30**

Delayed Development **31**

Three to Six Months: The Juvenile Period **32**

Teething **33**

Dealing with Frustration—Yours **33**

How Does My Puppy Grow? **36**

The End of Social Attraction **38**

Six to Nine Months: Adolescence **40**

Unhelpful Human Habits **40**

*Expect Behavioral Trial
Balloons* **41**

*Helpful Habits to Build: Living
Successfully with Your Older
Puppy* **43**

Nine to Twelve Months: Living with Your Pupteen **46**

Disobedience or Missed Obedience? **47**

Activities: Time to Go to Work! **48**

Handling: Keep It Up! **48**

CHAPTER 2 • UNDERSTANDING TRAINING

WHAT IS START ABOUT? 55

WHEN DO I START TRAINING? 59

UNDERSTANDING REWARDS 60

UNDERSTANDING CORRECTIONS 62

THE FIVE TYPES OF "COMMANDS" 64

DOG TRAINING: STOP THE INSANITY! 65

EQUIPMENT 65

COMMON COOKIE QUAGMIRES: HOW TO USE FOOD REWARD EFFECTIVELY 71

WHY IS ANTHROPOMORPHIZING BAD? 73

INTRODUCING THE COLLAR 74

INTRODUCING THE LEAD 75

WALKING ON LEAD: WHAT CAN I EXPECT? 76

CHAPTER 3 • START LEVEL I

MUTUAL AWARENESS 79

GETTING TO GOOD 79

PLAY PERSPECTIVE 80

COMMON LEVEL I
   CHALLENGES 80

SPACE: MINE 82

SPACE: OFF 86

TOUCH: PLACEMENT SIT 88

TOUCH: GUIDED DOWN 91

ATTENTION: LOOK AT ME 95

ATTENTION: CATCH MY DRIFT 99

REQUIREMENT: COME: BASICS 102

REQUIREMENT: STAY: BASICS 105

TRUST: NEAR IS DEAR 110

CHAPTER 4 • START LEVEL II

BEYOND BRACING 113

CONFIDENT LEADERSHIP 113

CONSISTENTLY CONSISTENT 114

COMMON LEVEL II CHALLENGES 114

SPACE: WAIT 116

SPACE: LEFT CIRCLES 119

TOUCH: CALM = RELEASE 122

TOUCH: GUIDED DOWN, THE NEXT LEVEL   124

ATTENTION: DOOR CHORES   129

ATTENTION: LEAVE IT   132

REQUIREMENT: COME: MAKING IT WORK   134

REQUIREMENT: OUT   136

TRUST: CHECK IT OUT   139

CHAPTER 5 • START LEVEL III

CREATIVE COACHING   145

WHAT IS YOUR INTENTION?   145

READY *AND* ABLE   146

COMMON LEVEL III CHALLENGES   146

SPACE: GO   148

SPACE: WAIT THERE   150

TOUCH: SIMPLE SIT   153

TOUCH: FACE IT   155

ATTENTION: FOLLOW THE LEADER   159

ATTENTION: BEAT THE
    CLOCK   161

REQUIREMENT: STAY II:
    WORKING THE 4 D'S   164

REQUIREMENT:
    NO EYE CAN   167

TRUST: SAY HELLO   169

CHAPTER **6** • SOCIALIZATION: DOMESTICATING YOUR DOG

WHAT EXACTLY IS SOCIALIZATION? 173

WHEN CAN I DO THIS SAFELY? 175

HOW DO YOU KNOW YOUR PUPPY IS STRESSED? 180

AT-HOME SOCIALIZATION 181

PRODUCTIVE PLAY 187

IN YOUR YARD 192

VISITING: GOING TO A FRIEND'S HOUSE 192

OUT AND ABOUT: THE REST OF THE WORLD 196

SCARED OF THE CITY 198

DOG PARKS 200

DOGGY DAY CARE 202

EXERCISE AND THE GROWING PUPPY 203

WALKING AROUND SUBURBIA 207

SOCIALIZING WITH OTHER PEOPLE 209

SOCIALIZING WITH YOUR CHILDREN 210

SOCIALIZING WITH OTHER CHILDREN 212

CHAPTER 7 · A CLEAN HOUSE: HOUSEBREAKING AND PAPER-TRAINING

HOUSEBREAKING: THE RULES 215

Rules of Supervision 215

Gates and Ex-pens: How to Keep Puppies Where You Put Them 218

Rules of Scheduling 219

Rules of Correction 221

Rules of Walking 222

Rules of Feeding and Watering 223

Crating 224

What Type? 224

What Size? 224

What to Put in It? 225

Where to Put It? 226

Introducing the Crate 227

Oh, Ick! Cleanup Hints 228

"Asking" to Go Out 228

Housebreaking: Problems and Solutions 229

After Spaying or Neutering 229

Bedding Is Wet and So Is Puppy 230

Can't Make It through the Night 230

Can't Hold It during the Day 230

Doesn't Poop First Thing in the Morning 231

In the Crate 231

Lifting His Leg Indoors   **233**

Leg Lifting Outside: Endless Hiking while Hiking   **233**

On Your Down Comforter   **235**

On Your Bed   **235**

Out of Sight   **236**

Peeing When Excited or Anxious   **237**

Peeing Small Amounts Frequently   **238**

Suddenly Peeing Large Amounts in the House   **238**

Peeing When Left Alone   **239**

Mistakes When on Medication   **239**

Won't Go Outside   **239**

PAPER-TRAINING: THE RULES   241

Paper-training: Problems and Solutions   **243**

CHAPTER 8 • COMMON PROBLEMS, EASY SOLUTIONS

TEN KEYS TO PERFECT PUPPY PROBLEM SOLVING   248

DEMOTING DEMANDING OR DIFFICULT DOGS   254

Barking: At People   **260**

Barking: In the Crate   **261**

Barking: Out the Window   **263**

Barking: In the Backyard   **265**

Barking: In the Car **265**

Begging **266**

Bites at Feet or Grabs at
    Lead **268**

Biting **269**

The Daily Dozens: An
    Anti-Bite Protocol **272**

Body Slamming: Get Out of In My Way! **274**

Car Sickness: Help for the Queasy Rider **275**

Chasing: The Cat **276**

Chasing: The Kids **277**

Chasing: Cars, Bicycles, Joggers **278**

Chewing **279**

Countertop Cruising **280**

Demanding Dog: It's All About Me! **281**

Digging **282**

Don't Pick Me Up! **283**

Don't Touch My Collar, Head, Ears **284**

Drinks Too Much **286**

Eats Cat Food **286**

Eats Own or Other Dogs' Poop **286**

Eats Too Fast **287**

Fence Running **287**

Finicky Eating **288**

Food Bowl Issues: Mealtime Menace **289**

Garbage Hounds: Indoors and Out   **290**

Growls When on Couch   **291**

Growls When Someone Comes
   Near You   **292**

Growls When Woken Up   **292**

Haranguing during Hugging   **294**

Hyperactive   **294**

Introducing Puppy to Resident Dog   **296**

Introducing Puppy to Your Cat   **301**

Jumping on People   **303**

Mouthing   **305**

Poles: Tired of Tangles?   **306**

Possessiveness: Finders Keepers   **307**

Possessiveness: Guarding   **310**

Running Away: From You   **312**

Scratching at Screens and Doors   **313**

Separation Issues   **314**

Sensitive/Shy: Help for Our Wallflowers   **316**

Sneak Attack from the Rear   **318**

Whining   **319**

Won't Come Back Inside   **319**

WORDS WE TRAIN BY   321

RESOURCES   323

INDEX   331

Pip and my first meeting. Pip approaches then rolls over, so I chat with her until she feels more confident. MELISSA FISCHER

Soon Pip makes friends. MELISSA FISCHER

We take a walk, Pip bounces along—I laugh. MELISSA FISCHER

I do a quick series of "puppy tests." Here I cradle her to see if she struggles. She does not. MELISSA FISCHER

MY SMART
PUPPY

CHAPTER 1

THIS IS YOUR PUPPY!

It is the evening on November 30, and we're about to get a new puppy! While scanning an Internet rescue site, a calm, intensely intelligent expression caught our eye. The fact that this puppy is also black, white, and tan, the color of our beloved late great Australian Shepherd, Caras, means we are hopelessly biased in her favor. Brian had to be in New York City on business, so I am driving out to Fishkill, New York, to meet this little one and her foster mother. As I pull into the parking lot of our meeting spot, I can see the puppy sitting next to a woman's feet. She is smaller than I thought, which is good. She sits there, watching the world parade by, neither leaping at passersby nor shying away. I like her from thirty feet away and it only gets better. Sidling up, ears back, she greets me softly, politely. She is incredibly cute. Once we've met, we go for a little walk together. She bounces everywhere without mouthing. When a shopping cart rumbles by, she startles then walks behind it, curious. Excellent! She is charming. She is adorable. Flipping open my cell phone, I place the call to Brian: She is perfect! And Pip has found her home.

Dogs have entered our lives many ways. Brian got his Rottweiler, Beau, from a top show-dog breeder and judge. PJ, our "well-mixed" terrier, was a foster puppy who stayed. We found Caras in an ad in a dog magazine. Good dogs come from many places, each arriving with his or her own blend of instinct, personality, and experience. You and your puppy are embarking on an adventure, one that has been repeated millions of times over thousands of years and yet one that will be uniquely yours. If you pay attention on this trip, you will learn more than you ever expected about yourself, relationships, and communication.

Where do we begin this journey? Where every such journey begins, with understanding the other. This chapter is about what you need to know about your puppy before you move forward with his or her education, socialization, or housebreaking.

TEN KEYS TO UNDERSTANDING YOUR PUPPY

1. Each Puppy Is Different

Even within a single litter of pups, there can be extreme differences, from outgoing and friendly to withdrawn and aloof. Are you and your siblings or cousins exactly alike? Neither are pups. This puppy of yours will be different from any dog you've had or will have. He has his own personality—with features that amuse and parts that annoy, a total package. And as the old saying goes, the trick to being happy is not to get what you want but to want what you get. Your job, as his leader, is to build on his strengths while minimizing his weaknesses.

2. Your Puppy Is Not a Blank Slate

Your puppy arrives in your arms a package of instincts and hardwired behaviors. In some, those instincts/ behaviors border on compulsions. Border Collies can stare obses-  sively at movement, Labradors may lose their minds over tennis balls, some Terriers bark almost nonstop. Your pup doesn't even, *can't* even, know there are other options. Saying "No" to a dog in the middle of an instinct-triggered behavior often doesn't help or if it does, it won't for long. "No" simply doesn't compute. "No" tells your puppy you are upset—nothing else. He needs alternatives, which you must supply. You must teach your Border Collie that he can look away, your Lab that he can leave the ball on the floor, your Terrier that he can sit quietly . . . as these ideas will never, *ever* occur to them.

3. Your Puppy Needs More than "Love"

Actually, love may be all your puppy needs, if love means meeting your puppy's emotional, mental, and physical needs, even when you don't especially feel like it. But if by "love" you mean meeting *your* emotional needs first and foremost, even when that conflicts with the puppy's needs, then that is not enough. What we say to clients is "Do you love your puppy or do you love loving your puppy?" If you love your puppy, doing what he needs is second nature. If you love loving your puppy, you will do what *you* want to do while complaining about your puppy. For example: Puppy urinates in kitchen overnight. Easy solution: Your puppy sleeps crated in your bedroom. If you love your puppy, you do that because you know it will help the puppy learn. If you love loving the puppy, you'll refuse to take that action because "you don't like crating her," and then you'll create a problem

4. Minor Moments Matter

Every interaction you have with your puppy teaches her something. There is no "small" interaction. If your puppy steps in front of you and you move out of her way to avoid bumping into her, she learns that she can make you move. If, instead, you kept your feet low, your knees bent, and shuffled on through her, she learns that you can make her move. You may think, Who cares? Your puppy does and therefore you must. In social mammals, leaders walk and followers get out of the way. This is true in people, horses, and dogs. Those many minor moments teach your puppy who you are. If you teach her to push you around, walk all over you, and ignore you, it can create problems later. People often say that problems "came out of the blue!" but they are often the result of months of dismissing or missing the meaning of those minor moments.

5. To See It Is to Mouth It

Puppies explore their world with their mouths which, until about four months of age, contain tiny, pointy, needle-sharp teeth. Pups mouth things that move, like your cat or your pant leg. They gnaw on things with the same predictability with which young human children attempt to stick things up their nose. It's just going to happen at some point. This is not a "bad" puppy; this is a normal puppy. Plan for normal events to happen, so you can supervise, teach, and redirect to a better option. Avoid thinking that normal things like this won't happen and then being annoyed or surprised when they do.

6. Puppies Do Not Understand Risk

First off, a three-month-old puppy has been on our planet for only ninety days or so. Nature has given him speedy mobility but little time for experience. You must protect your puppy as he will swallow, chew, leap off, and careen into slippery, sharp, and dangerous things. Sarah remembers all too well watching five-month-old Bracken, her German Shepherd Dog, race up the back steps and vault off the three-foot-high railing, arcing upward toward a bird on the back fence. As she landed she dropped some six feet or so to the ground without incident, but was that anticipated? No. You can never anticipate everything. So, when considering risk, ask yourself not what you think might happen, but what *could* happen.

7. Puppies Love Pleasing You

Anyone who has ever seen a puppy sporting a delighted, open-mouthed grin when his person praises him knows that dogs of all ages enjoy it when we enjoy them. They want that connection—

it is one of those things that makes dogs dogs. They get a kick out of us!

It is in vogue in some circles to talk about how dogs have no desire to please. We feel sorry that anyone in the dog community could live with dogs and not experience that warm, mutual connection. In some circles, touch and praise are billed as "distractions to learning." As if a relationship were a "distraction." We have dogs *because* of the mutual relationship we can share with them. What a sad, cold world it must be to treat a dog as if he is incapable of deep connection and to then be treated in the same way by the dog.

My Smart Puppy people do not have to live in that distant world. You will build a relationship with your puppy, seeing his or her joy in our joy. In order to see this, you must learn how to praise your puppy warmly and sincerely in a way your puppy enjoys. Show your puppy through touch and voice just how fond of him you are and you will see him respond in kind.

8. Puppies Need *Lots* of Sleep

Humans take around fifteen years to grow from infancy to sexual maturity. Your puppy does it in under one. She may start life at one pound and bite into her first birthday cake at seventy-five pounds. That is an extraordinary rate of growth. A large-breed puppy may, at the peak of growth, put on nearly a pound *a day*. To accomplish this feat, your puppy needs rest and a lot of it. Expect your puppy to log nearly eighteen to twenty hours a day for a few peak-growth months. Just like children, overtired pup-

pies can become cranky, pushy, whiny, or otherwise frustrating. It is your job to recognize those signs and tuck the pup into his crate for a nap. This is especially important in households with children, where a puppy can be kept awake and active for too long.

9. Puppyhood Is Messy

In every sense. Not only will you be dealing with physical by-products—urine, feces, vomit, hair, dirt, and in some breeds drool—but learning is messy. Think how difficult it is to communicate clearly between people. Now try between *species*; you are trying to communicate with a species that has no clue about what you're trying to teach. Sometimes your puppy will be confused, sometimes you will be, sometimes you both will be—that is *normal*. The way through it is productive practice. Avoidance, frustration, or "putting it off" never trained a single puppy. You *can* do this! Nothing has to be perfect—as long as you are consistent and persistent, your puppy will learn to understand you.

10. Puppyhood Is Brief

Hallelujah and darn—all at once. You would not be human if you didn't think from time to time, When will this end? We can tell you when it will end: very quickly. Use these months. You cannot ever get them back. Train, play, socialize, explore—prepare your puppy for a long, happy life as an adult dog. Along the way, take pictures, find ways to have at least a little fun with your puppy every day, and have patience with normal mental and physical canine developmental stages. They are as precious as they can be annoying.

DOG-TO-HUMAN PICTIONARY

Dogs "speak" clearly, though we humans do not always hear them. In our opinion, human lack of understanding causes many of the dog bites in the United States. If we "heard" dogs better, we would be bitten less. This section can save you and your loved ones from trouble with dogs. Our goal: to prevent the bite long before it happens. Please read it carefully, and look at the pictures, then, if you have questions, come to www.MySmartPuppy.com and ask!

When reading any dog, check their T.E.E.T.H.:
Tension, Ears, Eyes, Tail, Head

Weight back, front legs out-stretched and together, often with a big yawn—this is a dog stretching.

This puppy has turned away from me, base of his tail is straight up, body tense—this pig's ear is his!

Ears sideways and tense, eyebrows pinched, nose low-ered, looks motion-less—this dog is frightened/worried.

Open mouth, relaxed face, bright eyes—this is a laugh in any language.

Weight forward, front legs akimbo, tail often wagging, mouth open, often barking—this is a "play bow." A canine invitation to a game.

Tipping over, tail tucked, ears back—this is a fear-ful, anxious, or naturally submissive dog.

Which dog is in control? The one making the other move more and holding his tail the highest. In this game Milo, our Beagle, is making Yoshi, a Vizsla pup, move and his tail is higher. He's in charge.
SARAH WILSON

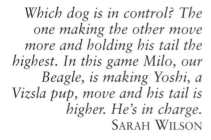

This young Irish Terrier is all bold from a few feet away from some dogs: Tail up, ears up, leaning forward, looking right at them. When he is released, he changes his tune: Tail down, ears, back, leaning back, trying to avoid eye contact with two dogs who are more assertive than he is—the Bernese Mountain Dog and the middle English Cocker Spaniel, both of whom are looking directly at him.

MYTHUNDERSTANDINGS ABOUT DOG BODY LANGUAGE

A Wagging Tail Is Always Happy

This is usually true, but not always. A wagging tail, like the human smile, can mean many things. A tail that is straight up, stiff, and vibrating back and forth? That is excited and stimulated, but not "happy." This dog could be moments away from aggression. A tail tucked all the way under the dog's body could wag at the very tip. This dog is frightened but trying. Do not press her. A tail that wags level with the spine or a bit above or below spine level in large, sweeping wags? *That* is a happy dog.

Showing Teeth Is Always a Threat

Most of the time it is, but some dogs actually smile when they are excited to see someone. This is pretty disconcerting until you know what is going on. Breeds known for their toothy grins include Dalmatians, Doberman Pinschers, Australian Shepherds, and

Greyhounds. If the dog's ears are back, the tail is wagging low, and you see a flash of front teeth, chances are you've just seen a grin!

Hackles Raised Means the Dog Is Aggressive

Hackles (the hair along the back) can piloerect (raise up) when a dog is excited and unsure. Sometimes it is a warning sign of aggression, but in puppies it is more often a sign of excitement, concern, or worry. Many dogs will hackle slightly (or not so slightly) when they enter a dog run, only to shake it off (literally— dogs often shake when they have calmed down a bit) in a few minutes before settling down to some serious play.

Cowering "Proves" He "Knows What He Did Wrong"

Nah, cowering "proves" he knows you are about to be angry, and those are two entirely different things. If your roommate came home once or twice a week, opened the door, and attacked you for no apparent reason, you might cower or leave the room when the door opened at night, too. That would not prove that you "knew what you did wrong."

THIS IS YOU! HOW PEOPLE IMPACT PUPPIES

Temperament is often in the eyes of the beholder. Variations in human temperament are numerous and affect how the puppy's temperament is perceived. One person's wonderfully "perceptive" puppy is another's "wimp." One "good watchdog" is someone else's "aggressive puppy." There are homes that will adore most puppies for who they are and homes that may dislike them for exactly the same reasons.

Now, what about us? What do we bring to the table as teachers and trainers? To understand who you are likely to be as a teacher, look at how you were taught. Until we consider the impact of how we were taught, we often are left repeating or completely avoiding our history. Taking a look at our inner teaching model allows each of us to make better choices about how we want to behave as teachers.

Example: We have a friend who attended a strict Catholic school where the nuns were harsh. If she didn't know an answer, she was punished. If she gave the wrong answer, she was punished. Since not knowing and giving wrong answers are a normal part of learning, normal learning was made frightening and stressful. How did that impact her as a trainer? She became increasingly anxious whenever the puppy did something "wrong." She was both quick to punish harshly and quick to have a growing sense of panic inside herself about not "doing it right" with her puppy. She didn't like being harsh, so she often felt helpless to control her puppy, allowing all sorts of behavior until she got frustrated and became harsh. The guilt was overwhelming. She would "apologize" to the puppy with excessive attention and asking for little in the way of self-control until the puppy's behavior frustrated her again and the cycle continued.

When this cycle was brought to her attention, it was a huge relief for her. She was able to start making different choices: redirecting her puppy sooner, setting clear, unemotional boundaries regarding what she wanted and didn't want as well as taking a break when she felt the frustration welling up. Her puppy calmed down considerably. Life got a lot better for both of them.

Is our friend a "bad" person? Not at all. We are all products of our history, but we don't have to be victims of it. We can learn to behave differently when we get support for doing so. There are no "perfect" puppies and there are no "perfect" puppy trainers. We're all just getting better and better as we go along. We all start as beginners. We all bring inner baggage—some of which makes us more effective and some of which makes us less. That is normal. Aim for steady progress and you'll do just fine.

During Sarah's master's degree research, she found that often people seemed to define "loving" their pup as giving the puppy what that person felt they were missing in their own childhood. Example: If you were raised by busy parents, you may believe that giving the puppy buckets of attention is being "loving." Below is a quick overview of a few possibilities. We just wanted to give you a place to start thinking about these things.

Past	Possible Impact	Result for Puppy Person	Options
Busy Parents and/or Many Siblings	Feeling unattended to.	Puppy gets non-stop attention; person feels stressed when puppy is not getting attention. If anyone suggests too much attention is being given, person has strong emotional reaction.	Realizing that learning to entertain oneself is an important life skill—for people and for dogs. Start to reward independent play and separate from demanding behavior.
Yelling/ Verbal Intimidation	Feeling intimidated into silence.	Person attempts to be endlessly patient and tries hard never to get upset. Because early boundaries can't be set for the puppy, puppy's behavior becomes more pushy and demanding. Person finally loses patience then feels terrible about self. Tries to be "better" by never getting upset.	Caring for a puppy is going to be frustrating and annoying at times. Learning how to reclaim sensible boundaries without yelling will allow you to be the sort of trainer and coach you want to be.

Past	Possible Impact	Result for Puppy Person	Options
Physical Abuse/ Threat of This Abuse	Feeling frightened of the parent; feeling intimidated almost all the time.	Similar to the above. Because boundary setting has been linked to abuse, never setting any seems like the loving and safe thing to do. Being abusive is often feared, so all confrontation is avoided. When confrontation happens and temper is lost, person feels great guilt. Tries to be "nice" all the time to the puppy.	Childhood trauma is not something easily dealt with alone. One of the main reasons this is true is that it is very hard to unravel (or even see) certain patterns from the inside. Finding a good counselor/coach to give you new insights and tools can be the key to being truly free. Boundaries were not the enemy in childhood; it was how they were set that caused the problem.

Past	Possible Impact	Result for Puppy Person	Options
Emotionless/ Depressed House	Fear of assertiveness, inability to assert self calmly.	From lack of experience, among other things, people who grew up in unemotional homes may find themselves overwhelmed by emotion in the course of raising the puppy. They may attempt to stay calm at all times and usually, being human, will fail. Guilt follows and the cycle continues.	Practice calmly asserting yourself. Understand that this will feel both weird and very possibly dangerous (since it was presented as "bad" in the childhood home). Expect successes and failures, as both are a part of the normal learning process.

Past	Possible Impact	Result for Puppy Person	Options
Abandonment/ Loss/Divorce	Fear of being left, fear that the other's behavior is somehow your fault.	May have a deep emotional reaction to the puppy not wanting to be near them all the time or sleeping away from them. May be afraid to tell the puppy to do anything for fear he will hate/leave them.	Experiment with teaching your puppy things—have fun doing it. Truth is, your puppy will be more attached to you and spend more time with you the more you ask of him.

PUPPY PERSONALITY PROFILES

Your new puppy is like no other—ever. She is her own special blend of behaviors, instincts, and tendencies. Understanding who she is makes it easier for you to be an effective leader who brings out the best she has to offer. Keep in mind that most puppies are a combination of temperaments. They may go through one (or more) changes as they mature and will display different personality traits in different situations. Your puppy who is Appropriate/Social at home may be Sensitive/Shy the first week of puppy class. Your job—and it can be a challenging one—is not to judge these normal shifts but to help your puppy at whatever stage or phase she is in. Understanding a little about the major temperament categories will help you do that.

Assertive/Pushy

Your puppy seems to be constantly in your way and underfoot. There is much grabbing at pant legs, leads (or leashes), or hands. Tug-of-war is his favorite game, though he does not release easily. When you take his collar or pet his head, he mouths you. He chews toys in the center of the room and may freeze (stop chewing and glare at you) if you walk by. Hard jumping, where he leaps against you with straight legs using you as a backboard, hurts and almost (or does) knock people over. He wants to be out the door

Tail straight up, head up, ears up—this puppy is feeling bold and confident! Not unusual for a Schnauzer pup.

first, to grab whatever you're carrying, to have his nose in your plate, and to sit with you or on you on the couch.

What Helps

- Space Games—early and often. See Chapters 2 through 5.
- Remember that Minor Moments Matter—do not let things slide with these puppies!
- Develop a light "Oh, darling, you must be confused" attitude so you can be assertive and clear without being aggressive or confrontational.
- Practice The Daily Dozens: An Anti-Bite Protocol (page 272).
- Getting to Good. It is easy to lock horns with these pups. Don't. Always focus on what you *want* instead of what you don't want.

What Hurts

- "Oh, he's just a puppy," "He doesn't mean it," "He's a baby," and any other excuse. Puppies do not grow out of behaviors nearly as often as they grow into them.
- No "No!" Avoid arguing with these pups. Instead, set your boundaries and create compliance by directing them to what you want.
- You are teaching him how to treat you right now. Teach him to push you around and he'll be more than happy to oblige you. Teach him now to respect your space and your person, and some ugly behavioral dragons may never rear their heads.

- Be cautious with dog parks or day care. Just as with people, daily activities become habits and if he gets to slam, push, and harass other people and dogs daily, what is he learning? Don't leave him where assertive, bullying behaviors are allowed or encouraged.

Independent/Aloof

You think he may have a hearing problem (to be sure he doesn't check page 30). He often lies by himself across the room, rarely leans against you, paws you or nudges you for attention. He walks off or turns away almost the moment you start to pet him. He's not a big tail wagger—he wags for a few people and that's about it. After the initial sniff (if that), he shows little interest in strangers. He is prone to wandering off without a look back and rarely "checks in" with you.

What Helps

- Having him work for everything he gets—either you become relevant real fast or your puppy learns to ignore you. Your choice.
- START training. Focus on the entire Level I course as described in Chapter 3. It all helps this type of puppy succeed.
- Making your attention brief so it (a) doesn't overwhelm your puppy and (b) stops before he disconnects.
- Keep treats in your pocket and give one anytime the puppy happens to come up to you, look at you, head your way. When you walk past him, toss him a cookie.
- Ignore the puppy a lot, especially if he decides to lie down close to you. Too much attention can send him to the other side of the room, so give him brief verbal praise then let him be.
- Move away from your puppy before he moves away from you. By creating a situation where he follows, you build his desire to do so.
- Start the Placement Sit and the Guided Down (pages 88 and 92) as quickly as you can so you can insist when he doesn't quite feel like it, which may be often.
- Take him to new places where you are his safe harbor.

- Establish a crating routine where he looks forward to being with you.

What Hurts

- Too much attention, too often—anything that encourages him to disconnect.
- Anything that drives your puppy away from you.
- Allowing him to "do his own thing."
- Be careful with Space Games as such pups are often sensitive to these since they have little attachment to begin with. Use partial body pivots, no staring, smiling, verbal praise, and immediate backing away to help them learn without disconnecting.
- Thinking that not making demands will make him "like" you more—it is just the opposite with many such dogs.
- Being inconsistent is a big mistake with these puppies. They are barely interested at best; don't give them cause to think that is right.

Appropriate/Social

Mouth open, body relaxed—this Petit Basset Griffon Vendeen puppy is having a ball!
LISEL DORESTE HAMILTON

This puppy loves people. He sometimes hesitates for a few seconds before approaching but he always approaches, often with ears back and tail wagging at level of the spine or slightly above or below. He takes a moment to start to explore new places and avoids the center of a new room for a bit, sticking closer to edges but not always underneath things. This puppy jumps up but not at you, licks as much as he mouths, and responds to an upset human with an ears-back apology.

What Helps

- Enjoy them! Count your blessings!
- Reward what you want, starting as soon as possible.
- Develop his self-control, as good self-control will make your life easier and his world safer.
- Socialize. This is easy to skip with the easy pups, but every puppy needs it.

What Hurts

- Using their sweetness as an excuse not to teach or to allow bad habits. We call this the "He's so good" excuse. That is something like saying my child is so nice and sweet he doesn't need manners or school.
- Giving him too much freedom too fast—indoors and out. He's still a puppy; he needs time and practice to learn to be well behaved and consistent.

Reactive/Energetic

This puppy leaps, spins, races, barks, and jumps—all at once. When you try to calm him down, he does more—and starts mouthing. He's hard to pet, as he squirms and mouths whenever you touch him. You've pretty much stopped having guests over because it is just too embarrassing and difficult. Other dogs seem to hate him on sight and are aggressive or pin him all the time.

What Helps

- Calm. Acting the way you want him to act is not optional.
- Get to Good! Focus on rewarding what you want rather than on stopping the "bad" stuff.
- Encourage self-control. Holding him back on lead only creates more frenzied behavior.
- Make every interaction count. These dogs are usually extremely bright. Using that mind tires and calms these pups in a way that physical exercise simply cannot.

What Hurts

- Getting angry or intense. These dogs react to your emotions. If you want a calmer puppy, become calmer yourself. And if *you* have a hard time doing that, imagine how difficult it is for your puppy!
- Rough, wild play—he doesn't need to practice this; he needs to practice self-control.
- Most day cares and dog parks will only encourage the worst in him. Handpick calm companions for him to play with and make sure he cannot intimidate or overwhelm them. Older dogs are usually the best bet.

Sensitive/Shy

Your puppy has a hard time meeting new people. He tries to come closer but can't quite make it, or he comes up slowly, ears back, tail and head low. New sights and sounds frequently scare him—and it takes him a while to calm down enough to explore them. In new places, he stays with you or explores by sticking close to a wall or edge. He is very sensitive to people with loud or angry voices or who move in ways he isn't used to. When frightened, he runs to you rather than running off by himself.

Hiding behind his person, this Schnauzer peeks out. Tail down, ears out of sight—this puppy is overwhelmed.

What Helps

- Check It Out (page 110) and Near Is Dear (page 110) and a lot of both! You need to create then practice confidence.
- All the Trust and Attention Games (see Chapters 2 through 5).

The more you carefully expose your puppy to, the more confident he will become.

- Classes, especially a small, well-run puppy class.
- Socialize, socialize, socialize—in small increments. See "Sensitive/Shy: Help for Our Wallflowers" (page 316).

What Hurts

- Avoiding new things because they scare the dog. Avoidance will never teach your puppy to be more confident—in fact, it leaves him wallowing in his fears. To be more confident, practice confidence.
- Don't use a lot of loud sound corrections with these puppies. They may work—too well. They need to be made more confident about sudden noises, not made fearful of them.
- Babying your pup. Since you get what you pet what are you creating by constantly petting a fearful, anxious, or worried puppy?

Avoidant/Fearful

Unlike the Sensitive/Shy puppy who is well attached to you but unsure of the world, the Avoidant/Fearful puppy doesn't trust you much and others even less. When nervous or unsure, he moves away and hides rather than coming to you for comfort. PJ was this sort of puppy. She, like many in the category, had little human handling during the first two months of her life. Job one with these puppies is to get the bond going with you. This can be a difficult but rewarding task. Some puppies can never be brought around fully, and what can be done may take months, or even years, to do well.

What Helps

- Exposing them to new things often and in small doses so they are successful.
- Reward every social interaction he has with you with a treat, then move away before he has a chance to leave on his own. We want to stop him from practicing retreat while not forcing

him to stay near to you. So treat, then walk away. If he follows, great! Well done! Now do it again.

- Hand-feed, if you can, always backing away a few steps after each handful—keep feeding then backing away.
- Be careful with Space Games, which are outlined in Chapters 2 through 5, as these pups are often extremely sensitive. Use partial body pivots, then immediately move away to help them learn without retreating. Stay relaxed, smile but no staring.
- Trust Games are your main focus. Do everything suggested but spend more time on those than on any other.
- Keep the pup on lead with you as much as you can.

What Hurts

- Lots of bending over, grabbing and overwhelming the puppy.
- Trying to "make" him be friendly to others by forcing interaction, staring at him, reaching toward or coming forward when praising him, or allowing him to practice disconnecting and backing away instead of you backing away before he does.
- Rewarding hiding with attention.
- Giving up. You are his only hope of becoming more social— don't give up! It can take some time, but every tiny step forward is a step in the right direction.

Your puppy, like ours, is as unique as a snowflake. No one single category will ever describe each one completely but having guidelines gives you a direction to take and things to avoid. Remember, potential is in the eye of the beholder. Use labels to inform but not to imprison; we've seen puppies labeled all sorts of things grow beyond all possibilities with a dedicated person in their corner.

PUPPY AGES AND STAGES

Now that you have some idea of who your puppy is, let's look at the normal stages of canine development. This way you'll know what to expect at various times along this journey.

How "Old" Is My Puppy?

Each year in a dog's life is not equal to seven years as we used to think. The chart below is the new comparison between dog and human ages. It is amazing how fast they mature! So next time your five-month-old puppy tries to grab something from your hand, ask yourself, What would I do if my ten-year-old child tried that?

Dog's Age	Human Equivalent
5 months	10 years
8 months	13 years
10 months	14 years
12 months	15 years
18 months	20 years
24 months	24 years

Birth to Three Months: The Age of Attraction

Puppies are born deaf, blind, barely mobile, and unable either to warm up or cool off on their own. Within the first month, their eyes open, their ears open, they begin to be able to regulate their own temperature, and their baby teeth arrive.

In the second month of life, puppies become learning machines. They are now walking, running, and jumping with the brain functions of an adult dog. The play and bickering with siblings teaches puppies critical life lessons. Those sharp baby teeth help bring home important rules about how and when to use aggression as well as how to inhibit it. Momma dog will begin setting rules, which she should be allowed to do.

The third month is all about learning through play, interaction, and exploration. Things that get done and shown in this time period (and things that don't) can impact your puppy for his or her lifetime. That said, please don't panic if your puppy's early life was less than ideal. Every puppy has some good and bad things happen when growing up, just like every person. The stable, resilient, and/or bold pups bounce back pretty easily. The reactive, sensitive pups can take longer and may need you to help them.

PJ came to us after September 11, 2001, when many New York City shelters stopped taking in dogs and cats as they braced themselves for what they feared would be thousands of animals left behind by people who perished in the towers. By the time PJ made her way to us, she was about nine weeks old, and had rarely been handled by people; she

Like ducklings, little puppies follow during the age of attraction (or at least most do most of the time). This will fade later, but taking walks in safe areas early is great fun!
CJ PUOTINEN

had an extremely low opinion of us as a species. It took a long time to help her over the biggest of her doubts, but we would not trade our funny, quirky, brilliant companion for anything. She is unique. She is PJ.

The age of attraction, which runs from about two to five months of age, is when the instinct to follow and be submissive to the family adults is strongest. Wandering off or losing track of the group could mean death in the wild. Your puppy will probably try to stick with you and will get nervous when he can't. He will be at his most willing to comply with your wishes and his most eager to be with you at this stage. This passes, so enjoy it (and use it) while it is here.

Remember through this time period that by the end of it, your puppy will have been on the planet fewer than 100 days! That's 100 days that included birth through family life through leaving home, adoption by people he never met, and a new life with new rules. This is pretty amazing and pretty amazingly stressful. Keep learning light and fun; he hasn't been here long and is just learning the ropes.

Sensitive/Fear Period

Somewhere between seven and twelve weeks of age, most puppies go through a sensitivity or fear period. This too is normal, and served good purpose in the wild, where a little caution was a protective thing as the pups explored outside of the den.

This stage usually passes on its own in a few days or a few weeks, though for some puppies it can take a month or longer. During this stage, your puppy may have bigger reactions to smaller things. A sudden noise, a piece of trash, a strange dog walking toward him may send him flying backward, yipping as he goes. Just last week, Sarah had Pip at a pet-supply store buying kibble. When she dropped two large bags on the counter, the sound frightened Pip, who blamed the people next in line. Suddenly she found them frightening, backing away, and trying to run. Sarah laughed and practiced some Check It Out (page 139) until Pip calmed a bit. Things like this are going to happen. Your puppy who feared nothing yesterday may jump at a leaf blowing today.

Want to help your puppy during this period? Act the way you want him to act. Be casual, confident, and calm. Smile and laugh, have fun, model a nice relaxed response. This may or may not help immediately, but it helps over the long haul. Some pups need a bit of calm, relaxed stroking or massage to regroup before continuing on. This can be done with a "You're fine—let's get on with it" attitude—not one of fear, worry, or concern.

What will confuse matters? You acting frightened and upset too. Then your puppy may look at you and feel, "Right, I *should* be frightened—look at my person!" So no collapsing into a pool of oohing, ahing and nervous petting. Not sure what to do? Keep moving away from the source of the stress. Encourage his best, even if he is creeping next to you. If he can take a treat (and he's not that frightened if he can), do some sits and tricks for a cookie. Basically, get his mind off his fear. If you cannot, get him out of there calmly. If you can't leave, then massage and hang out with him. Do your level best to encourage confidence in your buddy.

Sarah was just at the veterinarian's with our young Beagle, Milo. He got frightened and started to shake. Sarah stayed relaxed, keeping her breathing normal and her body at ease. She massaged him down the back when he sat next to her. She praised him calmly if he explored. She gave him slack in the lead to go and sit next to the vet. She supported him in any confident moment he had. Was this a cure-all? No. But fear isn't fixed in one session or five. It was a good visit, and next time will be even better.

During sensitive/fear periods, try to avoid new and potentially scary places. This is *not* the time to take your puppy to a fireworks display (a place most dogs should never go) or local street fair. This is a wonderful time to play the Trust Games (in Chapters 2 through 5). These will build your pup's trust in you, as well as teaching both of you what to do when he becomes frightened. This phase often passes as suddenly as it arrives.

Special Circumstances

Singleton Puppy: This is a puppy who was the only one in his or her litter. Caras, the wonderful Australian Shepherd we had for over fifteen years, was a singleton. His breeder made special efforts to handle him often, tucking him into her shirt as she went around her home. She took him everywhere, let her older, sensible, gentle but savvy dogs interact with him, and gave him one positive experience after another. Doing all this gave us a

human-focused, adaptable, stable, extraordinary dog. We miss him daily.

If he had been left in the box by himself, handled very little, never exposed to different dogs, and raised by an indulgent or novice canine mother, we could have ended up with a fearful yet pushy puppy who was quick to use his mouth when frustrated and generally a handful to live with.

Flattened on the wall, paws tucked under, not moving, whites of eyes showing—this looks like a puppy saying "Don't bother me" or "Where am I?"

Sick Puppy: Some puppies arrive at your home sick with parasites or kennel cough, or they injure themselves soon after arrival. Doting over such little ones is totally understandable, but it poses some risks. A puppy doesn't know you are doting because they are sick; they simply know that you live to serve them. All the attention sets them up potentially to become quite bratty as they recover. So, as soon as you can and as soon as your puppy is able, start to work on basic commands and fun tricks. Get yourself into a working dynamic with you leading the team as quickly as you can. While all START games will help, Space, Touch, and Requirement Games are key.

Older Puppy from Limited Environment: You've just gotten an older puppy from rescue, a pet store, or, sadly, some puppy producer (we don't flatter these people by calling them breeders) who never took the puppy away from home. These puppies have a great deal of catching up to do. If they have been urinating and defecating where they have to live, housebreaking may take a while to get started. Housebreaking is founded on the puppy's desire to keep her bed clean. If that desire has been eroded, our first task is to get it back. (See "In the Crate" in "Housebreaking: Problems and Solutions" page 231.)

Such puppies can be frightened of new places, people, and things, requiring extra effort to bring out their confidence and curiosity. Things can and most often do get better. How much better is generally a combination of how much effort you put in, how much skilled advice you receive, and your puppy's genetic temperament. But we've seen near-miraculous turnarounds in puppies because of the deep dedication their people had to their progress.

Special Needs Puppy: Blind, deaf, three-legged, neurologically impaired—many conditions can count as special needs. What you need to understand is that this puppy has no idea he is special needs. He does not feel sorry for himself or bemoan his state. A deaf puppy can't imagine hearing. He doesn't know what he misses or that anyone experiences the world differently, which is probably why such pups can cope amazingly well.

Some white Boxers can also be deaf.

Deaf puppies are easily trained to hand signals; blind ones to words and sounds. The three-legged puppy won't be slowed down much, but we would minimize rough play, especially with larger dogs as injury prevention is key. Playing with other dogs can be complicated for deaf or blind puppies, who cannot hear or see the signals the other dog may give them. The other dog assumes the puppy is ignoring the clear signal and aggression can result. Choose calm, friendly, easygoing play partners.

IS MY PUPPY DEAF?

The most commonly deaf dogs are all white, or they have a white head and, most importantly, white ears, or they are merle (a splotchy color pattern) pups who are born to two merle parents. Puppies with a pink nose, pink eye rims, and pink skin are at greater risk. Why? Because myelin, a compound that colors skin, is necessary for the auditory nerves to work. No myelin, no hearing. Breeds most often affected include Dalmatians, Australian Shepherds, Bull Terriers, and Boxers. If you ever have to wake up your puppy when you come home, be suspicious. An easy home test is to stand around a corner, then call your puppy, shake a biscuit box or squeak a toy. A hearing puppy will usually come running; a deaf puppy will not respond. No response? Time to talk to your veterinarian.

Separated Too Early or Orphaned Puppy: Puppies need to stay with their litter for at least seven weeks. We much prefer puppies going to pet homes to be ten to twelve weeks of age if the breeder is knowledgeable about socialization and training. In an ideal world, puppies would arrive at your home crate trained; well on their way to being housebroken; knowing Sit, Down, and Come; comfortable on a lead; experienced with riding in cars and exposed to people of various ages and races and of both genders.

A puppy removed from a litter too early is not only much more difficult to care for because of how young he is, but he can have profound behavioral problems depending on how early he was taken away. Puppies separated before six weeks require work, and puppies separated before four weeks demand excellent handling and socialization to avoid possibly becoming quite aggressive when frustrated as they mature. This puppy is even more at risk than the singleton because he doesn't have his mother to teach him to be polite, inhibit his aggression, and mind his manners.

Littermates and Momma teach puppies how to cope with frustration and annoyance and how to moderate their aggressive reactions. Too often, people raise such young pups with large doses of love and mixed messages. Puppies separated early benefit greatly from being around an older, sensible dog who can pick up where Momma left off. We humans can try hard, but we'll never be as good at raising a puppy as another dog.

If such pups reach four or five months unable to restrain their reactions to frustration (they become frustrated, then snap or bite hard), it can be extremely difficult to instill inhibition successfully. Some people do manage to avoid frustrating the dog to some degree, but never mistake avoiding a dog's triggers for "fixing" the problem. Life is inherently annoying at times, for all of us, and it will happen. When it does, this puppy can bite hard and fast without regret or hesitation.

Delayed Development: Neglected and/or fearful puppies can be too hesitant to explore their world as a confident puppy might. As they settle into your home and you start helping them feel more confident and less stressed, they may proceed through the normal stages of puppyhood—just later. You might see a previously nonjumping puppy (who was "polite" not from understanding but from being too frightened to have contact that way) start leaping for all she is worth. That is *great*! Congratulations! Now you can start training your puppy through these issues as everyone else did: step by step, setting her up for success, and pretraining the right answer before you ever allow her to ask the question.

IS MY PUPPY CRAZY?

Twice a day (sometimes more, sometimes less) your puppy will go a little nuts. Ears back, she will race around your home, barking and spinning, leaping and careening into things. What the heck is going on? This is what we call a FRAP—a frenetic random activity period. Coined by a client years ago, this term aptly describes the puppy crazies. You can stay out of the way, put your puppy in the backyard, put her on lead and do some fun training, have her log some crate time with a delicious chewy, or just wait it out. This stage passes, but it is mighty cute while it is here!

Three to Six Months: The Juvenile Period

Oh, such a fun age! Full of exploration, enthusiasm, energy—and almost no inherent self-control. These three months encompass rapid growth on all levels: his adult teeth come in; his tail, feet, ears, and muzzle reach nearly their adult size; his weight surpasses half his adult size; and much more! Can you imagine growing to half *your* adult weight at four to five months of age? That would be like you going from 8 pounds to 80 in under 150 days! Extraordinary!

It is easy to forget that your growing puppy has so little life experience. He makes up for it with enthusiasm, though, which can be a trying combination. So don't be surprised if you become a bit frustrated from time to time. This is normal; just take a break—and reread the "Dealing with Frustration" which appears on page 33 of this chapter.

Teething

Just like human children, pups get two sets of teeth. Their "baby" teeth come in while they are nursing on their momma just in time to start solid food (and to encourage the start of weaning—ouch!). These needle-like sharps fall out

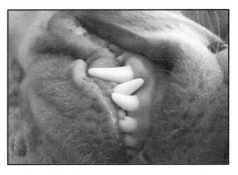

around sixteen weeks of age, though they can start as young as twelve. First the tiny front incisor teeth exit, followed around the mouth to the molars. Last to fall out at around five and a half to six months of age are the longest teeth, the four canines (long fangs up front). While teething, your pup's sore mouth will bleed. You'll find blood on his toys or playmates. His breath may really stink. He may not want to eat dry food, so soaking it in a bit of water will make things easier. All this is normal.

Pups can get fussy when they teethe. They may have some soft stools, run a slight temperature, or be a bit lethargic. While any or all of these may be normal, ask your veterinarian if you have any concerns, doubts, or questions.

Note for Toy Breed/Mix Owners: Sometimes the baby teeth don't come out when the adult come in. You'll know this has happened if you peek in his mouth and see two rows of teeth. These baby teeth, usually the canines, can easily be removed during neutering, so speak to your veterinarian.

Dealing with Frustration—Yours

When will this end! The peeing the pooping the yipping the gnawing the chewing the jumping the spinning the dragging the constant energy? It's time for any My Smart Puppy person to pop puppy into his crate with a favorite toy and take a break. Go out for a walk, lie down and read, take a long shower, phone a friend—whatever. Now breathe—we're not kidding. Take thirty seconds and just breathe—deeply—in through your nose and out your mouth. Feel better?

Things to remember:

Your puppy isn't perfect and neither are you.

Perfection is neither required nor possible. Aim for progress—you'll be much happier.

Your puppy can understand only what you teach him understandably.

If he isn't responding the way you want, you have to fix it. Your puppy simply cannot get better unless you get better first!

Trying everything you know isn't trying everything.

There are so many different methods and philosophies out there. Many turn out a well-trained dog, so find one that fits your personality. We collect methods like chefs collect recipes. Be open minded, learn many things, apply what works for you.

If your puppy isn't a stellar student, become a better teacher.

How much are you actually practicing with him? Are you setting him up for success or waiting for his mistakes? Is his tail wagging, is he looking at you, does he want to be close to you or far away? Is he calmer after a session or more crazed?

Petra pulls to say "Hi" to Sarah. Melissa sees this as a chance to practice "Come" and "Sit" so she backs up and calls Petra to her, making an impulsive moment a frustration-free chance to learn. Excellent job! SARAH WILSON

Bit-by-bit brings you better.

Nope, he's not trained yet. That takes a while. But is he better than he was last month? Last week? That's all we're looking for. If he isn't better, then try something new. If he is, great! You're on the right track.

One person's problem is another person's opportunity.

When your puppy doesn't come to you, you may think "This is terrible!" or "I'll never get this right!" because you don't know what to do yet. Turn this "problem" into an opportunity. Linda Parelli, a talented horsewoman, suggests: Instead of thinking "Oh no!" think "Oh boy!"

COPING WITH ANGER

Anger happens. It's what happens next that is within your control. Figure out your triggers. Being physically hurt, certain pitches of barking, frustration, exhaustion, feeling incompetent, social embarrassment, hopelessness, hunger, loneliness, eating the wrong foods, and drinking are all possible triggers. There are more: everyone's got a few. Then develop a list of options for yourself: Crate puppy, call a certain friend, bellow at the ceiling (better than lashing out), go for a walk, consult cyber buddies, turn on some of your favorite music, breathe deeply, lie down for a few minutes, do yoga, whack a pillow. Whatever works for you that doesn't involve getting angry at your puppy. And when it passes, don't berate yourself for being angry. Congratulate yourself on how you handled it. And if congratulations aren't exactly in order, get more help until they are. You can do this!

The incredible cuteness saves them when they are incredibly annoying.
ROXANNE FRANKLIN

How Does My Puppy Grow?

How big will my puppy be? With purebred pups, you have a pretty good idea of what their adult size will be. Mixes are more of a surprise. Don't be fooled by "runts." The pup who was born half the size of the rest of the litter can grow up to be the biggest dog of all. A good rough guide of size is to double a pup's weight between four to five months of age, meaning if your pup weighs twenty pounds about then, she'll probably end up around forty at adulthood. Have a giant-breed puppy? Cut him plenty of slack; he may be huge but he's still very much a youngster. Giant-breed pups seem to mature mentally a bit slower than other pups, probably due to their extreme rapid growth between three to seven months of age. They catch up, we promise.

Why are my puppy's feet so big? A pup grows from the outside in. Their tail, ears, nose, and paws get to be adult-sized long before the rest of them does. So a pup with big feet and a big tail will probably grow into them—eventually.

What sort of coat will my puppy have? Fuzzy pups will probably grow up to be long-haired adults. Smooth-coated pups with tufts of longer hair behind their ears and slightly longer hair on their rear legs and tails will grow a longer and thicker coat as they grow up. Pups with just the hint of a mustache at twelve weeks may get wiry when full grown. Pups who are obviously wiry will have a fuller, fluffier wire coat when they mature. Pups who are slick and smooth all over will probably stay that way.

Will my puppy's ears stand up or not? That depends. Generally, if the ears were standing up before teething, they may well drop during teething. This often happens, though no one is exactly clear as to why. It could be stress, mineral depletion due to the teething process, or something else entirely. In any case, those ears that were standing will usually stand again after teething. If they were not standing before teething and are supposed to stand, watch for them to be making an effort to do so, standing up a bit more all the time. If they are not, or if they hang down like a Labrador's, either embrace this look as a unique aspect of your dog or ask your veterinarian how to tape them up to help them stand. No matter what you do, some ears just are not going to stand up. Oh well. It doesn't matter to your puppy.

Will my puppy change color? Often, yes—at least a little. Kerry Blue Terriers are born black, becoming their signature slate gray as they mature. Dalmatians are born white, with spots arriving afterward. If your pink-nosed puppy has even a few black dots on that pink, the black will expand over the first year.

He may even become a black-nosed puppy yet. Tan markings may darken to reds if your puppy has any red; look at the color right behind the ears. Black on the face or legs can recede; look for brown hairs scattered in the black. This is common in German Shepherd Dogs, and little Pip, though not a Shepherd mix, is lightening up already.

The End of Social Attraction

Somewhere around four and a half to five and a half months old (maybe a little earlier for toy-breed puppies, later for the giants) your sweet, loving, compliant puppy will have a thought and the thought will be, "No."

Instead of coming when you call, he will come close, then throw you a quick play bow and take off. Independent puppies may now start playing "Did you call me? I didn't hear a thing" in earnest. Reactive puppies may simply race on past "I came, I went" with lightning speed. All of it will add up to the same thing: They no longer come to you when you call them.

So, as with all such moments, when you don't have or have lost mental control over your puppy, you attach physical controls. In this case, allowing your puppy to drag a long line outside or a lead in the house can short-circuit these runabouts before they really get going.

Hint: Walk casually in the general direction of your puppy. Step casually on the lead. Count to five, then call your puppy to you happily. Praise! If he comes, great! If not, back up and pulse that lead until he heads in your direction. (See "How to Squeeze/Pulse" on page 96.) The moment he does, pause the pulse and praise! Pulse again if he wanders. Throw a praise party when he arrives. Soon he will start to get the idea that coming to you is not optional, but it is fun!

Head to Chapters 2 through 5, and focus on Come: Basics (page 102) and Come: Making It Work (page 134) to help him understand this better. Time to start your Space Games (same chapters) in earnest if you haven't yet.

OH NO, WHAT HAVE I DONE! THE FIVE-MONTH-OLD REGRETS

Five months seems to be the magic number. The pup is out of that cute cute baby stage; he is teething, active, pushy, and impulsive. This is not what you had in mind! This too shall pass, and sooner than you can imagine. Build up your Level I games (pages 82–111) like Mine, Off, Look At Me, and Guided Down, so you have a way to communicate with each other. Instill your daily routines such as waiting at the door, sitting for his supper, gently taking treats, and productive play. Make sure he gets the diet and exercise he needs to grow and by the time you've done that, your puppy will be growing into being your best buddy.

Six to Nine Months: Adolescence

This is a delightful age. Teething will be over soon if it isn't already, housebreaking is generally done, and there are fewer midnight walks and daily interruptions. You are getting to know each other better with more of the sweet, calmer moments you may have dreamed of when you got your puppy in the first place.

Your baby isn't a baby any longer. This is more like pre-teen/early teenage in humans. Questioning authority begins in earnest in many. Your dog may no longer be (nor should he be) as focused on you as before. He's his own dog now (or will be soon). It's a great age for having fun together, as he is more of a partner now. People often say this is a hard age because their dogs become stubborn or difficult. We don't think that way. What we do see is that whatever holes you had in your training and relationship with your dog in the early months will be in clear view now.

If you want your dog's responsiveness and connection to continue to improve, you need to change your focus a bit so you are training the dog you have now, not the cute, big-eared puppy you had a few months ago. If your dog is new to you, go through the initial training laid out in Level I (Chapter 3). But if you've been doing that work for a few months, then it is time to start putting away the treats and expect the behavior you have taught. At first responsiveness may drop as you both adjust to this new level, but it will rebound if you keep up your enthusiasm and follow through.

Unhelpful Human Habits

Repetition: You're so used to your puppy responding right away that his slow response confuses you. You start repeating the command to "give him another chance." Your puppy responds to this by waiting for you to follow through. Dogs learn to respond at the *moment* you help them respond. If you say "Sit" three times then make it happen, the command becomes "sit, sit, SIT!" The single best habit to develop right now? Say it once, then make it happen!

The Pause That Confuses: You say a command, then stare at

the dog. Will he do it? He stares back at you as if thinking, Are we doing something new? I guess I'll wait and see. You stare at each other, then the dog internally shrugs and may walk away or slowly comply. Sound familiar? At every level of training, the rule is the same: *Say it, do it.* If you do *just* that your dog will be reliably obedient.

Allowing Space Invaders: Allowing your dog to intrude into your space starts to have more obvious consequences now. You may get slammed in the dog park, scratched by a jumping dog who is "happy to see you," shoved off your own couch, or threatened over a toy. If you have not played the Space Games in earnest yet, today is the day. If you don't understand why these are important, play them anyway. We're betting it will become clear to you in practice. Do not allow yourself to be pushed around, walked on, or physically dismissed.

Expect Behavioral Trial Balloons

At this age, pups start testing the boundaries. A classic example is plate poaching: walking right into your space when you are eating. This is just as pushy in a dog as it is when a friend reaches onto your plate without permission for a french fry. Your answer should be casual but immediate. Play a round of Mine (page 82). Stand up and calmly but clearly block your puppy away from the table. Return and eat. Repeat every time your puppy intrudes. Do not hesitate, do not negotiate—just do it. Block him back until he stops intruding. Polite pups do not plate poach— period.

Most of these types of behavior could have been taught unintentionally but if a few are suddenly present or are suddenly getting worse, then your dog may be giving himself a promotion. Please read "Demoting Demanding or Difficult Dogs," page 254. Here are a few others to watch for:

• Slamming past you at doorways
• Not moving out of your way

- Not giving up sleeping spots (on couch or dog bed)
- Immediately taking your seat when you get up
- Whining at you to get you to move from your spot
- Getting up on the counter
- Lunging at things on lead
- Freezes and/or glares when you walk by him eating or chewing
- Growling (other than in play) or baring teeth at you
- Struggling, mouthing when handled

KEEP UP CONFINEMENT

Even though your pup's housebroken and done with teething, it probably isn't time to leave him free in your house when you leave. He's still young and will learn all sorts of interesting games if allowed, games like What's in the Couch? or 101 Things to Do with a Roll of Toilet Paper. The more active your dog's breed or mix, the longer he'll probably need crating. Most sporting breeds need one and a half to two years crated when alone before you can transition them to being loose. Some other breeds can start at a year, plus or minus. Either way, six to nine months old is too young for most dogs. Don't rush this part!

Helpful Habits to Build:
Living Successfully with Your Older Puppy

Raise the Bar. To keep your puppy interested, keep asking for his very best. When you are starting out, every tiny effort toward obedience is rewarded. Good puppy! But once a behavior is basically learned, it is time to raise the bar. Try these things: If you repeat yourself or physically help your puppy get it right, then no treat. Put that treat right to his nose then put it away. Too bad. Try harder next time. You're not angry, but he doesn't get a gold star for C-level work. If you want to encourage A's, make them the gold-star option. Save your treats for the best performance your puppy can currently offer. Give two or three small treats in a row for stellar moments. While you're feeding, smile and

Melissa raises the bar for Petra by practicing attention in a tractor supply store. Things go well and Petra gets lots of praise, petting, and a treat. Nice teamwork! Notice Melissa's slack lead!
SARAH WILSON

praise. Leave no doubt in your puppy's mind that you are delighted! At this age, it should work out to the top 25 percent of the best responses gets treats and praise, 50 percent of the standard, "okay" responses gets a treat and some praise, bottom 25 percent gets no treats and brief praise. In this way you are making it clear to your puppy what you like the very best. If his slow Sit after two commands gets the same treat and praise that an immediate Sit with full attention gets, how is he supposed to know which is better? If you want the best, reward the best with the best.

More Than Ever, Minor Moments Matter. Behavior is cumulative. The more intense and intelligent your dog, the more such moments add up. With our Pip, we have to be ready to redirect her to a better choice or respond to her choice at a moment's notice. She's not an easy puppy to live with, not even for us. How she goes through doors, takes treats, plays with toys, walks with us in the house, responds to directions are all watched carefully. We know that letting little things slide sets the stage for bigger problems later on. For us, it is not the size of the behavior that matters but the mental state behind the behavior.

Anticipation: Preventing and Redirecting Trouble. Again, Pip is a good example. Her terrier background means that she escalates from excitement into aggression quickly around the other dogs. Because we know this about her, we set her up for success rather than allowing her to practice this unwanted cycle. When we let all the dogs out, she is last, remaining crated until we can focus on her entirely. Then she must sit quietly at the door, not stand on her hind legs digging wildly at it while barking, which is her first choice. She must wait as we open the door instead of racing through the slightest crack. When we get to the side gate into the larger fenced area, we take her collar and ask for a quiet Sit again. She is not released until she is quietly restraining herself without any pressure on her collar. That's the link we are developing: Calm = Freedom. It is a link she will never discover on her own. Either we shape her choices now or we fight her tendencies for a lifetime.

Restraint creates resistance (and OH how we HATE the retractable leashes!). This is not teamwork or connection. Time to play games like Look At Me, Simple Sit, and Catch My Drift.
SARAH WILSON

Find and Use a Good Praise Level. Dogs believe us. If you are boring and lackadaisical in your praise, your puppy will be slow and lackadaisical in his response. Often people are embarrassed to really praise their puppies. Interestingly, they may have no problem scolding them. Think about that. Get over your issues with praise and use it. Be enthusiastic relative to your natural self, meaning you don't need to sound like a clown to get the message across; you simply need to sound warm, loving, and sincere. Watch for a soft look in your puppy's eyes, his ears back, his mouth relaxed—a happy expression. If you are too much for your puppy, he will look away, even turning or walking away, or he may start to jump up or mouth you. In some cases, the puppy will stop coming all the way up to you. If this happens, slow your hands and voice; touch him on his neck and body, not his face; stop and walk away sooner. Your goal is for your puppy to stay for the praise. If you aren't energetic or sincere enough, your pup may not wag or look at you at all. In this case, speed up your hands (still stay away from the face), be more enthusiastic and warm. Find what works—then use it!

Nine to Twelve Months: Living with Your Pupteen

Times they are a-changing. You remember that sweet little pup who followed you around and listened to your every word (or close to it)? That pup's gone. For good. People frequently call these dogs their "puppies." If you are doing so, stop. Call them your dog because that's what they are. It is time to put away puppyish things and start moving on to handling your maturing dog.

If you've recently adopted your dog, assume he has had little coherent instruction and is confused about the world and his place in it. Assume he thinks humans are, at best, incompetent, and, at worst, unreliable and frightening. With any adopted dog, always start at the very beginning of training, working on your START Level I basics and reading the sections that come before this one. Doing this will allow you to discover any holes in his understanding while showing him that this is a brand-new relationship, one without confusion or violence. If you've had your dog from the start, now is the time to step up daily structure and direction, to increase calm follow-through, further decrease food treats, and move into living with your mentally adult—soon to be physically adult—dog.

Disobedience or Missed Obedience?

Last night I was teaching puppy class and PJ was assisting. We were demonstrating Wait at the door where the dog pauses in front of an open door rather than rushing out. As PJ and I approached the sliding doors that lead to the outside, I said, "Wait." PJ sat beautifully as I slid open the door. We exited together. Perfect. Turning, I decided to show this coming back into the room. I said "Wait" again but this time PJ didn't pause a moment; instead she trotted through the door and into the room. Hmmm, I thought as I called her back out and tried again. Again, I said "Wait," and, again, she walked right past me into the room. Then I understood.

Is she being disobedient? Not on your life! She's being literal, as most dogs are. Since I had only worked PJ on Wait as I left the room, that's all she understood. So while I thought "Wait" meant pause at the doorway, she thought "Wait" meant pause on the inside facing out.

Her going back into the room wasn't "bad"; she was trying to get herself in position to do the command as she understood it. It wasn't what I wanted, but whose fault is that? So I set her up a third time and stepped in front of her, blocking her. She looked rather surprised but sat with an "Okay, this is different" look on her face. Good dog! From then on she understood.

Dogs learn exactly what you teach them. *Exactly.* I called a pup in class and the pup ran, tail awagging, to his mom and sat. Bad puppy? Not at all. While we know "Come" means come to the person who called, he knew "Come" meant run to Mom and sit. A few treat lures and a lot of praise later, he quickly got the idea.

Another classic is Sit. Mostly we humans teach Sit with the pup in front of us. Later when walking on lead, some owners are frustrated because every time they say "Sit" the pup swings in front of them instead of sitting by their side. Pup is just doing exactly what you trained her to do. If you now want Sit at your side, you'll need to teach that. Very often, what we humans are quick to label "disobedience" is actually us missing a pup's effort at obedience as she understands it.

Activities: Time to Go to Work!

At this age, dogs need things to do. Those can be things you want or things they want—your choice. Bracken, our eldest German Shepherd Dog, picks up food bowls for us at dinnertime. Sarah started asking her to do this when we had client dogs and the bowls were often left in the back of crates. Sending her in when the occupant was outside playing was easier than crawling in after it. Other dogs we know put their toys away on command, pick up laundry, find toys by name, fetch a can of dog food, or a roll of paper towels, carry a bag with tools or a note from one part of a large house to another to the person specified. Be creative! What a dog can do for and with you is limited largely by your imagination.

Handling: Keep It Up!

If you've been handling your pup daily since he was two months of age—great! Keep it up! If you haven't, now's the time to start. Every companion puppy in the United States should allow himself to be touched without concern or protest. You never know when glass will cut a paw pad, daily eye medication will be required, a stick will get caught in the roof of your dog's mouth, or he will need to be restrained at the veterinarian's. When those things happen, you want your dog to trust human hands on his body. Some accept handling immediately, others need our help. Either way, practice ensures success. This is so important that we have included Touch Games as a part of all the START Training in Chapters 2 through 5.

Handling also builds bite inhibition, making your puppy a safer pet. We adults tend to touch our dogs in very predictable ways. Enter someone new or a child who grabs or hugs or does something unexpected and your dog might react with surprise. This is much less likely if you've made handling his body a part of your daily life together.

You can be playful—grasping his tail suddenly but gently, lifting both ears up or folding them down, holding a paw gently. In each case, waiting patiently until the dog is calm before releasing makes your point. Drying paws after a wet walk, brushing all over, gently massaging his neck and down his spine, learning how to stretch your dog safely all help to build mental as well as physical compliance.

HOW TO PLAY TUG

Another way to improve self-control when your dog is excited is to teach her how to play Tug properly. This is not a free-for-all. Most pups will get overstimulated by this game if it is played improperly and end up jumping at you, mouthing, or generally blowing a small (or a large) canine gasket. If you see that about to happen, stop. Down your dog. If you can't Down your dog verbally, leave a lead on her flat collar and use the Guided Down as taught on page 92. Foot on lead, let her calm down. Then start again more  slowly. This gives her a chance to learn how to listen when excited and you a good way to practice this important skill together. But, if she cannot calm down, quit for the day. *Note:* If you have small children, skip this game until they are older.

Properly played:
- Dog sits.
- You present a toy to the dog and wait. Use a

large one that you both can hold at the same time. She must not leap and grab. If she does, simply lift it out of her way as you do with Sit for Your Supper (see page 267). In fact, playing that at every meal this week should help your dog's self-control here.

- You tell her to start by saying "Get it!" and play at an excitement level your dog can handle. No whipping her head back and forth roughly. That can be risky physically and behaviorally. We allow the dog to tug us forward as she tugs straight back. This makes the game a good rear and back workout for your dog as well as being fun.
- You stop playing—do not pull on the toy—say "Out" (or "Drop"—the word doesn't matter).
- If the dog removes her mouth, praise.
- If not, try reaching under and putting your hand under her jaw. Don't squeeze. Just place your hand on her jaw. Many dogs release at this touch.
- If not, go work on your Out (page 136) until she releases reliably.
  - If your dog needs to build her confidence, then let her "win" the item often. If your puppy has a bit too much confidence, then don't let her get the toy much, if at all.

What the heck is THIS?
SARAH WILSON

Eeep! Looks dangerous!
SARAH WILSON

I will bark at it fiercely, that will scare it!
SARAH WILSON

CHAPTER 2

UNDERSTANDING TRAINING

Pip settles into being her true self within days. Then she is a couch-leaping, cat-chasing, crate-barking, shoe-stealing, rocket-launched puppy. None of this concerns us. We know she is just what she is: an uneducated herding-and-Terrier-mix puppy with a lot of potential. So we get right down to business. On the first day home, Sarah did Sit for Your Supper (page 267). Within less than a minute, our little ball of poor impulse control was sitting—vibrating with anticipation but sitting. Next we worked on the Off game so we'd have some way to tell her not to ricochet off us. She is, as most puppies are, incredibly responsive to calm "cause and effect" work. To us her speedy learning is nothing new. It's what we do many times a year with puppies of all ages, breeds, mixes, and sizes. The games we teach you here are so easy—easy for you to teach, easy for your puppy to learn. It makes things fun and it will lower any anxiety you may have about whether you can handle this or whether your puppy is smart. You can and she is! We're going to teach you what you need to know—beginning right here!

Each level contains the five START categories: Space, Touch, Attention, Requirement, and Trust. Each category at each level contains two games for you to play with your puppy except for Trust, which has one. You can teach an entire level at once then move on to the next one, or you can proceed through the Level III Space Games while you are working on Level I Requirement and Level II Touch. We do suggest you start at the Level I exercises regardless of your previous training as this stuff is different and the learning is cumulative for both of you.

START Games	Level I	Level II	Level III
Space	Mine	Wait	Go
	Off	Left Circles	Wait There
Touch	Placement Sit	Calm = Release	Simple Sit
	Guided Down	Guided Down II	Face It
Attention	Look At Me	Door Chores	Follow the Leader
	Catch My Drift	Leave It	Beat the Clock
Requirement	Come: Basics	Come: Making It Work	Stay II: Working the 4 D's
	Stay: Basics	Out	No Eye Can
Trust	Near Is Dear	Check It Out	Say Hello

WHAT IS START ABOUT?

Space

Dogs do "speak" to each other with body language, energy, intention, and intensity. If you want to communicate quickly with your puppy, learn his language. The good news is you already know it. We use the same way of communicating all the time with each other, but we use it so naturally we don't even think about it until someone breaks one of the commonly held rules. For example: A friend approaches you, then stops six inches from your face. Depending on your temperament, you might stand still wondering what the heck was going on, step back to give yourself more room, or step forward to ask your friend to back up and give you space.

Dogs do the same. Space is their primary language, overriding expression, body postures, and vocal cues. Because of the relationship we have with our dogs, we allow them more access to our personal space than anyone else. Doing so can create no end of confusion in the dog.

To deal with some of these confusions, we have developed a whole new series of games that are easy to understand, teach, and use. They may seem simple, but they quite simply can change the relationship between human and canine without confrontation, confusion, or conflict. Puppies become more compliant and responsive within minutes without fuss or force. These games are the foundation upon which all else is built. For novices and experienced alike, this training is fun, effective, and darn close to magic.

Touch

A dog's natural response to pushing or pulling is to strain in the opposite direction. That urge to fight the pressure by pulling away is called the opposition reflex. And we all have it.

Have you ever been given a Chinese finger puzzle? If you're like us, you peered into it and saw nothing dangerous, so you did as instructed. When you tried to get your fingers out, the paper

Jack, a young Boxer, leans in toward and looks up at Brian. He loves this petting. Touch is a powerful way to communicate. SARAH WILSON

tightened and you were stuck. This has been funny for about 3,000 years because when most of us get our fingers stuck our first instinct is to pull harder to get free. That only makes matters worse, which generally makes you pull even harder.

Remember that puzzle the next time you think, Why do dogs pull so hard on the lead? They are choking themselves! If they just slowed down they would be fine. A walk on lead is basically a doggy finger puzzle, only it is on their neck. All they are probably thinking is Get away from this! Our job—your job—is to teach your puppy how to soften to you, mentally and physically, rather than to brace/pull/push against you. That's what the Touch exercises are all about: softening to you in every way.

PETTING 101

How you touch your puppy can calm him or make him into a mouthing monster. To get good results, follow these guidelines:

- Stroke with the hair, not against it
- Slow hands = Calmer puppy
- Fast hands = Mouthing puppy
- Hands around face = Mouthing puppy
- Do not rub or buff your puppy
- Watch for him turning his head or walking away; this generally means he doesn't like what is being done
  - Try to stop before your dog walks away—as the saying goes, "Leave them wanting more!"
  - Scratching the chest helps puppies sit up instead of lie down
  - If your puppy mouths you when you touch his rear, talk to your veterinarian—your puppy may be uncomfortable

Attention

In social mammals, the lower-ranked animals in the group watch the higher-ranked ones. We are no different. When someone we revere enters a room, we pay attention. Everyone pays attention. In fact, not to pay attention would be quite rude. And so it is with dogs. But this is not the same as staring; this is who keeps whom in their awareness and sight. So, if as you walk along you stare at your puppy, you are "telling" your puppy that you are following him. Why should he pay attention to *you* if you are paying attention to *him*? Glance at him, keep him in your peripheral vision, look at him briefly when you praise him, but when you walk, look where you are going. You lead, he follows—puppies pay attention to their leader.

Requirement

Here we deal with spoken commands: Stay, Come, Out. These are three critical commands for your puppy's safety. Sit, Down, Wait, Off, and much more are covered in other areas. In Requirement, we focus on being able to get your dog to you, stop him, and get him to spit things out of his mouth. We call them a requirement so you get the idea that this isn't an optional program. For us, training offers

your puppy freedom and safety. In order for training to offer safety, your dog must respond immediately and reliably.

Trust

There is much in the world your puppy doesn't understand and never can understand. He or she will have to depend on you to deal with many of these things. If your puppy depends on his own instincts, he may panic, which launches all sorts of behaviors, from flight to aggression. If he depends on you, then you can help him handle a situation by giving him options and rewarding different choices. This can be practiced, and practicing it is what the Trust exercises are all about. When you and your puppy have learned how to handle frightening moments as a team, you will more easily handle whatever life sends your way.

These five categories of exercises and games are given to you in Level I, Level II, and Level III. It isn't necessary to go through each level entirely before moving forward, but do start at the beginning of each category before moving to the next one up. These are presented in an order with a purpose. They work best done in this progression. Have fun! Go train!

WHEN DO I START TRAINING?

Right now—the first day! Whether you want to be or not, you *are* training from the first moment you touch your puppy. You get what you encourage. If you play roughly, you encourage roughness. If you squeal excitedly when your puppy mouths you, you encourage mouthing. What you don't want to do is to frighten your puppy. That's not the plan. The plan is to be a team, you and him. Treat him like what he is—your future teammate—and you won't go too far

Giant breed puppies, like this six-month-old Newfoundland, take longer to mature mentally. Even though they are huge on the outside, they are little on the inside, needing extra patience and praise during early training. SARAH WILSON

wrong. Training simply means knowingly influencing your puppy's behavior and that starts right here, right now!

Something we hear often is: I don't have time to train! But really, you don't have time not to; developing good habits is so much easier than trying to remedy bad ones. Training is a time saver. Consider this: Do you have a minute? Do a sixty-second session. When you get good at this you can do ten Sit or Down or Come exercises with time to spare. You could play a few rounds of Look At Me. Practice bite prevention with Mine or challenge yourself to see how many things you and your puppy can do well in a minute. If you trained *just* during TV commercials, you'd have one of the best-trained puppies in your neighborhood in no time.

UNDERSTANDING REWARDS

Brian throws Hazel a praise party. She loves it! Having fun with your puppy is a terrific reward—for both of you! SARAH WILSON

A reward is anything your puppy enjoys. That can be you touching him, looking at him, or speaking to him, being given freedom to play, being near you, stepping away from your puppy, giving him slack on the lead, or a treat. Each puppy loves different things—Pip loves a good romp, Milo adores stroking and praise while PJ prefers a really yummy food treat. What each loves doesn't matter to us; delivering their preferred rewards does. Try to praise or reward about ten times more often than you correct and you'll both have a grand time!

Here are rewards we use in this book:

- Petting
- Praise (speaking to him)
- Laughter (which most dogs love)
- Looking at him

- Smiling at him
- Delivering toys
- Tossing a ball
- Allowing him out the door (Door Chores) or the crate
- Allowing him to eat a meal (Sit for Your Supper)
- Removal of spatial pressure (Off)
- Removal of physical pressure (Guided Down, Placement Sit)
- Play (Tug)
- Moving away from something scary (Check It Out)
- Freedom (Calm = Release)
- Food

YOU GET WHAT YOU PET; YOU RAISE WHAT YOU PRAISE

Last night in puppy class, a young mixed-breed puppy started to bark. Her owner, a bit embarrassed by the noise, reached her hand out to scratch her chest. Her obvious hope was to quiet her puppy. What did the puppy actually experience? That barking causes petting. As the barking continued (you get what you pet), the owner started to talk to the puppy, trying to soothe her. What did the puppy learn? Barking causes praise and since we raise what we praise, you know what happened next: bark, bark, bark. What worked? Giving the puppy other things to do, shuffling into her when she barked thereby forcing her to move then, when she was quiet, giving her a bone smeared with some cheese on the inside. Barking became less fun, so she focused on the bone. Perfect!

UNDERSTANDING CORRECTIONS

Corrections are anything your puppy doesn't enjoy. How you teach impacts how your puppy accepts correction. The more consistent you are in word and deed, the clearer your intention to cause change, the more sincere and abundant your praise is, the more responsive your puppy will be to subtle corrections. The goal though is always to be effective. What is effective? Effective is as gentle as you can be, as firm as you must be—both—at the same time. Too firm and you lose your pup's willing participation, too gentle and your pup soon ignores you. Here are our thoughts on useful correction:

- Corrections should work. You should see steady improvement in what you want, or your puppy should be responding better to your direction.
- Corrections should "get to good." Useful correction creates opportunity to reward—that's the whole point. Puppy jumps up: you signal Off and step into his space (the correction). Puppy sits: Good puppy! Wanted behaviors can and should be pretrained whenever possible. Work on the START Level I Games at home, where things are quiet. Practice until your puppy responds well consistently, *then* use them in real life. Homework first, then test!
- Corrections should help your puppy. A useful correction helps a puppy understand what you want, calming the puppy as it does so.

Here are corrections we use in this book:

- Removal of petting
- Removal of eye contact
- Going suddenly silent (Near Is Dear)
- Speaking in a startling way ("Ouch!")
- Acting in a startling way
- Eye contact (Out)
- Startling sound (Used for countertop cruising)
- Turning away (Wait There)

- Stepping forward into the dog (Off, Go)
- Stepping back away from puppy (Wait There)
- Lead pressures (Guided Down, Simple Sit)
- Physical pressure (Placement Sit)
- Stopping Play (Used in managing mouthing)
- Sending from the room (to stop begging)
- Putting in the crate (to stop barking at you)
- Pulse/squeezing the lead (Follow the Leader, Look At Me, Leave It)
- Removal of meal (Sit for Your Supper)
- Removal of food (Raising the Bar)

WHAT IS ABUSE?

Abuse occurs when an interaction is overwhelming, unpredictable, inescapable, unstoppable. Here's an example of abuse: An owner came home and found trash all over the kitchen. He yelled at and hit the dog and kept doing so. The dog, frightened and having no clue why his owner was attacking him, ran into his kennel which infuriated his owner. The man took the kennel apart in order to continue to hit his dog. The dog bit the man (no surprise there). All four criteria of abuse were met: The situation was unpredictable and emotionally overwhelming to the dog. The dog could not escape or stop the attack. The man had lost control and that loss of control was all that was happening. Anytime you're doing something *to* your dog in anger instead of *with* your dog with the goal to teach, you're headed to (or knee-deep in) the dark side.

THE FIVE TYPES OF "COMMANDS"

There are five simple ways to "give" commands to dogs and those are: spoken, sensation, spatial, situational, and signals.

Spoken is what you are probably familiar with: You say "Sit," your dog sits. These are the most common of all commands and the hardest for dogs to comprehend.

Sensation simply means using touch to "command." Example: Your friend comes up behind you, places a hand gently on your upper arm, and gives the lightest of pressures away from her. You step aside with a smile. She "asked" you to step aside; you did. Some people link "pressure" with "force," but teaching your puppy how to respond to gentle pressure is no more "aggressive" than your friend touching your shoulder to guide you.

Spatial means using space to "command" your dog. Your dog rushes for the door. You step in front of her and she stops and sits. You blocked her, "telling" her to stop with your body, and she did.

Situational commands are habits. You meet someone: he faces you, smiles, and extends his hand—you don't need to be told to extend yours and shake his hand in return. The situation tells you what to do. Many other situations control our behavior: you see a red light, you stop (hopefully), you walk up to an elevator door, you press the button.

At first, we had to be taught with words and touch what to do but later it all became automatic. So it can for your puppy. Teach your puppy that sitting makes good things happen and soon he will sit at curbs or doorways, around treats and toys—all of that can become nearly automatic. And what a joy it is when it does!

Signals are easy for dogs to learn and we'll use them. The Off hand signal is a good example. Their limitation is that your puppy must be looking at you to "see" you, but signals are lots of fun to teach and use.

Throughout this book, we'll be teaching you spoken, sensation, spatial, situational, and signal "commands" that will make your life with your puppy easier, safer, and more fun.

DOG TRAINING: STOP THE INSANITY!

First, there are many, many ways to train a dog and all of them work for someone. Apply any method consistently and the dog will figure it out. Everyone has favorite (and least favorite) methods. We're attached to what works for both the dog and the human. Avoid methods that make your dog look miserable; equally avoid methods that make your dog look like a junkie angling for his next fix. "Crazed" is not "happy." Also, skip trainers who claim to be "all positive" with the dog (no such thing) but are downright mean to the human end of the lead. If "all positive" really worked then they would use it with everyone.

EQUIPMENT

Oh how we *wish* there was some magic piece of dog-training equipment that instantly trains a dog but there isn't, any more than buying a certain hammer is going to guarantee you a perfectly built house. Both are tools. No tool trains a dog—the human mind does. The good news is that almost every tool has a use. Your job is to (a) find out what tools your puppy needs in order to learn, and then (b) use those tools. Since you're not the one being taught, your opinion of the tool matters little. What you want to find is the thing that makes it easiest for your puppy to learn what you are teaching.

The bottom line? All young pups should be started on a wide, flat or martingale collar. As your puppy matures, use the tool that allows you to use the *least* force to accomplish your goal. If a Triple Crown collar allows us to get an older puppy's attention with a finger flutter as opposed to a flat collar that the puppy flails against full throttle, we use the Triple Crown collar. On another puppy, that same collar might be too much. There is no single answer other than "Look at your puppy."

Stop what doesn't work, no matter who is giving you advice.

Tool	Best for:	Bad for:	Warning!
Flat Collar	Sensitive puppies, young puppies, holding dog tags, off leash work, playing with other dogs.	Teaching leash work to most adolescent or older puppies and many strong pulling, physically insensitive puppies.	Is very comfortable for many dogs to pull against. Because of this, it can effectively teach puppies to pull.
Martingale Collar	Works well for not-quite-so sensitive puppies, leash work with sensitive dogs, for pups who slip out of their flat collars.	Dogs who have been pulling, touch insensitive dogs.	Same as the flat collar.
Head Halter	Puppies much stronger than their handlers; puppies walked by children; low-to-the-ground garbage hounds; possessive aggressive puppies; mouthy puppies. Good for pups who are tracheally sensitive (cough on flat collars).	Puppies with little or no nose; reactives who are slow to accept this tool.	Must use a backup collar with this as occasionally one slips off. *Never* use with a retractable lead!

Tool	Best for:	Bad for:	Warning!
Triple Crown Plastic Prong	Many puppies who do not respond well to a flat collar or martingale collars, respond to gentle use of this collar; good for people who don't like the look of the metal prong. Good for pups who cough on flat collars.	Very touch sensitive pups who can be physically overwhelmed by this tool. Can be hard to get on or off.	Play a little Look At Me indoors to introduce him to this tool. Reward all attention. Must use nylon or chain slip collar with this as occasionally one comes apart.
Metal Prongs	Older pups much stronger than their owners; pups who do not respond to the other tools.	Young puppies. Can be hard for some people to get on or off.	As with the plastic prong collar.
Clicker	Shy dogs, young and undersocialized pups; teaching behaviors that are hard to create (such as sneezing on cue). It really can be "quicker with a clicker" and it's an	Used exclusively, runs the risk of creating pushy animals that have extreme reactions to even low levels of frustration or restraint. This can easily be countered by	In recent years, some dangerous adolescent dogs have come to us from clicker classes. They are great on their basic obedience— when they feel like being

Tool	Best for:	Bad for:	Warning!
Clicker (cont.)	excellent tool for honing your training skills, getting you positively focused, and having some fun.	daily handling and using guiding placement.	great. They are also hectic, assertive, and growly when handled in even the most basic way.
Slip Collar	We use over-sized slips as backup for head halters and prong collars—nothing more.	Use another tool.	There are better tools that are more effective and easier to use properly.
Front Clip Harnesses	Haven't found a "best use" yet. We're not fans.	Aggressive dogs; dogs at risk for elbow and shoulder problems; dogs who know how to back out of a collar.	Appears to encourage pulling, have yet to see a dog on one with a loose lead. Easy for a dog to get out of if they back up. Does not control head.
Under Forelegs Harness	Can be helpful for dogs with neck injuries or sensitivities.	Can chafe under arms; most come with soft covers for the cords.	Can be complicated to put on at first, but you'll manage.

Tool	Best for:	Bad for:	Warning!
Tie-to-Your-Waist Leads	*No one!* These are dangerous tools!	Everyone. A well-trained puppy doesn't need one and an untrained puppy should not use one.	*Never* tie your puppy to you to go for a walk. This is a recipe for the nastiest sort of physics lesson.

If this puppy bolts, that little girl's hand could be cut to the bone. We know more people and puppies seriously injured by retractable leads than all other training tools, combined!

Some people hold their training beliefs as passionately as others hold their religion. We call them "true believers," and, like all true believers, these folks seem to think that they have found *the* answer and want to give you that answer right away. Here's what we truly believe: There is no one way. If you get a method and it doesn't work, find out how to use it differently or find a different method. The goal is the response from your puppy, not to uphold the theory or the belief. The only dog-training experts that matter one whit are the dogs. The rest is just conversation.

WE'RE INTO LEATHER . . .

Leads, that is. After training many thousands of dogs, there is just nothing that competes with a good-quality leather lead. We use four-foot leads, as we find that is plenty of length for walking and stationary work without giving people too much lead to wrestle with. We're fans of the smaller clip size. We watch those big clips on the nylon leads smack puppies in the face on an almost weekly basis. They also weigh down the collar more than we like, muddying the line between slack and pulsing. For the vegetarians out there, our second choice is a small clipped cotton or hemp lead for ease on the hands and nylon for strength and convenience. We do not use or recommend chain leads as they have no give, are hard on your hands, and can yank out a baby tooth if the puppy grabs it with his mouth. If your puppy is a lead chewer, please see page 268 for answers to that common problem.

This huge clip will smack this puppy in the face. Use leads with smaller clips.
HEATHER WHITE

COMMON COOKIE QUAGMIRES: HOW TO USE FOOD REWARD EFFECTIVELY

Food is one of the most wonderful training tools around, and it's one that can cause no end of trouble when used improperly. It is reinforcing for the people because the puppies appear to learn quickly. But puppies can also quickly learn that cookies make the world go round and soon no cookie can mean no response.

Pip has that potential. She is more than willing to work for food—downright enthused actually—but it wasn't impacting her connection with us much. She wasn't softening or becoming

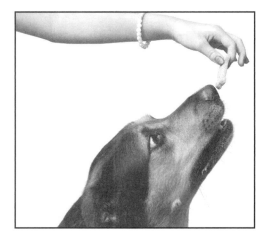

more attentive—quite the opposite. When we noticed this, we put most of the treats away for a few weeks, working with praise, touch, and space. This had the desired effect of making us the focus instead of the food. Sarah still used treats for some work that she wanted to get Pip started on, but the bulk of our training was done food free in weeks 18 to 20.

Here's the common progression: The cookie rookie usually starts out just fine. She gives one treat for each behavior the puppy does. This is being a "soda machine." You put your money in and you get a soda—virtually every time if the machine isn't broken or empty. You never put in money and get a jackpot or a surprise. Its beauty is its predictability. This is just the way to start building a behavior with a puppy.

But once the behavior is well started, continuing to be a soda machine leads to puppy boredom. They know exactly what is coming, with many pondering, Hmm, am I more interested in the cookie or in doing something else? When the answer is "something else," your puppy is gone. To keep a puppy's interest as training progresses, you need to become a "slot machine." Your responses vary; cookies become harder to get. Maybe your puppy will get a belly rub or a game or a toy or even a several-treat "jackpot." Or, if things were mediocre, the puppy gets nothing. Now things are interesting! He never knows what you're going to do, so he pays more attention. He finds out that cookies come to those who listen, so he starts to listen more. Well done!

THE SCOOP ON TREATS

Whenever possible, use your puppy's kibble. We know it is balanced and good for him. When you measure out his food in the morning, put some aside for training. If you use other foods as treats, pick mild things in small pieces. Avoid tummy upset by avoiding rich foods such as freeze-dried liver or huge amounts of anything. Watch his waistline. You want your puppy lean.

OUCH! MY PUPPY GRABS AT TREATS!

If your puppy is a good weight, fed a premium puppy food in the right amounts, and is free of parasites, then it is time to work on some manners. Put the treat between your fingers. If you feel puppy teeth on your hand, do not give the treat; instead push the treat steadily—not suddenly—toward your puppy's nose. Push steadily enough that he moves his head back a few inches. Remove and offer the treat again. Do this "cause and effect" cycle until you get gentler interest—when that happens, give him the treat. This method assumes that the grab hurts but doesn't cause bleeding. If your puppy is really being fierce instead of simply overeager, please seek hands-on help from a qualified dog professional.

WHY IS ANTHROPOMORPHIZING BAD?

Anthropomorphizing is a big word for something we all do, at least a little: treat our puppy like a person. Now, dogs aren't humans but humans are, so we humans tend to relate to dogs like other people at first. Many people have said this is bad. It isn't. In fact, when you do that, *really* do that.

People who smile and pet a dog who comes up and nudges

If you had the same expectations for polite behavior from your dog as you did from another good friend, you'd be a better trainer and have a happier puppy.
SARAH WILSON

them aren't anthropomorphizing. If they were, they'd probably tell the dog to knock it off. If a child came up to you and nudged you for attention with the mandate of "Look at me right now!" we bet after a time or two (probably the first time for many parents) you'd say some version of "Excuse me? That isn't polite. Wait your turn." Or, if you are Sarah's mom, you would simply raise one eyebrow slightly, make very brief eye contact, then turn away. Unmistakable.

Can you imagine if you were walking out of your house and your spouse/friend raced up full speed and slammed into you to get out the door? How about if she or he ran across the room and leaped into your lap? (Might be fun the first few months of dating but after that, we bet you'd set a boundary but fast.) How about if someone came in and threatened your spouse with a knife for stepping close to you? Some ill-behaved dogs do this by snarling or growling when one family member approaches another. Would that knife threat be "cute"? Would you laugh and say "Oh, that's just Uncle Tommy—you know how he is!" So *please* anthropomorphize—then see what happens!

INTRODUCING THE COLLAR

Your pup's first collar should be a wide, non-tightening buckle collar. It should fit so only one or two fingers can be slipped underneath it. If it's too loose it could slide off or your puppy could get a paw or his jaw caught in it. Ready to introduce the collar? Good. Put it on. There, you've done it.

Most pups will scratch at it a bit, then ignore it. A few have a bigger reaction, rolling in protest or freezing in place, but they generally adapt if left alone to sort things out. If you want to go slower, you can put it on before each meal for a few days, letting him eat with the collar on, but generally this is not necessary. Puppies cope quite well given the chance to. *Hint:* Big-necked dogs like Bullmastiff, Bulldog, or Pitbull pups may need a martingale-type collar because flat collars sometimes slip right over their heads.

INTRODUCING THE LEAD

Many people recommend letting the pup drag a lead around to get used to it. We don't. We want the pup to learn immediately that her job is to move into any pressure, toward you.

- Got treats? Arm yourself with good treats, go to a quiet indoor area where *you* are the most interesting thing in the room and practice. Clip the lead to that wide, non-tightening collar. Now back up and apply light pressure toward you with the lead. Most pups will pull away. Hold steady. Do not add or subtract pressure. Do not drag the pup toward you. Just meet her pressure with yours. Squat down and encourage the pup to step toward you by speaking kindly and patting your leg.
- Slack is reward. When the pup leans even a bit in your direction, release all pressure, let the lead

Walking on lead is a skill every dog deserves to have. It keeps him safe and allows him to accompany you everywhere.

go slack and praise! (Verbally. Do not go to the pup to pet her—praise from where you are.) Good puppy!

- If the pup comes to you, great—praise and treat her! If she doesn't, that's fine too, she will in a second.
- Now gently take up the slack again, nice and easy so you apply pressure gently until the pup resists. Hold there. Again, do not add, do not subtract—just hold. When the pup steps toward you, give slack and praise! Soon your pup will be stepping toward you anytime she feels any pressure on the lead. Excellent! That's going to be a big help!
- Practice this daily until your pup walks all the way to you as soon as she feels any pressure on the lead. This is one of the few times in our training when you will hold a steady pressure. The purpose is to train your pup to step toward you when she feels slight pressure, rather than to pull away.

WALKING ON LEAD: WHAT CAN I EXPECT?

Expect to be doing a lot of teaching at first. Your puppy will be busy exploring, reacting to new sights and sounds, trying to greet (or avoid) every person on the sidewalk and generally being a typical puppy. What should you do? Well, do not follow obediently after a puppy who is dragging ahead of you like a lead dog on a sled team. Practice your Come (page 102) and Catch My Drift (page 99) everywhere you go. Use fences and buildings to practice Throw Your Wait Around (page 118). Do Look At Me (page 95) and Leave It (page 132). Guided Downs (page 92) are a start to having a good "emergency brake" Down later. Practice Left Circles (page 119), work a few rounds of Mine (page 82), notice with a smile and a treat any time your puppy looks up at you. Work your Simple Sits (page 153) at curbs and randomly on your walks. Place your puppy gently when he isn't responding. All of these games begin to develop good walking habits, which you can build on as your pup matures both mentally and physically. Alternatively, walk your puppy on a head halter for a few months as you do your homework in a quieter spot. As

The only way a dog can pull like this is if you pull back—you need to back up, squeeze/pulse and practice when he is calm. But, if you dress your puppy like this, we don't blame him for trying to get away.

you both improve, start asking for more on your walkabouts.

When Pip hit the streets with us soon after we got her, she was all over. Pulling ahead, lagging behind, cutting across our legs—normal, normal, and normal. We just started educating her. Now, she is walking happily at our left side on a loose lead. All the time? Usually, but when she has an impulsive moment, we just handle it, then start again. No big deal. We know this is a process. Our goal is progress, not perfection. We use skills you are about to learn—onward to Level I!

PUPPY PUTS PAW OVER LEAD

There are a few versions of this. First, the puppy gets tangled in the lead. This will happen. You reach down, untangle her and move on with the walk. Next, the puppy gets tangled the same way, the same foot, a few times every walk. This is a puppy who has learned to get your attention by getting tangled. Generally, if you simply keep walking, your puppy will untangle herself just as adeptly as she tangled herself. When she does, smile to yourself and proceed. When it stops working, she'll stop doing it.

CHAPTER 3

START LEVEL I

Level I can be started at any age. We start in small ways from the moment we meet our puppies, then add more games daily as the puppy settles in to a new life with us. Why? Because the puppy is learning his foundation habits right now anyway, there is no reason to let him learn unwanted ones. If he already has picked up a few less-than-ideal habits—leaping up on you, grabbing at things on the floor, struggling when being brushed, or shoving you out of the way at the door—you're not alone. Most people and puppies are in exactly that same spot. Start new ways today! The sooner you start the better! Here are your goals for the Level I Games:

MUTUAL AWARENESS

What do all good puppy/person teams have in common? They are constantly aware of each other. The puppy's awareness of where the handler is creates a puppy who is safer off-lead, who responds to Come quickly and consistently and who walks on lead without pulling. Puppies who aren't keeping their person in mind drag and run in all directions. Your awareness of your puppy prevents problems by helping your puppy make better choices.

GETTING TO GOOD

We want you to be positively focused, to watch for any bit of effort or good behavior on your puppy's part, and to pounce on it with praise, petting, treats, play, or whatever else your puppy enjoys. In any situation, ask yourself: How can I get to "Good!"? Then work toward that. Teach your puppy what you want, cause that behavior to happen, then reward what you caused! Your clear intention of having fun with your attentive, obedient puppy sets the stage here. Know what you want and then go for it!

PLAY PERSPECTIVE

Sure, some of this is work, but do you have to tell your puppy? When we humans work we tend to get serious, error focused, and dull in our emotions. When we play we smile, and we become focused on progress rather than problems. Our energy level rises. Develop a play perspective with your training. It is completely contagious; dogs "catch" our attitude as easily as our other good two-legged friends do. Joy is a goal: go for it!

COMMON LEVEL I CHALLENGES

Expecting Too Much

Think back to when you learned a new sport or watched some-one else learn it. Did you do it perfectly the first time at a tee, in a pool, on a basketball court, or sitting at a piano? The tenth time? The twenty-fifth? Probably not. And you had some idea of what you were trying to accomplish. Your puppy has no idea, and he has a novice teacher. When in doubt, cut your puppy slack!

Getting Frustrated

If you start thinking words like "stubborn" or "stupid," *stop!* You're getting frustrated. Go relax for a second and think about how confused both you and the puppy are. Just because you know what you mean to teach doesn't mean you're a great coach yet. Being a great coach takes time, so for now, have sympathy for and patience with your student.

Skipping Practice

Practice doesn't make perfect. Practice makes for better and better behavior, and that is what we're aiming for. Your puppy only learns when you teach. Period. So if you want your puppy to change his habits, you have to change yours first. How are you doing with that?

Going Too Fast

Sometimes when we humans get nervous, we speed up. Our hands, voices, and bodies move faster and all that movement confuses, stimulates, and distracts the puppy. So if your puppy is having trouble, slow down. If your puppy is too excited, calm down. Take a deep breath and let it out, then start again. Go slowly and watch for any effort in the right direction. When you see it, *praise*! Good job!

Being Too Quiet

Praise is free, so don't dole it out like gold. Shower your puppy with it; any small effort in the right direction gets a *"Good puppy! What a Smart Puppy!"* Stay quiet, then praise when your puppy gets it right! Make it crystal clear exactly what you enjoyed. That makes learning faster.

Working Too Hard for Too Long

Learning is hard, and the harder it is, the more breaks we all need. Taking short thirty-second breaks to commune with your puppy, gently scratching his favorite spots and using long slow strokes on his sides gives you both time to relax and enjoy each other. Try it and see how much better the next part of the session goes.

SPACE: MINE

Goal: A puppy who sits and looks at you whenever you get between your puppy and something he wants.

Mine is your first spatial command, meaning your space in relation to your puppy is the "command." If you or anyone else ever steps toward something your puppy wants, he should back up, sit, and look at the person. Why use space instead of a word? Why not just say "Leave it"? Because your friends or a visiting child might not know to say "Leave it," but they may still reach for something your puppy covets. Backing off when a human appears near something on the floor needs to be automatic. Mine is also a safety command. Our clients have been able to keep their puppies away from spilled medications, a broken jar of spaghetti sauce, and a dropped pot roast simply by stepping in front of their puppy.

- Put your puppy on lead. Face the puppy. Show the puppy a large but relatively uninteresting item—a toy or a big dry biscuit. Toss that well behind you and play goalie! Your task is to prevent the puppy from reaching the item. Use your body to block the puppy if she dives for it.
- Try not to let your puppy push you backward—don't lose ground. Block side to side. If you bump her, you bump her—she should get out of your way. Look for the moment the puppy hesitates, even the smallest amount. Praise and reward with

Pip jumps at the English muffin I toss down, but I quickly move to block. The moment she pauses, I praise and give her a treat! My Smart Puppy! ELI ORLING

a better treat from your hand. Good puppy!

- As soon as the puppy is noticeably slowing when you step in front, praise and have her sit. Then deliver the better treat.
- When puppy is stopping and sitting quickly, praise, speak her name, and be a bit patient. Wait for her to glance up at you. Good puppy! Excellent!

Having Trouble?

Puppy bulls past you to grab treat

Tether your puppy back or practice this in a doorway where it is easier to block effectively and play for success! Keep your knees bent and play as if you're blocking your puppy away from poison. Play with that intensity and you will succeed.

Puppy lunges for temptation item when you reach down to pick it up

Quite common. Place your foot between you and your puppy as a block. Don't snatch up the item; pick it up normally. If your puppy moves as you bend over, stand up, and step in front of her, making her back up a step or two. One or two steps are plenty—this is not a big deal.

Puppy pushes through legs

Close your knees on her and hold her there. If she backs up, good puppy. If she doesn't, wiggle your knees as you hold her. If she backs up, good puppy. If she doesn't, start shuffling forward. If she backs up, good puppy. This is to hold, not to hurt. Effective pressure will vary; less is more. Ramming between your legs is unsafe for you and for her, and for men it can be downright life altering.

Puppy walks away

She may be a little confused or overwhelmed, so try again. Now, try a more tempting item to toss and praise her more quickly for her first attempt at pausing. Reward her fast with a yummy treat and she'll start to hang around more.

Puppy does not look up

If your puppy is pausing well but not looking at you, be patient. No biggy; it's easy enough to fix. Say her name gently, try shuffling into her a bit—the moment she even glances up—praise, and treat. Soon she'll find you riveting.

You end up standing on item

Use a line of tape on the ground and stay on it. Do not get pushed around! Practice in a doorway or tether your puppy back if you need to, but don't get pushed back. Deal with this at fifteen pounds because you don't want to get body slammed when she is seventy-five pounds.

Puppy doesn't even try for the cookie, but sits and looks up right away

That's not a problem—that is success! Praise—yeah! Excellent! What a polite puppy you have.

HOW TO TETHER

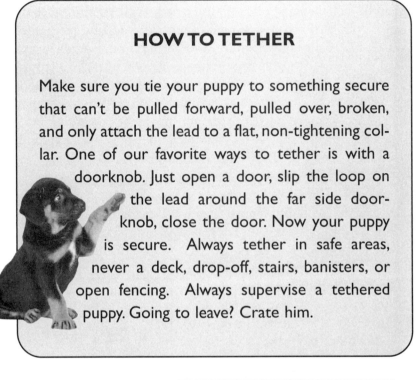

Make sure you tie your puppy to something secure that can't be pulled forward, pulled over, broken, and only attach the lead to a flat, non-tightening collar. One of our favorite ways to tether is with a doorknob. Just open a door, slip the loop on the lead around the far side doorknob, close the door. Now your puppy is secure. Always tether in safe areas, never a deck, drop-off, stairs, banisters, or open fencing. Always supervise a tethered puppy. Going to leave? Crate him.

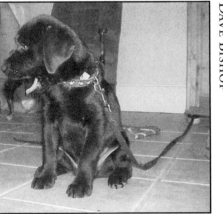

DAVE BISHOP

SPACE: OFF

Goal: For your puppy to keep four on the floor when you ask him to.

Jumping up is one of the most common puppy-owner complaints. It can be a challenging one because it is (a) a very natural behavior for your pup and (b) we tend to reward it at least every once and a while. First task: clean up *your* act! From this moment forward, be clear—stop rewarding jumping. Don't "try" to stop—stop. If you reward him just a little bit, say every third or fifth or tenth time, you've become a slot machine, and even puppies play the slots. If you're unclear how you might be rewarding your puppy for jumping, please see "Jumping on People" in Chapter 8, "Common Problems, Easy Solutions" page 303.

- Teach the Off signal. The one we use is a hand open in front of us, toward the puppy's nose. Think "stop" signal. Practice this with your puppy on lead. Back away from the puppy. As your puppy approaches you, put the flat of your hand out toward his face while taking a half step forward (putting your space in his face, as it were) and saying, Off (not "Down," "Down" means to lie down on the floor).

- Most puppies will rock back, surprised, and sit. Good puppy! Praise and treat. Excellent job!

- If your puppy jumps on you, go back and work your Mine and Wait Games some more.

- Still jumping? Try changing your level of intention. Next time you do this, imagine that he will be hurt if he jumps up on you, that his paws would burn if they touched you. Now block him as if you were saving his life. How'd it go that time?

Brian steps forward with a clear Off hand signal. Liz rocks back into a sit. That's good practice for when this bouncy puppy jumps up. SARAH WILSON

Having Trouble?

Puppy turns away

This may be more respect than lack of attention. Try a little less of a step forward and a bit of a slower hand signal, then praise warmly and be quick with the treat. That usually helps.

Puppy keeps right on jumping

Do more work on Mine until your puppy pays attention when you appear in front of him. This is important. If he's ignoring you now, don't expect him to become more compliant as he grows up. Press him off you with an open, flat hand directly against his nose. Press him—do not hit him or smack him—in one even, smooth motion. You stand upright. You're simply outlining your space. Nothing more. Nothing less. Once off, praise him warmly and give a treat. Or leave his lead on when you're home so you can step on it when he starts to jump. Step with your weight on the leg that is on the lead, and keep your knee slightly bent. Hand signal him Off, stay calm, wait for him to settle himself. Then praise verbally as touching or bending may start him jumping all over again.

Puppy jumps up and sits immediately

Oh, you two almost have it right! Past rewards have taught your puppy that jumping then sitting is what you want. So, play a new game. If his paws touch you, put a treat right to his nose, then put it away. Try again, stepping forward more boldly, and do so when your puppy is farther away from you. See if that works better.

OFF MY PLATE

Leaders own their food. Followers' plates get picked. If you relentlessly endure your puppy's assault on your food, you are training your puppy to see you as his follower. Use the Off hand signal you just taught. Sit on a chair with an unadorned bagel or piece of bread on a plate. When the puppy investigates, put your hand straight toward his face and lean forward. If he keeps coming, pulse your palm toward his nose. Is he still coming, pushing past you as if you're an obstacle in his path? Press him back, palm to nose and lean forward. If you need to, do a few rounds of Mine using a plate as the temptation, then try this again. When he backs off, briefly praise him verbally then pretend to eat. Do not stare at him or give him treats. Message? Don't bother me when I am eating.

TOUCH: PLACEMENT SIT

Goal: For your puppy to sit when you apply light pressure.

One of your primary tasks during puppyhood is to teach your little one that you are 100 percent consistent with your words, actions, and expectations. To us, a command—any command—is a promise to your puppy. When you follow through, you are keeping that promise. But you need a way to follow through that asks for your puppy's participation. This method does.

I apply light pressure, Pip moves away from that pressure into a sit and I praise. She doesn't much like that touch at first but that is just something to work through. Touch is a part of a companion dog's life. Soon she's used to it and responds quickly.
ELI ORLING

- Take your puppy's collar in one hand. This prevents your puppy from walking away. With your other hand make a "U" between your thumb and another finger and put that U just in front of your puppy's hip bones. Now, apply about the same amount of pressure you would to pick up a ripe peach. Hold it steady and pause.

- Ideally your puppy will stand for a moment, then move away from the pressure by starting to sit. Allow your puppy to move out from under your hand by sitting (or starting to sit). Good puppy! Now do it again. Soon your puppy will be sitting at the gentlest of pressures. *Note:* Only use a wide, flat, buckle collar.

Having Trouble?

Puppy doesn't sit

Be patient. Don't move your hands around. Say "Sit" as you apply the gentle guiding pressure. With a small percentage of dogs who really lock up, rocking the hips a bit side to side as you add a bit more pressure down and back can help them unlock. A bit. It is better to wait than to wrestle.

Puppy spins around

Some puppies will squirm at any touch. Stay calm, keep your hand on the puppy, and wait for the slightest move toward a sit. Release. Good puppy! *Note:* If you feel anything "moving around" in the hip area or hear anything, talk to your veterinarian.

Puppy lies down

Smile, take a few steps forward, encourage him to follow, and try again. Next time reach down to his chest and scratch it as he sits; this helps prevent lying down.

Puppy walks off

Got your hand on the collar? Then don't move! If your puppy is too strong for you, work him on lead in a small room and learn to control your puppy. He's not going to get any weaker as he matures.

TOUCH: GUIDED DOWN

Goal: For your puppy to lie down immediately when you apply light downward pressure.

This is one of the most useful exercises. Once you and your puppy understand each other, you'll be able to take him more places, control him better when he's distracted and, in general, manage him without argument or debate.

- Start on tile, linoleum, hardwood, or some other uncarpeted surface (if you can). Your puppy should be on lead and you should have treats in hand or within easy reach.
- With the pup sitting, hold a yummy treat in the hand closest to his head. Rest the other hand on his shoulders. Don't push; just rest. Put treat to your pup's nose, then slowly lower it down between his front feet. Slowly now—you need that nose. Once the nose is near the floor, slowly pull the treat away from the pup. Slowly. The complete move looks like an "L." As your puppy follows the treat into a down, say "Down."

- Do this for five or six sessions until your puppy responds happily and immediately to the lure.
- Now take your hand that was on his shoulders and add a *slight* downward pressure on the lead *as* you lure him into the Down. With slight pressure, you are making a suggestion to your puppy, not pulling on him. You apply enough pressure to feel your puppy—keep it there.
- Apply light pressure, say "Down," and lure all together at the same moment (or as close as you can manage). The *moment* your pup starts to Down, release the pressure. Release. The instant you release is the instant your puppy says "Oh, *that's* what she wants!" If you continue to apply the pressure all the way down (baby-sitting your puppy in the process, which is not what we want; we want the puppy learning to do things himself), then how does your puppy know when he has made the right choice?

As I lure Pip down with a treat, I add slight downward pressure on the lead. This links the act of lying down with that light pressure. When Pip lies down she earns praise and a treat.
ELI ORLING

• Now we move from luring to reward, meaning have a treat nearby but out of your pup's sight. Say "Down" as you apply the light pressure and make a hand motion as if you have a lure. When he follows your empty hand into a Down, praise him and give him the treat. Good job! *Note:* Lures appear before the behavior, rewards appear after. Start with lures but move to rewards as quickly as possible. If you stay with lures too long, the lure becomes the "command," and when there is no treat you get no response!

Here I apply light downward pressure without the lure. It takes Pip a moment to figure out what I want but when she does she earns praise and a treat. Good girl!
ELI ORLING

Having Trouble?

Puppy consistently pauses halfway

While we reward best efforts, we also need to be working toward what we want. So if he continually pauses, hold the pressure there—do not add or release it. Hold. And wait. Chances are good that in a second or three, he'll lie all the way down. You need to breathe and stay relaxed. Many times people start chanting the command, moving the lead around, or applying more or less pressure, all of which confuses the puppy. Stay calm, let him think it out, have faith in your puppy. There is no rush! Take your time, have some fun, and you both will get it!

Puppy fights pressure

Fighting is usually a sign of too much pressure downward. Remember, you are not pulling him down—you are teaching him a subtle cue that means Down. Also, *only* teach this on a flat buckle-type collar, nothing that tightens or has prongs. There is no discomfort with this, simply some gentle pressure.

Puppy not following treat

Use a better treat, slow down, reward his best effort. Try again! Reward what your puppy willingly gives you, then ask for more. Some puppies need to get treats for just lowering their head at first, later lowering it more and then lowering themselves.

Puppy stands up

Slow down. Usually this is because your hand is moving too fast or you're not lowering it straight down between the front paws first. Other trade secrets: Use a better treat or work on a slippery floor.

WHY DO I NEED THIS? MY PUPPY DOWNS FOR A TREAT?

Because one of these days, your puppy won't Down for the treat. Your puppy will be distracted or full or just not interested. At that moment you'll be left with few options, none of them good. You can repeat yourself until the puppy does it, which trains her to ignore your first command. You can wait until the puppy feels like doing it, which trains her that she doesn't need to respond quickly. Or you can get a better treat, which trains her that ignoring you brings improved rewards. "Down" is your puppy's emergency brake. Emergency brakes must work—all the time, every time.

ATTENTION: LOOK AT ME

Goal: Your puppy looks at you when he feels a squeeze/pulse on the lead.

Teaching your dog to look at you around distractions is the foundation of coming when called, dealing with distractions, and off-lead obedience—and it's so easy to teach!

• Start by putting a four-foot lead on your puppy indoors. Take a handful of treats and a mildly interesting item. Place the item—a toy maybe—on the floor, and have a couple of treats in your hand.

- Have your puppy Sit several feet away and say your puppy's name warmly as you squeeze/pulse the lead. This is one where you can repeat her name a few times if you need to at first. When she looks up, *praise*, smile, and hand her a treat as you back away from the temptation. Good job!
- Now go back to where you started, have her Sit, and play again.

Hazel, a delightful five-month-old Saint Bernard, gives Brian lovely attention as they work in a local parking lot. What a team!
SARAH WILSON

HOW TO SQUEEZE/PULSE

This is a foundation skill you need to learn. We use this because steady pressure on the lead easily creates steady resistance when walking. Put the thumb of your left hand through the loop of the lead and fold up the slack. Your lead is the correct length when the clip hangs down freely with your arms at belly-button level. There should be a slight "U" in the slack of the lead. Too tight and the clip doesn't hang down, too loose and the puppy can step over the lead. Now practice without your puppy at first. Open and close your fingers as if you were squeezing water out of a large sponge or making and unmaking a fist. This communicates with your puppy but doesn't hurt him in any way. You will use it many times throughout this book.

Having Trouble?

Puppy doesn't look at you

Start farther away from the distraction, praise more quickly, reward more quickly, squeeze/pulse the lead, pick a quieter area, wait until she is hungrier, use better treats— set her up for success! This can happen if you give a command only when your puppy is looking at you. Once the puppy learns this connection, he may avoid looking at you. His ears are not attached to his eyes, so say the command. Go to "No Eye Can" (page 167) for help with this.

Ready to Advance?

- Play this near her empty food bowl. Put a treat into her bowl, ask her to look up at you. When she does, smile, praise, then tell her "Get it" and point to the bowl. Let her get the treat out of the bowl.
- Toss a toy. Play Look At Me: When she does, send her to get it! Now you're on your way to having a puppy who looks for your permission before she chases after something. How nice!
- Play Look At Me outside or anytime your puppy is mildly distracted: Stop, Sit, expect her attention. *Praise* and *treat* when she looks up. Be enthusiastic when she looks your way!
- Play the Look At Me Game, then let your puppy go to greet your friend. Great start to gracious greetings! We want the message to your pup to be: Want *wonderful* things to happen? Then look at me!

SARAH WILSON

DARE TO BE EFFECTIVE

A young Golden Retriever slammed into a weekend class recently, flinging himself against the lead at full Incredible Hulk force. His owner dragged behind, making no effort to stop him. When we pointed out that following him rewarded his pulling, she said she knew but didn't know what to do. When we suggested pretraining attention with games like Look At Me (page 95) and Catch My Drift (page 99), she said she was uncomfortable using the lead in that way. When we pointed out that the yanking he was doing was uncomfortable for *him* and that what he did to himself was far more pressure on his neck than we would ever suggest using, she replied she could see that but what he did to himself was okay with her but she could not *intentionally* pulse the lead. We suggested a head halter. She said she was uncomfortable with them. So off they went, both the dog and the owner at physical risk because she refused to be his teacher, refused to be effective. If that lead breaks, she will not be able to get him back. He will not be welcome at her friends' homes. He will be no fun to take on long walks. Her "beliefs" will quickly become his prison.

ATTENTION: CATCH MY DRIFT

Goal: For your puppy to move when you move and stop when you stop automatically without any spoken command.

Do you dream of walking *with* your puppy instead of being walked *by* your puppy? Of walking through a field off-lead with your puppy paying close attention to where you are? Of walking past distractions with complete puppy attention? This game can help make that dream a fun reality. Enjoy!

- Play this in a quiet area with your puppy on lead. Praise him warmly as you start to walk. When he drifts (or shoots) past you, back away from him in a straight line, squeeze/pulse the lead, and say his name. When he looks at you, smile and praise him. If he comes to you, hand him a treat.
- If he stops to sniff, keep walking while you squeeze/pulse the lead. Do not stop unless your puppy is actually going to the bathroom.
- Now drift slowly to a stop. This is a game of connection, not of "faking out" your puppy. When you stop, your puppy should stop. If he doesn't (and few pups do at first), back up, squeeze/pulse the lead until he looks up at you, then smile and praise calmly. Then drift to a stop again. Repeat until he stops when you stop. When he does— praise and give him a treat.

This talented young handler is backing up, with a loose lead and a grin. Her Shiba happily matches her step-for-step. They are dancing! ROXANNE FRANKLIN

- If he loses focus, do something—turn, shuffle into his space, do several Simple Sits (page 153) but act. Leading and following are the goals here. It is your puppy's job to watch you, not you to police him. When he does focus—smile, reward, and praise him. Good puppy.
- Start off with ten second sessions and work up to a game you can play for a minute or more. You'll be amazed just how clear you get with your body language when you stay silent.
- We don't say "Let's go" as much anymore, because the "command" for good on-lead behavior is being on lead.

Having Trouble?

Puppy won't follow

Keep moving, pulse the lead, and move. Do not drag but do not hesitate either. Pulse and *go!* Remember, pups follow moving feet. If your feet aren't moving, your puppy cannot follow. When you stop stopping, your puppy will stop stopping.

Puppy gets distracted

A light collar squeeze/pulse while picking up your speed and sounding more excited will bring most pups back to attention

Restraint creates resistance. Pulling back on a puppy only makes the puppy pull forward more. Catch My Drift, Simple Sit, and Look At Me could help this pair get to good. SARAH WILSON

easily. If your puppy is distracted often, do shorter sessions, pick a quieter area to work, use treats your puppy finds fascinating, reward more frequently, or throw more praise parties. Your job is to sell your puppy on what fun you are having. So sell!

Puppy sniffs nonstop

First, does he need to urinate or defecate? If he does, take a potty break. Is this too distracting a spot to work right now? If yes, find a quieter location. If he is still sniffing, try this: When his head goes down, shuffle into his space. Keep shuffling, gently bumping him as you do so. When he looks up, stop, praise, and treat him, then back away to start the game again. Usually this gets a pup's attention.

KEEP TRYING!

Your pup is not stupid and neither are you. You're both learning, and one definition of "learning" is trial and error. You're in the error phase. Everyone passes through that—more than once. Don't give up. Find a new way, try an old way but do it a little differently, try focusing on a tiny piece of the larger behavior and rewarding that, try looking at things from your puppy's point of view, but keep trying! Effort is a far better indicator of success than innate skill. Don't give up!

REQUIREMENT: COME: BASICS

Goal: Your puppy links the word "Come" with good things near you!

A blazing off-lead Come when called is every owner's dream because it shows that their puppy will stay connected and attentive, even at a distance. If anything will save your puppy's life someday, it is this—a consistent Come. Like all off-lead work, such a wonderful thing is built on the basics. Here is where you start:

- With your puppy sitting in front of you, say "Puppy (use your dog's name) Come!" brightly and clearly. Give your puppy a treat. Repeat. What is the point of *this*? The point is we're linking the word "Come" with being fed a treat while sitting in front of you. And since every Come should end this way, this is a critical (and ridiculously easy) step. Do this before each meal, three to five times using his kibble. Total elapsed time: Ten seconds.
- Next, since Come involves your puppy turning back toward you, coming, and then sitting in front of you, practice that whole sequence on a four-foot lead. Allow your pup to wander a bit on lead indoors. When he is distracted (and really, when isn't he?), back up, squeeze/pulse the lead, say "NameComeGoodPuppy!" all in the same breath. *Praise* as you back up.
- As he approaches happily, slide one hand down the lead so that when he arrives you have good control over him. Reach in and handle his collar as you praise him and deliver a treat. What a Smart, Smart Puppy!

As Liz, a six-month-old Tibetan Terrier approaches, Brian slides his hand down the lead so he can make sure he "gets to good" quickly by helping her to remember to sit. SARAH WILSON

What nice attention and connection. Keeping that right hand lower and the lead slack would be better but, other than that, what a team!
ROXANNE FRANKLIN

Having Trouble?

Puppy doesn't look up at you

Are you delivering the treat to him when his head is turned away? If yes, then you've trained him to have his head turned away. Next time, put the treat to his nose, bring your hand slowly up to your belly button, and, as he looks up, smile, praise, and reward. He'll catch on!

Puppy wanders off

Have him on lead, back up a few steps, squeeze/pulse the lead, and call him again. Try a calmer location and/or a better treat. If these things don't work, try shuffling into his space and making him move out of your way. Often this will get your puppy to look up at you—at that moment, praise and reward!

Puppy doesn't come; he resists the lead

Are you backing up as you are squeezing/pulsing the lead? Move your feet when you want him to move his. So back up! Are you applying steady pressure on the lead, hauling on him? If yes, your puppy will resist coming forward. If you squeeze/pulse too hard, your puppy may be confused and back up. If you continue to squeeze/pulse *as* your puppy moves toward you, he may figure that isn't what you want and try something else, like resisting.

Puppy races to you and leaps up on or at you

Sliding your hand down the lead faster so he doesn't have slack when he gets to you should prevent it. Then work on your Off to teach him to respect your personal space more.

My puppy isn't wandering!

That is GREAT! Good for you—gold star! Back up and call him anyway. You're ready to work outside on lead a little bit. That usually gets a puppy distracted!

TWO-TREAT GAME

Here's a great Come game you can play from your living room chair. Take two small treats, have your puppy sit next to you, and take his collar with one hand then toss one of the treats several feet out in front of you. Insist that he Sit. When he does and shows even a second of self-control, release him with a happy "Take it!" Once he grabs that treat, call him back to you with "Puppy, come, good puppy!" As he comes to you, lure him to a sit with the last treat and give it to him as you praise! Good job! When this goes well, start adding a bit of Look At Me. After the toss, he must look at you to be released to "Take It." This is a fun sixty-second session that gives you practice on Sit, Look At Me, Take It, and Come that you can do from a chair during commercial breaks. Fun!

REQUIREMENT: STAY: BASICS

Goal: Stay right there until I return and tell you it is time to move.

Stay used to be a chore to teach and a bit confusing to the dogs, but no more. Even a young, active pup can quickly learn to Stay for brief periods using these methods. From there, it is not difficult to build a long, solid Stay.

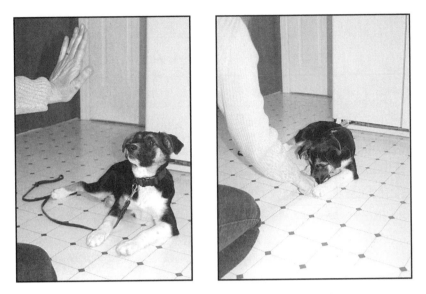

Flat of hand out toward puppy as I say "Stay" then a treat is delivered between the front paws. Pip thought this was such a great deal, she refused to move after the first few times.
ELI ORLING

- Tether your pup back (page 85). This must be done.
- Down your puppy. Say "Stay" as you use your hand signal (open palm toward face in a "stop right there" signal), then place a treat between his front paws. (Yes, between his front paws, not from your hand.)
- Repeat: Say it, Signal it, Reward it. Quietly verbally praise throughout, but avoid using his name. Use his name to get his attention or call him to you, not to praise him in Stay.
- We want your pup to link Stay with food between his front feet. It's a sweet deal: Lie there and I tell you you're great and you get goodies. Most pups start to enjoy this game quickly. If your pup is confused about where the treat is, point it out a few times—he'll catch on!
- After a few treats have been given, release him with a tap on his shoulders while you say his name. Why the tap on the shoulder? Because that is a clear signal to your puppy and it forces you to return all the way to your puppy. This makes

things clear to your puppy and helps prevent problems, such as getting up when you walk away from him, from developing.

Having Trouble?

My pup gets up before I release him

Stay calm and guide him back down—no big deal. If you react in any way, your pup may start to use movement to attract your attention when he is bored or you are doing something else. Nope, if he gets up, just calmly replace him. Say little or nothing. Once he's down, continue. Also, have you been backing away saying "Stay, stay, stay," then calling your puppy? This teaches your puppy that you want him to get up and come to you, and now he is doing just that. Have you been giving him treats from your hand? If yes, then you are training him to focus on your hand and he will be more prone to getting up as you approach.

He doesn't get up when I release him

This is a good problem because your puppy is basically saying "I love this stay game so much I'd rather just stay here." Excellent attitude and bravo to you! Now, tap him on the shoulder, say his name, then either toss a treat behind him so he gets up to go get it, or show him a treat and lure him up into a sit or stand. Praise! Good puppy!

Puppy crawls forward

This is why we use a tether. When tethered, your pup cannot crawl and so cannot learn that this is even possible. In the unlikely event that he starts, go back to the tether and be sure you feed from the floor, not from your hand. And then go find out who's been calling him out of Stay.

HOW "STAY" CAN BECOME A SCARY WORD

Sarah helps competitive-obedience people fix their Stay problems. Maybe their dog crawls toward them on the Stay, pants or drools, shakes, or tries to leave the ring. In most cases, Stay has become stressful because it became a no-win situation for the dog. Instead of teaching small pieces with success, Stay training went too fast. The dog got confused, and got up (often to come to the handler for reassurance) only to be corrected back to Stay. This stressed the dog more, caused him to want to come to his person even more which, led to more correction and soon the dog comes to fear/hate Stay. As far as the dog is concerned, their human becomes cranky and unpredictable around Stay. Turn it around. Create a "no mistake" setup, allow the dog to "get to good," and dogs are often more than delighted to Stay.

- After a few seconds, step back out of sight. When you do, go silent, look away, drain all the energy from your body. Become hugely boring. Count to ten and start again.
- Repeat this pattern until your puppy is excitedly focused on you when you step back into view of this distraction. When will that happen? Who knows? It might take one session, might take several. It doesn't matter. This is not a race. When your pup is relaxed and happy, then move a little closer.
- You'll know you have succeeded when that car that used to make your puppy erupt into barking now makes him look up at you with a "Gotta treat?" look on his happy face. Well done!

Having Trouble?

Puppy isn't making progress

Are you too close? Could you be more fun, more enthusiastic, when you're feeding? Are you playing this like a game? Too often people defer to the puppy, getting quieter as the puppy gets quieter. That's no help. Act the way you want your puppy to act!

Puppy pays no attention to the distraction

Is this still working? Yes! Well done! Go a little closer next time and see if things stay relaxed.

Puppy was doing great but is now getting worse

Maybe you moved a bit too quickly. Go back to where you are successful. Work there, have fun, see if your puppy improves. If he does, then you probably went a bit too quickly for him.

TRUST: NEAR IS DEAR

Goal: Your puppy relaxes quickly when around exciting/scary things.

Whether your puppy wants to chase cars, bark at the neighborhood kids, or hide from your guests, Near Is Dear gives you a way of changing your puppy's mind. Our job is to change his emotional reaction to one of calm acceptance.

- Put puppy on lead, grab a handful of really good treats, and step into view of whatever your puppy wants, barks at, runs away from, or chases. When you step into view of it, at a distance where your puppy is aware of it but not overwhelmed, you smile, praise, and treat, treat, treat.

I put down the bread and hold on tight to Pip. Even though my hand is out to block, Pip dives for the food the instant she is released. I block—pressing her away. This is not violent, this is definite. The message: Do not push through me. When Pip pauses, I praise and treat (from the hand not used for blocking). I set it up again and now Pip pauses. Smart Puppy! Total training time: less than 2 minutes! ELI ORLING

CHAPTER 4

START LEVEL II

ongratulations! You've made it through Level I! That makes you one of a special group of dog lovers: people who want a deeper connection with their puppies and who understand that training is the way to freedom. At Level II, you will build on the skills started in Level I, moving you toward a connection that goes beyond equipment, treats, or location. You will start some hands-on handling work and develop a reliable Out. Here you will really start to understand what we mean by *"It's not the lead that connects but the connection that leads."*

BEYOND BRACING

A dog—of any age—can brace against you physically and mentally. Our Level II goal is to help you recognize bracing when it happens, to get your puppy past it and into mental participation with you as quickly as possible. As a My Smart Puppy person, you know to stop everything else you're planning and deal with the brace when it happens.

CONFIDENT LEADERSHIP

As your skills improve, your confidence will increase. As your confidence increases, your puppy's confidence in you increases accordingly. Be your puppy's best coach. Make things fun, have high expectations while holding the thought that you may well be the root of most of the confusion. Work on clarity of intention; have a picture in your mind of exactly what you want from your puppy. Then try things. If they don't work, try again or try something new. Lead! Your puppy will love you for it.

CONSISTENTLY CONSISTENT

If you think it is hard to remember the right word or action, imagine what it is like for your puppy. She's only been on this planet for a few hundred days or less, she's not our species and she has no inkling of what you might want—that puppies learn at all from us is a *miracle*. Being inconsistent is a type of cruelty, like some nasty older sibling teaching a toddler the wrong words to use or changing the rules midgame then yelling at the toddler for getting it "wrong." The more control you have over another's life, the bigger your obligation to make sense, be consistent, and be kind. Being consistently consistent isn't easy, but it makes things so much easier for your puppy!

COMMON LEVEL II CHALLENGES

Hesitation

In Level I, you actively caused behaviors to happen. Because things were new and you were new at them, you were attentive and followed through quickly. As your puppy's skills grow, you may have started expecting responses a bit prematurely, waiting to "see what he was going to do" rather than making sure he did it. This waiting causes hesitation. Since puppies respond at the point when you cause the behavior to happen, your puppy starts to hesitate right along with you. Your puppy always reflects his or her current understanding. If you don't want your puppy to hesitate, follow through promptly.

Magic Thinking

If your puppy has stolen your toast from the coffee table several times why would you leave some there again to answer the phone, thinking he won't take it this time? That's magic thinking. Reality-based thinking dictates that you would expect that

These two Samoyeds, one of them a six-month-old puppy, wait patiently for a cookie because that's what they've been consistently taught to do. Good job!
SARAH WILSON

your puppy will do what he is being trained to do. Trained? You say, I am not training him to steal my toast. Oh, yes you are. You are setting up the situation, he is getting a major reward for doing what you set up—that is training. Stay reality based; your puppy will, too.

Thinking That Dog Training Is about the Dog

Nope. If you want your puppy to change what she is doing, you must change what you are doing first. There's no other way to do it—sorry. When you embrace your role, your puppy will change—faster than you can imagine.

Relentless Understanding

Sarah's mother ran schools for years, and what did she teach Sarah about parenting? To guard against "relentless understanding," or the urge to love the child by constantly excusing all behaviors as endlessly acceptable. With no boundaries, the child flounders. His floundering causes a flurry of new "understanding" and the child is caught in the vortex of parental confusion. The same cycle can happen with puppies. "She had a bad life," "Her breed/mix can't do that," "She's upset or excited," or "She doesn't like it" or—Stop! Have rules and enforce them calmly, kindly, but consistently. The result? A balanced, happy dog who is a joy to live with.

SPACE: WAIT

Goal: A puppy who stops and sits when you pivot in front of him.

Teaching your puppy to wait—pause for a moment until further instruction—is basically a moving version of Mine. Use this around open doors, getting out of cars, at curbs before you cross the street, and when she sees something distracting during a walk. It also starts to teach your puppy how to walk next to you on lead rather than to pull ahead. Yeah!

- Find a barrier you can work along: a couch, a coffee table, a row of chairs, a fence, the side of a building, a wall. Walk so your puppy is between you and that barrier. Now pivot in front of your puppy, blocking his path. Think of your body as a door closing in front of your puppy. Your puppy should stop and look up at you. Praise! What a Smart Puppy!
- Work along barrier. If the puppy tries to rush, pivot in front, then shuffle into her, making her back up a step or two. These are penalty yards for playing off sides.

Having Trouble?

Puppy doesn't stop, but pushes right on past

Do more Mine and Off work from Level I. Play this until the puppy consistently stops and looks at you without touching you

There are moments when Wait *is more than important.*

at all. Warm up with a couple rounds of each, then try Wait again. That should help.

Puppy is never next to you, instead is always ahead

If she does this you can back up and practice Come, you can hold a delicious treat in your left hand feeding her when she appears in the correct position, you can get in front of your puppy and shuffle into her, backing her up a bit, or you can do Wait every step or two at first. Is your lead too long? Try shortening it up a bit.

Puppy is always cutting in front of you to the right

Take your treat out of your right hand. Don't feed her from your right hand. Hold the treat or the toy in your left hand instead.

Also, make sure you're leaving enough room for your puppy. Herding breeds who tend to feel closed in can scoot forward out of the pressure. Left Circles, the next exercise, can help a lot with this as well.

Puppy is nervous to step into the space

Some dogs are more sensitive to close spaces than others, herding dogs often being the most sensitive of all. If your puppy lags behind, not wanting to step up next to you, then dashes forward through the open space, step to your side and give her a bit more room. Make this a game, praising her happily when she braves this new experience! You may walk within a foot of the barrier with a tiny toy-breed puppy, but with a herding-breed youngster you may need to be three or more feet off to the side.

THROW YOUR WAIT AROUND

"Wait" teaches your puppy that you need the space right in front of his nose. That explains to him better than most things exactly why walking next to you makes sense. Want to create walking on a nice loose lead? Then Throw Your Wait Around! Work along a fence or wall. Start with a Wait every couple of steps. Smile, praise, and reward your puppy well each time. As he starts hanging back a bit, ready for the next Wait, take a few more steps. Soon you'll be walking a hundred feet or more with your puppy relaxed and in perfect position. Now that's a great start to great walking!

SPACE: LEFT CIRCLES

Goal: For your puppy to stay out of your way when you walk.

Doing Left Circles with your puppy has many wonderful benefits and one common problem. The benefits include teaching
your puppy to walk in the traditonal left-side heel position, to
give ground when you cut in front, and to pay attention to you.
The one common problem is that if you look down at your
puppy nonstop, you'll get dizzy. Eyes up! Look where you are
going!

- Find large things you can put on the floor in a line for you to
  circle around. Chairs are great, but people have used cans,
  buckets, boots, cones—whatever. These are really just physical
  targets for you to circle around. Start off with your puppy on
  your left between you and the item you're circling. Walk
  toward the chair, then circle to the left, counterclockwise,
  around it. Look where you are going. Be sure to leave enough
  room for your puppy.

*Using a chair to work
around, I start my Left
Circle. This delightful
Shiba Inu puppy is paying
close attention!*
ROXANNE FRANKLIN

Brian and Liz work Left Circles around a cone. Her job is to stay out of his way and she is. Good puppy! SARAH WILSON

- Hold the lead and a treat in your left hand. Put the treat to his nose quickly so he knows you have the treat there. This can help him stay focused on your left. If you carry your treats in your right hand and/or feed with your right hand, your puppy will cut in front of you to get to the treat. Not at all helpful here.
- Start off with a few Waits, then move to some Left Circles. If he pulls ahead, he will get bumped as you turn left. Cause and effect. You did not seek to bump him; he was in your path. You simply allowed the natural result of that choice to happen. Notice the word we used: bump. Not kick or slam or ram. We are aiming for annoying, not painful. You walk normally. The exception? Toy-breed puppies. For them, keep your feet close to the ground and shuffle on through.
- Avoiding your pup won't help him learn. Bump him in the course of your normal turn. When he gets out of your way, praise him. Once you complete one circle, head toward the next target.
- Play this game indoors until you both can manage a Left Circle without bumping into each other.

Having Trouble?

Puppy continually bumps you

Next time it happens, pivot in front of him, shuffle into him making him back up a step or two. Those are penalty yards for being off sides. Your puppy still bumps you? Pivot in front of him and back him up with clear intention, then you turn and resume without comment. Be ready to praise when he gets out of your way next time! Still happening? Work your Mine and Off some more. This puppy needs to learn to respect your space.

Puppy cuts to your right

Normal (and smart). Make sure you are leaving enough room between you and the chair for him as well. If there's no room for him, he has to go somewhere. Herding breeds/mixes can need more space than others, sometimes needing up to a three-foot space to feel comfortable. If there is plenty of space, then do you have a treat in your right hand or pocket? If you do, he may be cutting to those. Get them into your left. You can try luring him a bit with the treat in your left hand. Stop and reward every step or two he makes. As he understands the game, ask for more. Or, if he cuts behind, you can keep walking as you pulse the lead forward with your left hand. This will bring the puppy back around to your left side. When he's there, release any pressure on the lead and praise!

Puppy grabs lead

First, make sure it isn't dangling in his face. Shorten it up so the lead has a little slack when your puppy is in the correct position. Spray the lead with an anti-chew product. Do that daily. Are you holding him tight all the time? We see many puppies protest this with a lead grab. Or, using a breath spray, spritz the lead where his mouth is holding it. Don't go at him or spray his face—just spray the spot on the lead where his nose is and continue.

TOUCH: CALM = RELEASE

Goal: For your puppy to stay calm and relaxed when handled.

We want you to be able to touch your puppy at will without being mouthed, head butted, scratched, or having to wrestle. To make this a reality, handling needs to become a daily habit. Not the petting you are already doing—that doesn't count. Passive restraint means that you keep your dog in a position for as long as you wish while being as calm as you can be.

- Sit with the puppy between your knees, facing the same way you are. If you can't kneel easily, sit on a low bench or some pillows. If that doesn't work, use a couch or chair that your puppy cannot back underneath.
- Giant-breed and older puppies, whose heads are close to your head level when you kneel, should be handled from a chair or couch to prevent skull-to-face contact if the puppy swings her head up and back.
- Hook your thumb of one hand through the collar, and keep that hand by the neck/jaw area. This hand controls your puppy's mouth if she starts to protest.

Skippy, a Collie, naps blissfully as he is gently restrained and massaged. If he is ever injured or needs help, he can now get it without a battle. Well done! BARRY ROSEN

- Do not lean over your puppy when she struggles, as we do not want you smacked in the face if her head swings around. Breathe evenly, be as relaxed as you can be. Most puppies settle quickly after an initial burst of activity.
- Your other hand scratches her chest and is ready to help restrain her if she bucks, squirms, mouths, yips, or otherwise complains. Stay calm. Your hands stay as relaxed as they can. Wait it out. When the puppy stills, you calmly release him without comment or fanfare. Lesson for the pup: Calming causes release. This lesson is best learned when your puppy is relatively small because it doesn't get easier as she grows bigger, weighs more, and gets more coordinated.

Having Trouble?

Puppy struggles a lot

If one hand is under his neck and on his collar, you should be able to prevent mouthing, but if you cannot, try using a head halter while you practice. Remember, keep your hands as relaxed as possible, slow and kind on your puppy. Say kind, calm things. Act the way you want her to act. Work when your puppy is calm. Pip is a sweet, sleepy pup late at night. We started Calm = Release then. Release when the puppy is calm for a few seconds—don't ask for more at first. Remember that all you're doing is asking him to sit and be stroked. If he's having a tantrum about that, this definitely needs work!

Puppy doesn't struggle at all

In most cases, great! This is not a problem. Just be happy you have such a relaxed and easy puppy. In some cases a shy puppy may be frozen in place, immobile from fear rather than compliance. If his body is tense, his head isn't moving, and/or his mouth is closed tight, keep things short and sweet. Lightly massaging down his back can help to reduce his stress. Your puppy should start relaxing soon.

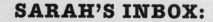

TOUCH: GUIDED DOWN, THE NEXT LEVEL

Goal: For your puppy to Down quickly and stay Down for longer.

Now you're about to get to the really useful stage of Down. You're going to learn how to get your puppy to Down quickly and to stay Down. This is most helpful when visiting friends, when you're trying to get something done, or when your puppy is just so silly, demanding, or annoying that you need him to stop for a few minutes. You have to have the persistence and the patience to allow your puppy to think a few things through, but once she has this useful skill, life gets much easier for both of you.

- You've worked the slight pressure on the lead exercise from Level I. Your puppy now Downs fairly quickly when you do that. Good. Now, take a seat. Your puppy is in her wide, flat, non-tightening collar, right?
- Now, while seated, slide your foot over the lead, and say "Down," as you slowly tighten the lead until you feel light resistance. Hold it there. Your puppy may be confused by this at first. Be patient. Stay calm. Lean your weight over the foot on the lead. Don't adjust. Don't stare at him. Just stay the course.

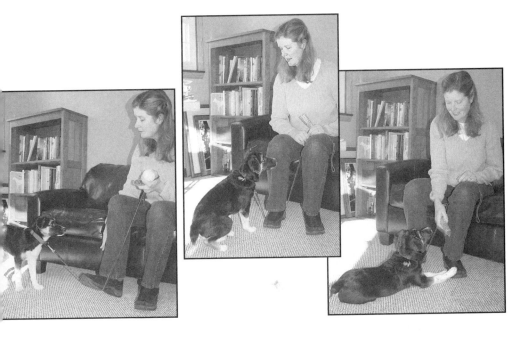

This is Pip's first lesson at this level. Because of the Level I pretraining we did, it all makes sense. She Downs quickly.
ELI ORLING

- If your puppy is still standing up after thirty seconds, take up another half-inch of lead. Wait. Take it up again, half an inch at a time. No rush.
- Should you repeat the spoken "Down" command? No need, just wait. Your lead is saying "Down" loud and clear.
- Since your goal is eventually to have a puppy who Downs at a distance, it is important that she starts to learn how to lie down without you bending over, pointing to the ground, or otherwise coaching her. Let the collar cue be the coach. She'll get it!
- When she does lie down, look at her, stroke her down her back, smile, put a treat on the floor between her front paws. What a good, Smart Puppy! Chances are good she'll try to stand back up again. When she does the lead will tighten again. Look away, get quiet, and let her work it out. When she lies back down, look at her, smile, and put a treat on the floor between her front feet.
- Start by keeping your toe on the lead for a minute at a time, working up to five minutes. Do this every day when you are eating a meal or watching TV or taking a break.

What lovely connection this young handler shares with her Shiba Inu puppy. She is praising his good behavior and he is loving it.
ROXANNE FRANKLIN

Having Trouble?

Puppy struggles

Do a few more sessions of the Level I lure plus slight downward lead pressure. Try again. Move to a more slippery floor like the kitchen or hardwood. Try less pressure, try calmly praising when the puppy is still, praise when he makes any move to lie down.

Puppy sits there looking around

Give it a minute. If she's looking around, she's not overly stressed. If she stays there for a minute or so, take up a little more lead so you apply a little more pressure. Pause there for a minute or so. Soon she will tire and lie down. Next time it will take about half the time it did the first time, then half again, then half again, and then it will be done. Forever. So relax.

Puppy wanders about

Stand still. If you shift around, your puppy may mirror you and move with you. If this is hard for you, try sitting in a chair. If the puppy still wanders, chances are you need to shorten the lead. Do so slowly, a bit at a time, until you feel your puppy resist slightly. Pause there.

Lead is tight even when puppy is lying down

Loosen it up. You always want the correct response to be met with immediate slack on the lead. Not only because that slack signals success for your puppy but because you don't want to teach your puppy that tension means "Stay put" and slack means "All done." Although that is a common mistake, it is the exact opposite of what we want your puppy to learn. We need your puppy to know that slack means "Success, well done!"

This lead isn't holding Pip down but if she gets up the lead will cue to her down again.
ELI ORLING

DISTANCE DOWNS

Since Down is your puppy's emergency brake, it should work at all distances, but it won't at first. Remember, your puppy is a literal being. So far, Down has always meant lie down at my feet. Since that is what you taught, that is what he believes. Now we're asking him to Down at a distance. This can confuse a puppy as much as me saying "Hug me, but don't step any closer." You'd have no idea how to comply.

Start with your puppy tethered back. Have a second lead coming out to you. In a perfect world, your puppy has two collars on—one attached to the tether and the other to the long line. Set yourself up for success by starting off close to your puppy and running the long line under your foot. This way, if you need to assist, you can with ease. Say "down." If he does, praise him as you step back to him, delivering a treat between his front paws along with some well-deserved petting. If he is confused, slowly tighten the long line until there is slight pressure on him and wait. Do not attempt to force him down. This pressure is a reminder—nothing more. When he Downs, smile and praise him. Good job! Slowly increase your distance as your puppy is successful. As your puppy catches on, change locations, always using a tether, starting close, and rewarding him well for success.

This puppy is watching closely as she does her first Distance Down. Notice how she is tethered back and on a long line.
ROXANNE FRANKLIN

ATTENTION: DOOR CHORES

Goal: Your puppy waits for you before going through an open door.

We want your puppy to be safe. Running out an open door is dangerous so we want to stop that. We don't use a spoken command because people who don't know that command will open your door. Making this a situational command, where the open door is the cue to look at you before leaving, is the best choice.

- First, put the pup on a four foot lead. Say nothing, just open the door. The pup will rush out. That's okay, we expect that. As he steps north, you step south. Simply back up, squeeze/pulsing your puppy back into the house.
- Move with confidence as you back up. This is straight cause and effect. His bolting out the door causes you to back up into the house. When the pup is inside again, you praise him and smile. Then try it again.
- Soon, when you open the door your pup won't go out—he'll look at you. At that moment, praise him warmly and step through together, as a team. Good puppy! Better trainer!

Hazel pauses at the open door. Notice the slack lead, Brian is not restraining her. He is both ready to call her back if she wanders through and has his hand in his pocket getting a treat. SARAH WILSON

Well done Hazel! Time for a big smile, praise, and a treat! SARAH WILSON

Having Trouble?

Puppy continues to bolt out

Does she need to go? Don't try to train when a puppy is desperate to get out to the bathroom area. First things first. Train after she drains. Are you being clear? Back up more briskly, speed up your pulsing (faster, not harder), and insist that your puppy come several feet back into the house before you reapproach the door. Be as matter-of-fact as your puppy is. Most delays are caused by owners hesitating or waiting for their puppy. Nope. As always, you lead, puppy follows.

Puppy starts to avoid door

Then have him sit and treat him for sitting next to you. Take a little mental break then repeat the exercise. You may be too brisk for this puppy, in which case you need to slow down, reward the best effort, and reward more frequently.

STAIR SAFETY: THE SAME GAME

We know people who have broken arms, dislocated shoulders, smashed facial bones, lost teeth, and damaged their vision from dogs dragging them down stairs. This game prevents that. Once your puppy is waiting for you solidly at the door, apply the same game to the stairs. Start on a short set of nonslippery stairs. If your puppy races ahead of you, turn and walk back up the stairs—be brisk, have clear intentions. Pulse, don't drag. Try again. Soon your puppy will be making a real effort to stay closer. Much better!

ATTENTION: LEAVE IT

Goal: For your puppy to turn back to you the moment he feels the jiggle on the lead.

Leave It is a moving version of Look At Me. Since you've already done a great job with that game (if you haven't, go back and work on that before you attempt this), this is a logical next step.

- Toss a so-so item on the floor. The moment your puppy looks at it say, "Leave it," back up, and squeeze/pulse the lead. The *moment* his head starts to turn in your direction, praise him! Wahoo! What a Smart Puppy! Allow him to come to you for his treat—don't go to him.
- Anytime your puppy becomes distracted, say Leave It as you back up, squeeze/pulsing the lead. The moment—the *instant* — he glances back at you, throw a praise party! Allow him to come back to you and give him a treat. Stroke him and tell him

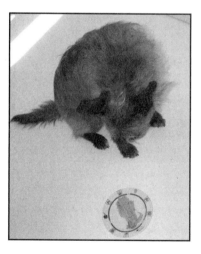

Leave It is one of the most useful commands. Here our PJ toughs it out next to a plate of ham.
SARAH WILSON

PJ looked (what dog wouldn't) but she didn't take any until I told her she could. This makes things easier for you and safer for her. Good dog, PJ! SARAH WILSON

how wonderful that was. Leave no doubt in his mind that you love that behavior!

- Repeat. When he looks back at you almost automatically, start to make the game a little more challenging. Put a toy on the floor and walk toward it. The moment his ears lock forward and he looks at the toy, say "Leave it," back up, and squeeze/pulse the lead. Keep backing. Keep pulsing. Look for that first glance—What a Smart Puppy!

Having Trouble?

Puppy doesn't stop looking at the item

The most common cause? You're not moving backward away from the item and/or you're not squeeze/pulsing the lead. If you don't move, your puppy won't break concentration on the item. If you don't squeeze/pulse, he will just lean against the lead and resist you. Next time, start backing up and squeeze/pulsing sooner or stay a little farther away.

Puppy won't look at item

Excellent! Well done! Now, try a slightly more tempting item, but always set yourself up for success.

Advanced Leave It Games: Two Fist Game

Sitting in a chair, put a small bit of a boring treat in each hand, and hold your hands out from your sides. Your puppy will sniff, lick, or paw at a hand. This is normal. Wait. The moment he stops, praise him, bringing your hands to your lap. Then lure him to that spot using the hand he was not sniffing, feed him from that hand, praising all the way. Now try again. As he gets better, start waiting for him to look at you before you feed. Always lure to your lap, and feed with the hand he was not sniffing. Soon he will stare straight into your face no matter what temptation is close at hand.

REQUIREMENT: COME: MAKING IT WORK

Goal: For your puppy to come immediately without any lead hints or help.

Now that your puppy is coming to you quickly on a short lead indoors and sitting in front of you consistently, it's time to take this show on the road.

- Work around more interesting distractions—on a sidewalk in town, outside an active playground, or even during puppy class. Be creative but log in many repetitions of this critical behavior.
- Anytime you have to use the lead to make it happen (and don't hesitate to do so), note that you would have been in trouble if your puppy had been off-lead. Since a rocketing off-lead recall is our ultimate goal, we need to get him to the point where he pivots and races to you—lead slack.

Phyllis, a charming Cavalier/ Bichon mix pup, does a blazing Come when called out in our fields. She was cheered mightily and got a few treats. She knows Come is fun!
SARAH WILSON

- At this level, if you must use the lead, then no treat is given at arrival. Give brief praise, put treat to nose, then put it away. You expect the best, you reward the best. There are no gold stars for less than the best at this level of work.
- Move to a ten-foot long line outside if you can. Start the session on a four-foot lead, then, if that is going really well, move to the ten-foot line. If it isn't great at four feet, no need to try ten.
- Set up all sorts of distractions. Play outside a playground, around squirrels, near a soccer game, put out some toys or food to tempt your dog—take each challenge as one you face together. Call your dog when he is just becoming distracted. Watch for his ears locking forward and him heading that way like an arrow.
- Focus on the moment your puppy decides to turn toward you. That is the moment you need to build on, so that it becomes as close to automatic as possible. The more clearly you can mark that moment, the more clearly your puppy will understand exactly what you want.

Having Trouble?

Puppy ignores you

Ah, then you are hesitating on the backing away and praising, or you need work on your Look At Me, Leave It, and Come: Basics. Or, as unlikely as it is, your puppy really does have a hearing problem (page 30). Be sure you aren't calling him to do something he considers unpleasant, like being crated before you leave for work. Go get him at such moments, don't call him. Try always to do something wonderful when your puppy comes to you.

Puppy won't listen when he's around X

X can be squirrels, my little brother, his best dog buddy, deer, motorcycles or whatever. Excellent! When you are done working this problem through, you'll have a much stronger Come. Persistent practice will pay big dividends! So, work at the distance you can be successful at, use extra yummy treats, and keep at it until your puppy understands that Come means Come. No matter what.

Puppy doesn't come all the way to you

Keep backing up, in fact speed up if you can and slide your hand down the lead as your puppy comes to you so you have better control as he approaches. Are you standing up straight? Bending over can teach puppies to stop three to four feet in front of you.

REQUIREMENT: OUT

Goal: Puppy spits anything out of his mouth when you put a treat to his nose.

Spitting out items on command is important for your safety as well as your dog's. You never want to argue with your puppy over the possession of things, whether it is leftover chicken bones from a park picnic spot, a pair of expensive reading glasses, or a bottle of pills plucked from a bedside table. This is a command often muddled by scolding the puppy *after* the puppy has spit it out. If you scold a dog after, then how is she supposed to know what you wanted? Your goal as a My Smart Puppy person is always to help your puppy get to good. No "Good!" is no good.

- Get an item your puppy is *mildly* interested in. Get some treats your puppy *loves*. Give the puppy the so-so item. Now, take yummy treat in hand. Put it right to his nose. Tell him "Out"; give him the treat as you take the so-so item. Good job! Now give that thing right back to him. What's the point? The point is you're teaching your puppy that "Out" means give up the item and get something better.

Now here is a puppy with ambition! Out will be key to living with this particular dog.

- The key here is that the yummy treat is put to the nose *before* the "Out" is said. *Never* say "Out" and then get the lure. That quickly teaches some puppies that holding on causes you to go get treats. Uh-oh!
- When that is going well, tether your puppy. Sit or kneel in front of him. Hand him something he likes but is large enough that he cannot fit it all in his mouth. A stale bagel works well, but then we're in New York and here those are easy to come by. Take hold of that item—do not pull on it. Simply hold it. Say "Out" clearly, really pronouncing the "T" sound. Be sure of yourself in voice and in your body. Confidence is critical here. If your puppy releases, *excellent*! Good puppy!
- If he does not release, do a quick downward pop with the lead (not the tether). Make sure you're quick—this is not about force, this is about surprise. Done well, this startles many puppies, who will then open their mouths. Good puppy! Make that a *big deal* as you feed yummy treats with one hand and move the item behind your back with the other.
- Or hold the lead with slight upward tension (but with puppy feet on the floor). Just hold it and wait. This is the cue for a Simple Sit, which is a Level II exercise, but most pups will also release what's in their mouths if you are still and patient. The moment he releases, praise as you kick what he dropped out of his reach.

- Start by using less tempting items. Then, when you have easy success, move to the more difficult challenges. Build on success!

BRIAN'S INBOX:

Bad Trade = BIG Problem!

I have been trading with my puppy, but he's getting worse and worse. He just will not release things at all now. I have tried everything—better treats, more treats but he's just getting worse!

Anytime a behavior is getting worse, *stop what you are doing*! Your puppy is confused. In this situation, one of two things is probably happening. Maybe the treat was not in hand when the trade was started. This pattern becomes: You ask for the item, the puppy clamps down, *then* you produce the treat. But, in the puppy's mind, what caused the treat to appear? Clamping down. Uh-oh. Or, worse: The treat was in hand but when the puppy did not release, his person went and got something better. This is like asking your daughter to take out the trash for a buck, and when she says, "No way!" you offer her a ten. What is the lesson? Resistance = Better Reward. Big uh-oh!

Having Trouble?

Puppy won't release

Did you set up for failure by using a very tempting item and only so-so treats? Always make sure you give better than you get. Start with things your puppy really doesn't care about so you can teach him why releasing is such fun!

Puppy runs off or puppy growls at you when he has something

If your puppy ever grabs an item and stares at you or tries to run off, growling, he is threatening you. Please go to "Possessiveness: Finders Keepers" (page 307) in Chapter 8.

Puppy won't release

Since you're failing the "test," do more homework. Work at Level I a bit more. Be sure you really praise that release! If you are angry, you may confuse your puppy, making it unclear that the release is the winning option. Use less interesting items to practice with, use better food rewards. In other words, stack the deck.

TRUST: CHECK IT OUT

Goal: For your puppy to approach new and unusual items confidently with you.

You want your puppy to be confident in the world, and when he's not confident, to look to you for help. This game exposes him to new people, places, and things while teaching you how to help him when he needs it. Teaching your puppy this spoken command will give you a way of defusing his doubt when it arises. And it arises in almost every dog at one point or another.

Brian and Hazel play Check It Out with a barrel that strikes the pup as a bit scary.
SARAH WILSON

Brian rewards Hazel for getting close then moves away with her. Notice the loose lead and the wagging tail (Hazel's).
SARAH WILSON

Brian then approaches again.
SARAH WILSON

Hazel seems over her worries. What do you think?
SARAH WILSON

- Start indoors, on lead, with a handful of treats and an unusual object. This can range from a box or a paper bag to an umbrella or a backpack. With your puppy crated (or held by a helper) put the object at the far end of a room or hallway.
- From a distance, happily say to your puppy, "Check it out!" and walk toward the object together. Reward with a treat when you are as close as you think you can comfortably get with your puppy. Look for willingness to go with you on a loose lead. If you get too close, your puppy will slow down, put his ears back, close his mouth, lower his tail, or even try to pull away. If you get too close, oh well, move away and try again. Never haul your puppy toward something he is scared of.
- After giving him the treat, turn and walk back to your starting point. No treats there. Now repeat. Approach on "Check it out!", treat partway, go back to the start. What this teaches your puppy is that approaching is good and that it is also safe because he won't have to stay there too long. This teaches him to look to you for help rather then bolt away on his own. If you have a sensitive/shy or avoidant /fearful puppy, this is *your* game.
- Some pups will walk right up to the item. If they do, praise them as you touch the object, then deliver a treat. Then move away. Repeat a few times. We want your puppy to react with a big grin and a wagging tail when he hears, "Check it out." That reaction will save you when he sees a garbage bag at night that suddenly looks to him like a puppy-eating monster.
- Your confidence, intention to succeed with your puppy, and sincere praise are your puppy's guiding lights. Praising effectively is hard for many people so borrow a pocket tape recorder and listen to yourself. Do you sound happy? Also, watch your puppy. Do you have eye contact from your pup, an open-mouthed grin, a wagging tail? Then you're doing it right! If not, keep trying!

Having Trouble?

Puppy doesn't care

That's okay. He's still linking the words "Check It Out" with approaching something and getting praised and treated. That's all good!

Puppy won't come anywhere near the item

Your goal is not to get close to it; your goal is to approach it with your puppy. So treat and retreat often, making it fun. Laugh, praise him, play it like the game it is. When he sees you happy, he will be happier. Don't try to get closer to the object, try to get closer—emotionally—with your puppy. The fastest way to get over fear is to take things slow.

Puppy drags you away from the object

That may happen the first few times until your puppy learns that you aren't going to overwhelm him or take him too close too fast. If it's been a few repetitions and this retreat is getting worse, then his stress is building. Stay confident and relaxed so your puppy has a role model in you. Take this retreat away as a signal to stay farther away, reward sooner, and be more playful. Try some Near Is Dear (page 110)—see if that helps relax him a bit.

Puppy dawdles near the "scary" object

Excellent! This is his signal that he now knows this is a rewardable spot and he's relaxed enough to hang out there, hoping that something else good will happen. Don't disappoint! Next time, approach a little closer, give two or three treats, then move away. Well done!

Petra has no idea WHAT the Jolly Ball is the first time she sees it. Typically "herding breed" cautious, she circles it slowly, then works up her courage to give it a sniff. Soon after, the ball became her favorite toy! MELISSA FISCHER

CHAPTER 5

START LEVEL III

Wow! You two are doing just great! Are you having fun? Are you creating the kind of dog/person team you thought only professionals could pull off? We are so proud of you! You're about to embark on your last START Level—what an accomplishment!

CREATIVE COACHING

At this stage, you are a team. Your job as coach is to keep things fresh while continuing to practice your developing skills. Doing the same thing over and over again won't keep you both motivated. Get creative! If you always ask for a Sit at the door—do a Left Circle or a Down instead. If your puppy does an awesome Look At Me from the left, try it from the right. Wow us with the fun you're having!

WHAT IS YOUR INTENTION?

The first step in training any dog for anything is to know what you want. Have a clear picture in your mind of exactly what you are going for—and then go for it. Brian often finds that a failure with the puppy is a failure in our intention. To lead well we need to be focused and confident, clear and energized. If your puppy is wandering, where are you? We're betting you wandered mentally first. Focus your intention clearly before you ever pick up the lead!

READY *AND* ABLE

Ready to reward and able to assist. You must be both—at the same moment. You're balanced on the trainer's edge: Reward or assist or both. If you are too heavy on the reward side, you will be slow to assist. Your dog will become confused about what is wanted. Responses will slow. If you are too quick to assist, you teach your dog that response is your job and he will leave it to you. Responses will slow, only happening when you make a move to assist. To train well, you must be ready *and* able!

COMMON LEVEL III CHALLENGES

Routine Training

Oh, we are such creatures of habit! We stop, we have the puppy Sit, we have the puppy Down, we walk around him to the right, we turn back to the left—your puppy knows you better than you know yourself.

If you want your puppy (and yourself) to stay engaged, you have to mix things up! Make up cards of behaviors to practice and deal yourself a hand.

Energy Drops

When we get bored or tired, our energy level drops. We praise briefly, we don't sound excited, we yawn. Your puppy takes his cue from you. You don't need to swing from the chandelier, but you do need to be sincere, warm, and genuine. Puppies, like children, absolutely know the difference. If you want to pick up your

This handler is beaming as she works on a Left Circle. That's the spirit!
SARAH WILSON

energy quickly, do one of Brian's favorite remedies: Praise your dog with the wrong words. Say "Bad dog" but make it sound happy. Say horrible things in the nicest way, and watch your puppy's tail start to wag as you start to chuckle. Never be afraid to have fun. Your puppy will never tell on you!

Not Raising the Bar

Once your puppy has the basics of a certain behavior down, make him work harder and harder for his reward. If you become predictable, he can weigh the known reward against a delightful distraction. Which is better: the cookie or chasing the squirrel? This is not a thought process you want to develop. Know what is and what isn't your puppy's best effort. Our general rule is if you have to assist your puppy (once he understands the basics) then no cookie. Better yet, take it out, put it to his nose—then put it away. Try harder next time! And he will! Your puppy can only be as good as you believe he can be.

Food Dependency: Yours

You are more important to your puppy than a treat. Really, it's true. And if you're not, change it because you're the one who taught him this. If you think he would dump you for a biscuit, then put treats away for a while and find other ways to reward your dog. Petting, play, certain praise tones—there is something else your dog loves! Go beyond treats. There is a whole other wonderful world out there waiting for you! (We use treats extensively at all levels of training but if we *have* to use them, we put them away. Something is wrong if your puppy has a stronger bond to a treat than to you!)

SPACE: GO

Goal: You can send the puppy from a room and keep him from coming back in, simply by body blocking.

It is both convenient and safe to teach your puppy to leave any room on cue, then to stay out until invited back in. Think of a moment when a water glass smashes on the kitchen floor or you're painting a room and don't need your puppy's "help," and you instantly see what we are talking about. It can also help cure demanding barking, begging, nudging for endless attention, stalking the cat, and any number of other puppy behaviors.

Why? Because it is a leadership move. Controlling another's movement is a power game in social mammals. Who moves and who gets out of the way is so basic that we don't think about it much until someone doesn't get out of our way or is pushy with us. That is irritating at the least and, in some communities, it can get you into a fight quickly. Teaching Go is easy, it just takes a little practice and persistence.

• Start with the puppy on lead and close to a narrow threshold between one room and another. "Narrow" is a normal door's width. In a perfect world, the flooring would be different as well and you'd be sending him from a hall into an open room, but any door will do. If the threshold isn't clear, lay down a piece of tape. He is out of the room when all four paws are behind that tape.
• Bring the on-lead puppy into the room a few inches, then step toward him as you point and look out of the room (but be sure

to keep your pup in your peripheral vision so you can see what's happening). Say "Go" as you block him backward. If you have to bump him, bump him. Start gently, as always. If he doesn't move, try a faster tempo and move your feet more, before you try harder. Once all four puppy feet are out of the room, stop. Relax your body. Praise calmly.

- When your puppy steps forward (and he will), stand up straight, say "Go," and block him back. Try to stop and relax instantly when his feet leave the room.
- When he accepts the situation by either Sitting, Downing, or walking away, praise him and let him come into the room by stepping to the side and saying his name. What a Smart Puppy!
- As his understanding grows, work from farther in the room, until you can stand anywhere and send him out the doorway, where he waits quietly. How cool is that?!

Having Trouble?

Pup pushes past you

Use the lead to prevent this. Cut in front of him faster. Back him out of the room. Practice more Mine and Wait so he learns not to cut around you.

Pup turns and leaves

Go slower, praise faster, smile, and be happy. For some dogs, this is a big correction. Cheer him past his concerns. That's a valuable lesson, too.

Pup is confused, lies down, doesn't move

Stop. Try this: Bring him into a room, hold his collar as you show him a treat, then toss that treat out of the room. Now, tell him "Go" and release the collar. Walk behind him as he leaves, praising him. Once he is out of the room, praise and treat him a couple more times. Repeat. Soon he'll Go with confidence.

Puppy keeps moving around

Are you antsy? Moving this way and that? All that extra movement confuses your puppy who doesn't know what signal to read. Take a deep breath, slow down, and try again. "Speak" clearly with your body; be crisp and definite. Does your puppy do better? We bet she will!

Pup moves to one side or the other

He's trying! He's moving out of your way, just not quite the way we would like. Persist in your goal—use the treat as above if that helps—stop and praise even a step in the right direction. Do that a few times and he'll catch on quickly.

Puppy jumps up—possibly mouthing

Think of this as if you asked a child to leave the room and, in response, the child came over and shoved you. This is often mental resistance. Did you skip the Touch Games because you didn't like making your puppy "unhappy"? If you did, this can be the result. You've taught him that resistance wins. Changing his mind now can avoid a host of problems down the road. Rework your Level I and Level II Space Games as you're focusing on your Touch work. That should help!

SPACE: WAIT THERE

Goal: For your puppy to wait calmly wherever you leave him.

This is an important canine skill, whether it is to stay quietly in a crate, peacefully in the car, or patiently behind a gate. This is a freedom skill, meaning he'll have more freedom in his life once he acquires it. This game also helps to inoculate your puppy against future separation problems, so play it often.

Teaching your puppy to wait patiently, like young mixed-breed Fudge here, will save your nerves (and your pup's) and your woodwork a great deal of wear and tear.
JACKSON YOUNG

- Set a chair, reading material, and treats at arm's length from the crate, ex-pen, or gate. Put your puppy in the crate or ex-pen or behind the gate. Read, making sure you are not facing the puppy.
- Ignore all whining, fussing, pawing at barrier etc. Exception? Climbing. If puppy starts to climb, reach over without looking or speaking and give the gate/ex-pen a shake. Alternatively, give puppy a quick spray of water from a plant mister—again without looking or speaking. We want this to be straight "cause and effect" with as little link to you as possible.
- When the puppy settles (often with a big sigh), look at, smile at, and calmly praise him as you go to him to deliver a treat. Make sure he is "four on the floor" when you deliver it.
- Go back to reading. If puppy remains quiet, repeat reward.
- As your puppy gets calmer, move your chair farther away from him. Wait longer to go back and reward him. Start having him Down before you give the treat. Soon you'll have a puppy who waits patiently for you. Bravo!

Having Trouble?

Puppy barks, digs, jumps, whines

Wow, he really needs your help. This is a harbinger of separation problems to come, so let's give him other options before things get worse. He can handle this and once he does, he'll be a more secure, confident dog.

Reactive dogs can cycle into barking with no idea how to stop. For them we might try a Guided Down (page 92)—pretrain this first! Use a long line attached to a flat collar and run out under the door of the crate (please don't do this with gates or ex-pens). If the puppy fusses, simply gently apply his Guided Down cue by tightening the lead. Do not look at him yet. Expect a bit of hesitation from your puppy as he figures this out. Just wait a moment and don't apply more pressure. Once Down, release any pressure, look at him, smile, and praise your puppy. Give him a treat through the bars and leave again. Your approach then retreat should get him fussing again. Good, you have another chance to teach. You can sit in a chair, read a book, and do this work. Soon he will do something amazing. He will start to fuss, pause, and then lie down. Go to him with warm smiles. Now he can calm himself. What a wonderful gift to have given him!

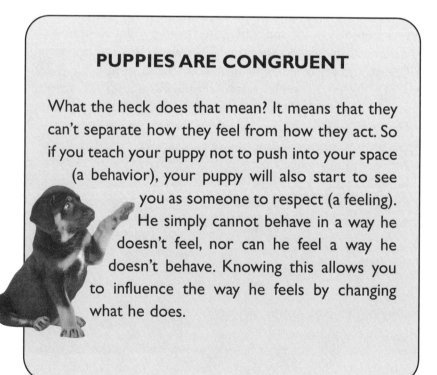

PUPPIES ARE CONGRUENT

What the heck does that mean? It means that they can't separate how they feel from how they act. So if you teach your puppy not to push into your space (a behavior), your puppy will also start to see you as someone to respect (a feeling). He simply cannot behave in a way he doesn't feel, nor can he feel a way he doesn't behave. Knowing this allows you to influence the way he feels by changing what he does.

TOUCH: SIMPLE SIT

Goal: For your puppy to sit immediately when she feels slight upward pressure.

This Sit is a sensation command where the command is a little upward collar pressure. We use this for all client puppies, as it is so natural for people to do it and so easy for puppies to learn that we finally figured: Why not make this really work?

Simple Sit is taught through gentle upward pressure with instant release. When you come to a halt, gently apply upward pressure on the collar, just enough that you feel a slight resistance on the collar. You're not lifting the puppy! Say "Sit," then give him slack the instant he sits. That instant release shows him what you want! Praise him as you scratch his chest. *Note:* People with show puppies should skip this one or your handlers will be annoyed with us. Everyone else: Do as we do. Teach it and enjoy!

- With your puppy standing next to you, apply slight pressure upward—and we mean slight! At no time should your puppy's front feet be lifted off the ground or even almost be lifted. This is to be a suggestion, not a punishment. As you apply that slight upward pressure, say "Sit." The *instant* he starts to sit, release the pressure and let the clip of the lead point to the ground.
- If he doesn't sit, you use your placement "U" you learned in Placement Sit in Level I to help him. Again, release the pressure the *instant* he starts to comply. Once he is sitting quickly for pressure + word, move on to just the pressure.
- Now, when you come to a door you're going to open, or a curb you're stopping at, or when you are pausing to chat with a friend, apply that light upward pressure. The moment your puppy sits, praise him, scratch his ear, give a treat, or just smile at him—take the time to really praise him. He'll get the message. This becomes a lovely way to gently get your dog to Sit without having to rivet your attention on him.

Pip and I are doing a Simple Sit demonstration for a humane group. She is a bit distracted by the seventy or so people sitting in front of us. I apply light pressure and wait.
MELISSA FISCHER

Pip has just sat so I open my hand, releasing the light pressure. The moment of release is the moment your puppy remembers. So release the instant your pup sits.
MELISSA FISCHER

Having Trouble?

Puppy struggles

Ack! You're using too much pressure, applied too quickly, or you aren't releasing fast enough. This is a four-on-the-floor game. If you're lifting his front feet off the ground, easy does it! This pressure isn't about "making him" sit, it is about gently suggesting that he sit. There is a big difference.

Puppy stands

Are you pulsing the lead? It's a common mistake. This is a steady, light pressure. It is common for puppies to take a few seconds to respond at first. You can say "Sit" or use your Placement Sit (page 88) to help him out but don't pulse the lead.

HOW TO CONTROL JUMPING USING SIMPLE SIT

Once your puppy sits quickly when he feels that little upward pressure, you can use it to control his jumping as well. If he jumps up, simply give that light upward pressure for a second or two—no more. Most puppies will instantly start to fold into a Sit, which you allow him to do while verbally praising him warmly (skip the petting for now). Excellent! Now you can have him Sit without you having to step toward him, look at him, or say anything. You can "talk" through the lead. As above, the pressure is slight and momentary. You are not lifting the dog up in any way! We often do this with one finger—this is not about force, but about redirection.

TOUCH: FACE IT

Goal: Your puppy stays relaxed when you touch her face, give pills, clean ears, or medicate her eyes.

Now that your puppy understands that Calm = Release, we're going to add handling her face and head. Most dogs initially dislike having their mouth messed with, teeth looked at, or ears handled. Teaching them how to accept it not only makes them safer and more tolerant companions, but it will teach you to be more confident handling your friend.

- With your puppy in your Calm = Release (page 122) handling position, go through your normal handling routine. Then, when your puppy is calm, take the collar with one hand as you rest the other over his muzzle (nose). If your puppy has no nose to speak of, then rest your fingers on his lips on either side of his nose area. Do not squeeze, simply rest there.
- Many puppies will fuss. Stay calm, don't squeeze, just stay with the movement until the puppy stops for a moment—a tiny moment. When he does, instantly remove your hand while praising calmly. Message is the same: Calm = Release.
- Next, open his mouth. With your hand over his muzzle, evenly—not suddenly—press his lips into the space behind his long canine teeth. This will open his mouth. When it opens, pop in a yummy tidbit, then let go. Repeat until he doesn't mind you opening his mouth. Be enthusiastic about how well he did. *Note:* Do not stick this treat down his throat like a pill.
- Work up to lifting up his lips to look at his teeth. This is a new sensation, which will start a new round of protest. But you know what to do now: Stay calm until he pauses, then praise as you remove your hands. Your calm will help him find his. When your puppy gets to the point where he is used to and trusts you to handle his mouth and face, you will have a puppy who trusts you to do many other things as well. And a special congratulations from us

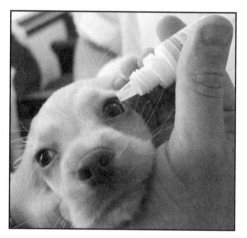

for doing what your puppy needs even if it isn't what he immediately likes.

Having Trouble?

My puppy doesn't like this, so why would I do it?

Because she doesn't like it. Life is full of things dogs don't like. Teach her to respond to such moments with calm, not struggle. Allowing her to fight you successfully now can set the stage for aggression later.

My puppy tries to bite

Is she mouthing (with her mouth on your hand, not bearing down, being wiggly and goofy)? Or is she biting (becoming motionless and/or snarling and/or grabbing hard)? Mouthing puppies can be dealt with in many ways: Work with them when they are calmer, release sooner for calm moments, have a friend feed treats as you handle your puppy, spray your hands with an anti-chew product, work on your hand placement so you can prevent this, put on a head halter so you can better control the mouth. Serious aggression (as rare as it is) needs professional assessment right away. If your puppy has orthopedic issues or

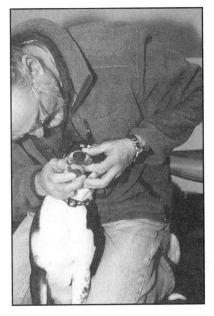

This puppy is learning to sit quietly when her human handles her. Giving pills, brushing teeth, removing things from her mouth will be easy after this. ROXANNE FRANKLIN

is ill (some tick-borne diseases can cause this), he may be snappish. Talk to your veterinarian. But if your puppy is just opposed to being kindly handled—do more Space Games, apply "Demoting Difficult or Demanding Dogs," do "The Daily Dozens: An Anti-Bite Protocol (see Chapter 8) as you get hands-on help from an experienced dog professional.

NO-STRUGGLE NAIL TRIMMING

Of all the injuries you're likely to face in your dog's lifetime, foot problems are at the top of the list. Paw pads get cut (and bleed profusely), nails get ripped, thorns get imbedded. Teaching your dog to allow you to handle his feet is best done *before* he needs your help. Start off just stroking his legs and paws as a part of petting. If your puppy stays relaxed, gently touch those toes. Good job. Do this in brief sessions in your Calm = Release position (see page 122). If you have a helper, have her give the puppy treats as you touch the toes—stopping when you stop, starting again when your hand is on the foot. The goal is: Touch foot = eat treat. Stay as relaxed as you can, breathing evenly with your body at ease. Your puppy will pick up on any tension, so keep both your hands and your voice calm. Going well? Then touch one nail with the clipper. Release and praise. Now, clip the very end of nail. Like humans, dogs have a quick in their nail, so just clip the tip. If you are unsure, ask your veterinarian to show you how. Well done!

ATTENTION: FOLLOW THE LEADER

Goal: Your puppy happily follows your every move with rapt attention.

This is how you will walk your puppy out on the streets. An advanced version of Catch My Drift, this is more forward motion than backing up. This is great fun played as a game. Let's get started!

- If your dog drifts forward now, speeding up, sharp turns, and crisper pulsing are the answer. You are more demanding, faster moving, and clearer. You move with intention, as if you're walking to catch a bus. Your puppy's job? To follow you. Your job? To lead!
- To balance the increase in demand, you must up your praise. Be happy, have fun, play this like a great game!
- Keep your eyes up, facing forward. Do not stare at your puppy at this stage; look where you are going. If you need to, pick a distant point and head toward it.
- Watch those corners. It's our tendency to slow down and watch our puppies as we turn. This slows you down, breaks the rhythm, and makes it harder for your puppy to follow. Turn and go. Don't

Leading with clear forward energy, this young woman leads the way, her puppy following perfectly. Her lead should be loose, but otherwise this looks great!
ROXANNE FRANKLIN

rush, you're not "faking" your puppy out. Just turn and go—expect him to be there!

- If you feel the lead tighten, pulse and speed up! Praise him when he catches up, which he will.
- Now you must allow slack in the lead. This is one of the hardest things for people to do because it feels weird not to "feel" your puppy every minute. Get over it. Otherwise you will be stuck with an on-lead dog forever. Tension on the lead teaches the wrong thing. It teaches the puppy that when he feels the lead he should listen and when he doesn't, he doesn't have to. We want him to think: If I feel the lead, I should look to my handler and when I don't, I am doing something right! This will get you to off-lead control.

Having Trouble?

Puppy sniffs

Has he peed? If not, potty him, then play. If he doesn't need to go, then speed up, sidestep, change directions, shuffle into his space—become very interesting very fast. The common human reaction is to (a) see what the puppy is sniffing (i.e., participating in your puppy's distraction) or (b) slow down (rewarding your puppy for sniffing by giving him more time to sniff).

Puppy distracted? Lead! Brian heads off, fully expecting the pup to keep up. If you wait for your pup's attention, you'll never have that attention.
SARAH WILSON

Puppy pulls ahead

Then go in some other direction, or Throw Your Wait Around (page 118) or back up and call him or do big Left Circles . . . but do something! Don't be where he left you when he looks back, and he'll start keeping a closer eye on you by walking at your side.

Puppy jumps up

Work your Off or Simple Sit then continue.

Puppy lies down

Pulse the lead as you move forward. He'll get up and when he does, praise! What a good, good puppy!

Ready to Advance?

It's time to start loosening your grip on the lead, to increase your trust in your puppy, to make sure your puppy isn't working off-lead tension, and to reignite your praise! When playing these games indoors or in safe areas, practice draping the lead across your palm while keeping your thumb over the lead. Keep your hands as relaxed as possible. If you close your hand on the lead, you must act! Squeeze/pulse, change direction, redirect—do something—then relax your hand again. When you can do complex patterns without ever closing your hand, you are ready for off-lead work!

ATTENTION: BEAT THE CLOCK

Goal: For your puppy to learn how to listen and respond when excited.

Many people have puppies who will sit in the kitchen with family but have no control when guests come over. Part of the rea-

Nice slack lead, wonderful connection and mutual attention, both are having fun, this is "Beat the Clock"!
ROXANNE FRANKLIN

son for this is that homework was never done when the puppy was all excited. To fix that, we have Beat the Clock, a game solely devoted to working those baby-dog self-control muscles.

- This is a treat-free zone. Your puppy's reward is a game with you. If your dog doesn't find playing with you rewarding, if a bit of food wins out over a romp with you—we need to work on that.
- With your puppy on lead in a quiet area, start by backing away or speaking excitedly. Reach in and touch your puppy's side or rear quickly if he needs to "wake up a bit." Be animated, have fun. When your puppy is prancing toward you, stop dead, say "Sit," and wait. Look away, say nothing. We want you to turn off like a faucet.
- The moment—and we mean the *moment*—he sits, the faucet turns back on. Good puppy, then back away! Be lively. We want as dramatic a difference between on and off as possible. The bigger that difference is, the faster your puppy will learn.

Having Trouble?

My puppy slams me, starts to grab me, gets way too excited

Then slow down and calm down. Start at a level you two can handle. That may be slowly walking backward as your puppy comes to you. Work there until his self-control muscles get stronger. Also, you can tether your puppy back at first if he is really too wild.

Puppy wanders off

Here you may need to increase your energy to get his attention. Back up faster, get a little bouncy, and sound excited. That should get his attention. Don't hesitate to squeeze/pulse as you back away. Avoid standing there begging your dog for attention. Get happy, stay happy, and insist that he follow your lead!

Puppy is frightened

Calm your hands, slow down. This is supposed to be fun for your puppy—not scary. Find a level of play your puppy enjoys. That may be very calm at first, but that's okay. This is now less Beat the Clock and more work on getting him over his fear, but both things are important.

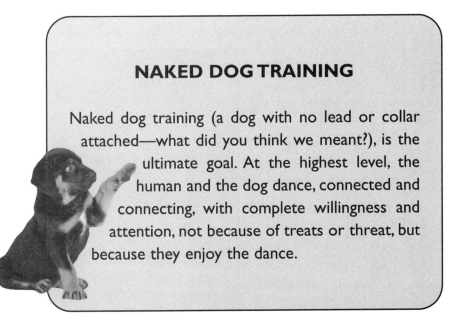

NAKED DOG TRAINING

Naked dog training (a dog with no lead or collar attached—what did you think we meant?), is the ultimate goal. At the highest level, the human and the dog dance, connected and connecting, with complete willingness and attention, not because of treats or threat, but because they enjoy the dance.

REQUIREMENT: STAY II:
WORKING THE 4 D'S

Goal: Your puppy Stays longer and better.

When you work Stay, you work four different variables: the 4 D's of Stay. Those are Duration, Distraction, Diversity, and Distance. Distance is the one everyone wants to work first but it needs to be done last. Why? Because you are too far away to return frequently to him to praise and treat or to replace him quickly and calmly if he rises. Avoid the ever-popular and problem-causing "Stay, back away, and call your pup" until you've done six months or more of successful Stay work. Otherwise, you risk teaching your dog he should get up when you walk away, and that is exactly what we are trying *not* to do.

- Work the D's one at a time. Start by building a little duration. Build your pup up to a couple of minutes in a relaxed, happy Stay. You want a happy pup with a wagging tail (ideally).
- Next, start on distraction. When you start with a new variable, always make the other ones easier. So more distraction means shorter duration at the beginning. Mild distractions include you moving a few feet in one direction or another (walking all the way around your pup is a big distraction—save that one for later). Squatting down, sitting in a chair, thumbing through a

Among other things, a good Stay allows you to capture lovely pictures, such as this one of Brian's Julia. She's gone now. What a gift that Stay whispered years ago gives to us still. SARAH WILSON

magazine—these are all distractions. Return to her frequently to praise and put a kibble or two between her paws. If your pup gets up (she is still tethered, right?), just Down her, and step off again. Make things easier so she can succeed by rewarding more often and releasing her sooner.

- Diversity is the third variable we add. When you change locations, even from one side of the room to the other, shorten up the duration and limit distraction. Basically, it is a whole new ballgame for your puppy. She'll pick up the game faster this time, but expect her to be the Stay newbie she was a couple of weeks back. When you move outside (always staying close to your securely tethered puppy) you can expect a response like "Stay? Have I ever heard Stay before?"

- The key to these games is that she succeeds much more than she errs. Aim for ten times as much success as failure. This will keep you working gradually with success as your focus. Once your pup can Stay in different locations for five minutes and can handle such things as dropped food or a toy, or you sitting on the floor or doing a few jumping jacks without a problem, then *and only then* can you start adding distance.

Having Trouble?

Your puppy gets up immediately

Brian Kilcommons

Go back to the hand signal then food between paws routine with your tethered puppy. Work on drawing out the time between hand signal and treat. Always deliver it on the floor between his front feet. When you move to the standing position, keep your toe on the lead. That way if your puppy gets up, he will cue himself to lie back down when he feels the tension on the lead. Be sure the lead has slack when he is down.

You are frustrated with Stay

And your puppy picks up on that, I promise you that. Work shorter sessions, keep him tethered, and set yourself up for success. If things are going downhill, take a break. Go do something fun. Come back to this later. You'll both get it.

Puppy won't get up after the release tap with word combination

Usually this is a grand "problem": the puppy likes Stay so much he doesn't want to get up. To help him out, tap and release, then use the lead to ask the puppy to follow you. When he gets up, praise him warmly. Walk around for a few seconds, then start again. You're doing great!

PLACE

Place simply means "Go to your bed and stay there until further notice." Start by making this a pleasant spot. Sit by it with your puppy near. Lure him (with a treat) onto the bed then drop a treat onto it. When he leaves the bed, ignore him for a few seconds, then use a treat to lure him back. If he stays there, drop treats every few seconds. When he likes the bed, start saying "Place" as you lure him onto the bed. From here on out he must lie down on the bed to get his treat. Do this by luring him onto the bed, then holding a treat on the bed. Wait. In a moment he will lie down. If he doesn't, add guiding collar pressure. When he Downs, release the pressure and give him the treat. Next have him on the lead, say "Place," walk him back to his bed, use the

Guided Down collar cue to Down him, then reward him. At this stage be sure you release him clearly with the shoulder-tap-and-name combo you would use for ending Stay. If he gets up before you release him, quietly take him right back, and use guiding collar pressure to Down him—no treat. Wait a few seconds, praise him, and release him. You'll soon have a puppy who can Place!

REQUIREMENT: NO EYE CAN

Goal: For your puppy to listen to you even when not looking at you.

One of the first and most powerful thing dogs learn from us: When a human looks at me, we are working; when she looks away, we're done. The trouble is, when we need them to listen *most* they will be looking at us least. If we want them to listen no matter what, we have to teach them.

When you need your pup to listen the most, she'll be looking at something else. Teaching her that listening isn't dependent on looking is an important step toward solid off-lead control.
Sarah Wilson

- Start with your puppy on lead in a calm area. Walk around then drift to a stop. Be sure your feet have stopped moving. Shorten up on the lead as you come to a stop, but don't apply pressure yet—allow that clip to hang straight down. Without looking directly at your pup (but while keeping him in view either out of the corner of your eye or in a reflection) say, "Dog, sit." If he does, praise and treat. Good puppy!
- If he doesn't (he's confused, not being difficult) help him either by placing him or with Simple Sit. Praise him the moment he complies. Praise but no treat. You can take the treat out, put it right to his nose, then put it away again. This tends to whet their appetite nicely.
- For Down, drift to a stop, give slack so the lead touches the floor, then slide your foot over the lead. This is more subtle than lifting your foot to put it on the lead. Say, "Puppy, Down." If he does, smile, praise, treat. If he doesn't, apply light guiding pressure and wait for him to comply. Pause, then try again.

Having Trouble?

Puppy doesn't respond to Sit or Down

That's perfectly normal. Just be ready to help her get it right through gentle, clear placement. Say it once, follow through. If you do just that, your puppy will be fabulously well trained in no time.

Puppy wanders around

Again, this is normal. You've taught her that when you are looking at her she is "on" and when you look away, she has "free time," so, as above, give the command then follow through. Easy while effective, kind while clear—leave no doubt about what you expect.

TRUST: SAY HELLO

Goal: Your puppy can greet people calmly and confidently.

This game involves four different behaviors, offering you a lot of practice packed into one exercise. It also conditions your puppy to expect to stop before greeting, which prevents the "haul to maul" greeting so common in young dogs. Here's the pattern: Sit, Wait, Say Hello, Come.

- Start by having your puppy sitting by your side about eight feet away from an assistant, ideally someone your puppy knows and likes. Smile and approach your assistant, who is standing or sitting calmly and silently. When you are still five feet away, pivot in front of your puppy for the now very familiar Wait. If your puppy stops, sits and looks at you—good puppy! Smile, praise, and give a treat. If he tries to push past you, shuffle into him, making him back himself up a few steps. Then do a left turn in front of him, go back to the start, and try again. The greeting only happens when the Wait is calm and collected.
- Once the Wait is solid, you instruct your puppy to Say Hello as you walk toward the assistant. Let your puppy sniff and wag for a moment (assistant stays quiet for now), then back up and call your puppy to you. Praise! You do this both to practice the fine art of quitting while

All puppies, but especially giant-breed pups, need to greet people without jumping. Here Brian encourages, then will reward, sitting.
Sarah Wilson

you're ahead and to practice calling your puppy away from a distraction.

- When your puppy can do this calmly, then have your assistant greet him calmly. For most puppies, you should be the source of any treats. We don't want your puppy rushing up to people expecting to be fed.

Having Trouble?

Pup rushes forward

In the cause and effect tradition you now understand, if your puppy rushes forward, you back up and call him to you. Proceed together or do not proceed at all.

Pup leaps up on person

Back up, call pup to you, try again. Exception: shy dogs. A really shy puppy who is coming up politely and gently can be allowed to do this for a little while, since her socialization is more important than her self-control at this stage of the game. Gently guiding her off into a Sit is fine as long as she doesn't show signs of stress when you do so.

Pup won't approach person

Be sure your helper isn't staring at your young pup, as that can frighten some. Play Check It Out on page 139. Never haul a puppy toward someone if the puppy is afraid (or allow a person to approach your puppy after your puppy has said "Uh-oh" by backing up, lowering her tail, shutting her mouth, or otherwise showing you she is distressed). That can make matters worse or force the puppy into defense. Better to stay at a bit of a distance, rewarding her for focusing on you. That is creating a positive association with being near a stranger rather than a stress-filled one. Be sure you stay happy; don't pick up your puppy's worry. Doing so won't help her at all and will probably make matters worse.

Pup won't come away from person

A friendly puppy is a fine "problem" to have—be proud. Now, have your assistant stand up, look away, and stop all interaction when you call your puppy. You back up and squeeze/pulse. Praise with enthusiasm while giving something extra yummy when your puppy arrives. This is excellent practice. If your puppy won't come away from a friendly person, he won't come away from a taunting squirrel either.

CHAPTER **6**

SOCIALIZATION: DOMESTICATING YOUR DOG

On our first walk in one of our large fenced fields, Pip was concerned about being outside. She noticed everything close up and at a distance. Stopping, staring, her tail was down. She was unsure. This told me she probably had never gone for a walk by herself with a human. She was running far ahead—a sign of her nerves or her confidence or both. I turned and walked the other way. She just stood contemplating me for longer than I would have liked before bolting to me to fling herself into my arms. Plan: More walks with me, use long line to teach her to respond sooner, bring food rewards to give her anytime she shows up at my side, and show genuine enthusiasm when she does.

Her doubt in the fields was well within normal. Reacting to various things with fear is an expected part of growing up. This does not make your puppy "shy" or "a problem"—it makes her a puppy. All pups have when they arrive in your home are puppy instincts, habits, and social skills plus whatever their previous experience has taught them. Since Pip and her brothers were abandoned by the side of the road in Kentucky, it isn't surprising that she has concerns about being alone outdoors. A few days of walking together and she is past her worries. She now rockets through our fields with abandon, not a care in her active little mind. If you hadn't seen that first day, you'd never imagine she ever had doubts. So don't worry about the bumps; concentrate on how to help your puppy become comfortable in his world. That's the answer and that's what socialization is all about.

WHAT EXACTLY IS SOCIALIZATION?

It is, quite literally, making your puppy social. Since your puppy cannot understand TV, conversation, books, or magazines, he has no idea what the world is all about. He cannot even under-

This pup is surprised by the plastic bag. Brian is going to stop and help this little one over this normal puppy moment. This pup is not "shy," he's just learning about the world.
SARAH WILSON

stand half of what he sees, whether it is cars, dishwashers, or elevators. The earlier in his life he experiences things, the more normal they seem to him. Conversely, the later in life he experiences things the weirder and scarier they are. It's just the same with us. If you were whisked off to some foreign land at two years old, a land full of strange-looking beings whose language, culture, or technology you could not understand, how long would it take you to accept this as the way things are? Now, what if you went there at twenty years old?

Your goal is to expose your puppy to as much as possible as soon as possible, without overwhelming him. For some pups, overwhelming is never a worry. For sensitive pups, you have to be more careful. Your goal is always the same: to keep your puppy safe, to give him as many positive experiences as possible, and to go lots of places to meet lots of people. Avoid doing too much too fast. A little that goes well is better than a lot that goes badly. Taking your puppy to the soccer field to pick up your daughter after a game: good. Taking puppy to a game with lots

A walk past a construction site is a fine trip, if your puppy isn't frightened. Hazel is relaxed, tail wagging, giving Brian good attention. She's enjoying her outing.
SARAH WILSON

of people wildly cheering: not so good. At least, not at first. Five to ten minutes in a new place is plenty for most young puppies. Avoid fireworks, costumes, motorcycle rallies (unless the pup was raised with bikes), trains and subways (unless you can keep a good distance from both as they come and go). But hanging out where people come and go, that is usually a great idea. What is socialization? It's immunization against later fear and stress. It is the gift of confidence so your puppy grows up into a dog who feels safe in the world he must inhabit.

WHEN CAN I DO THIS SAFELY?

Puppies need field trips early and often. Some veterinarians advise quarantining pups from the outside world until twelve to sixteen weeks old, sometimes even older. The hope is that this will keep them safe from disease, but unless you never, ever wear your shoes in your home, you track the world in with you anyway.

Quarantine may keep your puppy physically safer, but it puts him at behavioral risk. Those first sixteen weeks of life are the best time to socialize your puppy. Letting him sit at home all day every day does no good.

We always get our puppies out, as safely and sensibly and as soon as we possibly can. We avoid dog-frequented places like parks and well-used fire hydrants, trees or light posts, pet-supply stores, or any puppy playmate who has not been in his home for at least two weeks. When possible, we make appointments at the veterinarian for first thing in the morning, carrying the puppy in and out if we can.

We do go to local dog-friendly businesses. In our area, our bank, hardware store, small video place, Lowes home improvement store, The Home Depot, the photography store, and the local crafts emporium all welcome our puppies. We walk them on a local college campus, which generally has few dogs. We hang out in front of large stores and malls so the puppy can experience the automatic doors opening and closing, shopping carts rattling, and people rushing in and out.

If people want to stop and say hello, we hook a finger through our pup's collar to prevent jumping up, and praise calmly while treating her ourselves. We are the source of the treats, not the stranger. This minimizes over-excitement and mouthing, keeping your puppy focused on you.

If you're worried about having your puppy on the ground, you can carry her or use a car.

Carry

If you can, carry your pup places. Any disease is on the floor, so carrying is a safe alternative. A young pup can learn a great deal from your arms. But don't baby! You get what you pet and you raise what you praise. Don't raise fear!

Car

The car is a wonderful tool for socialization—when used wisely. We often bring a new pup to town or a playground, park the car and just sit with the pup. We say little, allowing the pup to watch or nap as she wishes. If the pup watches quietly from a window, we will offer praise and a treat as a way to reward curious, calm behavior. If the pup barks or shakes, we'll park farther away and work hard to praise and treat any quiet or comfortable moments. When Milo arrived, he was too frightened to get anything positive from a walk around town, so we drove. We put him in a

Letting your puppy watch the world go by is an excellent idea but keep his head in the car— when parked or moving.
SARAH WILSON

crate in the van, drove to a parking lot, popped open the back door, and sat with him. We put an open container of fresh roasted chicken bits in front of the crate door to whet this appetite. (*Hint:* If your puppy doesn't even take a sniff, he probably won't eat yet either. Try parking farther away.) Anytime someone walked by, a car door closed, or a truck roared past, we put a piece in his crate without comment—it was just cause and effect. Over time, when a person came into view he'd stay more relaxed, anticipating the delivery of an extra-special treat.

ONE, TWO, THREE, FOUR, GET THAT PUPPY OUT THE DOOR!

The next few months, you're going to be busy. This rather hectic time is an investment in your puppy's future. If your puppy is confident and calm in the world, she will have more freedom to do more things more often and more safely. Isn't that worth it? For every week between the third week after your puppy comes home and nine months of age, here's what you do:

- Meet **One** Unfamiliar Dog

Puppy class takes care of this! On-lead street inter-action is fine. Safety first, especially with the toy breeds.

- Go to **Two** New Places

This can be sitting outside the drugstore as your friend runs in to pick something up. You don't have to get fancy—just get out! Don't count places twice. A six-week puppy class counts as one place. Within two miles of our home we have a few friends' houses, a horse stable, a flock of sheep, two rivers, a concrete pad overlooking a river, a bridge, two restaurants, one deli, an auto mechanic, a store, and a honey farm with an actual bear. Every neigh-borhood is different but you will always have plenty of places nearby that qualify as an "adventure" for your puppy.

- Interact with **Three** New Things

Take a paper bag from food shopping and see if you can get your puppy to stand on it or put his head down inside (a treat helps with this). Or take a plas-tic shopping bag, wad it up, and pet him with it. Can you lure him under a curtain you make by draping a towel on a broomstick between two chairs? Out on your walks have him sit on top of a low wall, walk him in and out of some automatic doors, or do

Check It Out (page 139) toward a flapping flag. You don't have to be fancy, just be creative. Explore the world and make it fun! Show us your success: Send pictures to www.mysmartpuppy.com.

• Greet **Four** New People

This one should be easy when you're out at those two new places. The more diverse the better. Soon Sarah and Pip will make a foray down to New York City, taking the train to Grand Central then walking around from there. There is nothing like a large town or city for diversity!

Young Vio examines a feather. Everything is new to your puppy! SARAH WILSON

Taking your puppy with you is fun and good training. Go explore!

Puppyhood is brief. Once your dog is full grown, many things will be more difficult. Train early!

HOW DO YOU KNOW YOUR PUPPY IS STRESSED?

If your puppy is anxious or overwhelmed, she will give you signs. She may be panting rapidly when it isn't that hot out, holding her head and tail low, trying to bolt away from you, hiding, refusing to walk if she has been walking, holding her ears sideways or flat back, trying to hide under things, sticking close to buildings, shaking or quivering, growling at people and things, backing away, having sweaty paw pads (you'll see wet paw prints on the floor), "blowing coat" (suddenly and profusely shedding), freezing—complete motionlessness (frequently mistaken for being "stubborn"), crouching, closing her mouth tight, whining (although this can also be pure frustration—it has to be within context of all other signals). Or your puppy might start panic bucking and flying against the end of the lead. Any of these signs mean: Get happy fast to see if that can change her mind, give her something else to do, feed more treats more rapidly (if she will eat), or get away from this place now.

AT-HOME SOCIALIZATION

There is a lot you can do to prepare your puppy for the variety and surprises of life. Here are some suggestions.

Mix It Up

Routine, we're all victims of it. We walk, we talk, we move in predictable ways. At least adults do. Children are some of the great socializers since they can suddenly bunny-hop into the room, then spin, squeal, and throw a toy up into the air. A puppy raised only by an adult will be quite surprised by this. She might bark, run off, hide, or simply show curious interest. A puppy raised with kids won't even wake up from a nap. So take a cue from youth; be a little more unpredictable. Not only is it good for your puppy, but it's just plain fun, once you get over feeling silly. Do some yoga, stretch dramatically when you get up from your desk, skip into the kitchen, and gently hold your puppy's tail as he goes up the stairs. Wear funny hats, ponchos, sunglasses, whatever. Mix things up. Try to do one or two unusual things a day. If your puppy reacts, slow down a bit to a speed or a movement she can handle. Work there until she accepts this odd new human thing. Then take it back up to whatever speed your puppy can accept. A few weeks of this and your puppy will take ebullient Uncle Bob and limping Aunt Mirabelle in stride.

WHAT CAN FRIGHTEN YOUR PUPPY?

- A large backpack (to your puppy: new and alarming growth on your back)

- Diving mask (to your puppy: sudden reshaping of forehead; eyes look weird)

- Large, unusual (to your puppy) headgear (to your puppy: gross deformity of human head)

- Wheelchairs and walkers (to your puppy: a human with wheels or extra legs?!)

- Different skin colors (than what puppy is used to—it's not "racial" as pups may react to any skin tone if they've never seen it before)

- Ponchos

- Big glasses

- Large packages

- Uniforms

- Large boxes or bags in an unusual place

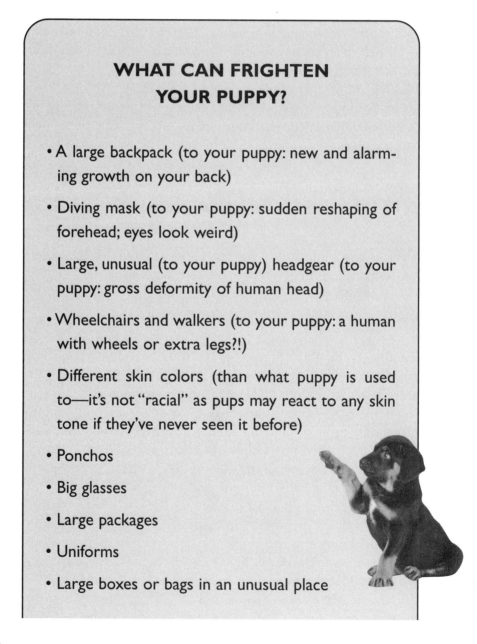

- Their own reflection (which they do not and cannot recognize)

- People on medication, drugs, or alcohol or people who have neurological problems as the different movement and, in some cases, the possible change in scent can throw a puppy off

- Someone you don't happen to like—wow, some puppies can really pick up on this!

Hi There! Now Is the Time for Guests

Have your children invite friends over, or invite some of your adult friends or neighbors over. Say "Hi" to the postal carrier with your puppy in tow. Even if they have no interest in petting your puppy, your puppy is still seeing someone in a uniform. Encourage calm interaction between puppy and people (and vice versa). Basic instructions to guests: Ignore my puppy for the first few minutes. This will help overly excited puppies calm themselves, minimize submissive urination puddles, and help shy pups accept the new person. If your puppy is really a leaper and grabber, try tethering him back nearby (see "Sit Is It!" on page 91 and "How to Tether," page 85) or crating him until you can bring him out on lead and under a tiny bit more control. Reward all good (or near good) behavior with a smile, praise, and a treat.

Expose, Don't Overwhelm

Exposure is where your puppy gets to experience something new at a safe distance. Overwhelming happens when your puppy

Taking a young dog into a crowded area can overwhelm some, though this young mix appears to be doing just fine. Maybe it's that plate of food in front of his nose.
BRIAN KILCOMMONS

can't get away from the new thing; it is too close and scares the puppy. Let's talk vacuum cleaners. Many puppies are understandably frightened by this roaring, moving thing.

A simple way to start: Turn on the vacuum in another part of the house just before your puppy's mealtime. Turn it off after you put down your puppy's bowl. It would look like this: Leaving puppy in kitchen, walk to other distant room, turn on the machine, walk back, praise your puppy as you feed him, walk back to the vacuum, turn it off. Your puppy shows no response to the sound? Excellent, that's perfect! Soon when your puppy hears the vacuum, he will look forward to something delicious. As your puppy adjusts, move the vacuum a few feet closer before each meal until it can run in the same room without your puppy being overly concerned. This all may take a few days to a few weeks. Who cares? This is a marathon, not a sprint. As long as you are moving forward and your puppy isn't frightened, you're doing great!

Handling Handling

Every puppy of every size and of every breed should allow handling by humans. Period. No debate. There are trainers these days who will tell you touching dogs slows their learning and is a bad thing. Nonsense! This theory is based on training marine mammals like dolphins, who do not sleep at the foot of anyone's bed. Even if handling does slow things down minimally, teaching a dog to accept handling without getting flustered or distracted is more important than any command you can teach. Dogs who live in our homes with us will be touched many times in many

Cuts on feet, ripped nails, sore spots are all common. Will your puppy let you help him?

ways every day. If you do not get them used to this early and often, you can run into trouble down the road. So get those hands on your puppy! Let's just do it in a sensible, productive way! The Level I Touch Games in Chapter 3 are a place to start.

Safe with Other Pets

If you want your puppy to grow into a dog who can be calm around your cat or bird or rabbit, start early. Have your puppy on lead, well away from your other animal companion(s). Practice Look At Me and Sit Is It! (pages 95 and 91) using plenty of calm praise and stroking along with treats to settle your puppy. Then move on to a little Near Is Dear (page 110). Proceed when you succeed.

Playing a few rounds of Mine using your other pet as the temptation (with puppy always on lead and other pets safe and secure) is also useful. This not

Here, young Greta shows that a well-trained puppy can behave around smaller pets. When in doubt, leave the lead on!
KAREN SAWDEY

only tells the puppy that this animal is literally yours, but it also pretrains him to back off and sit if you are heading toward him when he is near your other pet. Now *there's* a good thing.

PRODUCTIVE PLAY

Play can take the form of a game you play together or something your puppy does on her own. Since we are all what we practice, when you two play together we want you to choose games that build cooperation, connection, compliance, or confidence, not combat and competition. Pip versus the cardboard box is a confidence game as she climbed in and on the box, hauled it around, and pounced on it. This game went on for about fifteen minutes. We would not use any box that might have stored anything dangerous or was held together with staples, but other than that it is a harmless enough game. If she had started to eat it, we would have removed it.

Tricks for Treats

Bow

The universal canine invitation to play, teaching your companion how to do this on cue is a fine idea. This is a two-treat trick—one treat when he's bowing and the second when he stands back up. That second one will help prevent him from collapsing into a Down position.

With your puppy standing, take a treat toward the ground then move it slightly back, so it ends up between his front legs. If he bends his neck to follow it, treat him! Good puppy! Repeat several times. Many puppies at this point will rock back into a bow. Say "Bow" as they do so. Excellent—treat and then raise back up with the second treat. Good puppy!

If your puppy collapses into a Down (and who can blame him, since that's what we've been practicing), try putting your hand/arm under the belly. Praise and treat any effort in the right direction. Laugh, have fun!

Shake

The easiest way to teach this trick is to take a treat, hold it under your pup's nose at chest level, and wait. More often than not, your puppy will nose it, nose it again, and then, in frustration, paw at it. The moment that paw lifts at all, open your hand. The age-old, lift the paw and shake it gently as you say "Shake" works as well. Either way, have fun!

Belly Up

Exposing the belly voluntarily is a sign of surrender (in most situations). A dog who does this easily is usually more relaxed with humans leading than dogs who refuse. It's a good trick to work on, but don't force it.

For dogs who enjoy belly rubs, this is simple enough to teach. As you reach down to rub your puppy's belly say "Belly up," scratch her, then step away. Wait for your puppy to flop back over onto her side, then approach again, say "Belly up" again, and pet that cute belly. Soon, when your puppy hears those words she will flip her belly skyward!

The Prize Inside

Toys you can put food inside can keep a puppy well entertained and count as productive play. We suggest ones that are easy to clean. Our picks: Sterilized bones (smear the inside with a bit of peanut butter or cream cheese), Kong Toy (smear as with bone, or stuff with soaked kibble, freeze and give puppy as a meal), Twist 'n Treat for dry kibble. Go easy on the high-fat stuffings. Those extra calories can add up, especially with smaller breed/mix puppies. In many cases, a dab will do ya when it comes to making toys tempting. Some toys are easy enough to load but nearly impossible to clean. Since we had two food-cube toys filled with ants one year, we're sensitive to that problem.

Do Not Play

Light chasing

Chasing a flashlight or pointer-type laser beam seems like great fun and many puppies love it, until it becomes an obsession. Then sunlight on a wall or a flash from your watch face on the floor and you have a puppy chasing and staring for hours on end. It's best not to open Pandora's box.

Pounce on Feet

So cute, right? A puppy pouncing on your feet or hands, especially when you're under a blanket. Then one day you curl up on the couch to nap and, just as you drift off to sleep, your forty-eight pound ball of energy lands on you, chomping a toe. Can't fault him—it's what you praised.

Tug with a Doll

Ah, *no*. That goes quadruple for a doll that cries. This can confuse a dog should he ever come across a baby resting on a blanket on the floor.

HAVING FUN: THE WAY TO PLAY

Play is good for all of us, but when it comes to your puppy we want to start off right. Follow these simple guidelines:

• You start it, not the dog.

If you start to play when your dog throws a toy at you, barks at you, or grabs your hand, you'll soon find him persistently doing all three. If you "get what you pet," you *really* get what you play.

• You stop it and the dog stops.

This is a way to check just how in control of himself your puppy still is. Stop playing, your body relaxes, you breathe calmly, you look away— what happens? If your puppy slows within seconds, lowering his energy and stopping the game, perfect! You can play some more. If your puppy is so excited he races around the room, barks at you, races some more, jumps up—he's out of his own control. Game over. Add Beat the Clock (page

161) into your list of games to practice for the next week or two.

• It doesn't encourage bad behavior.

There is often some mouthing, some racing around, and the occasional bark, but nothing should hurt or be excessive. If you wonder if it is over the top, it is. Stop the game, and do some Guided Downs (page 92) and Simple Sits (page 153). Stop dead in your tracks, turn away if your pup does any of the above. Strive to be as crisp as possible. The more clear your actions are, the easier it is for the puppy to understand. You should turn off like a faucet. Leave no doubts.

• Now, go play!

Fun is . . . well . . . fun. Have all you like, just make it safe, productive fun. Late last night Sarah played some "football" with Pip in the living room. She had her sit, then she "hiked" a large stuffed sheep toy to her as if Pip were the quarterback. This was terrific Sit Is It! (page 91) and Wait (page 116) practice along with a little No Eye Can (page 167) thrown in for good measure. Pip thought it was a riot, Sarah laughed—good game.

If you cannot stop the game, then it is no longer a game.

IN YOUR YARD

Now is the time to start pretraining calm yard behavior. Many puppies never learn to listen in their own backyards because it is a place of freedom and play but never practice. If you want your future dog to be calm when people walk by, to be quiet when other dogs come into view, do your homework. You can play Near Is Dear with distractions beyond your fence. Step into view of them and reward, step out of view and go still. If your puppy is already barking, go as far away from the distraction as you can, then do Simple Sits, Guided Downs, Mine, Look At Me, and *lots* of Come into the house. Be persistent, then when he gives you a little attention when someone walks by, stop! Quit while you're ahead. Avoid that old "having achieved success, I rush headlong toward failure" pattern.

VISITING: GOING TO A FRIEND'S HOUSE

If you're like us, you want to take your pup with you as much as possible. And if you're like any new puppy person, you're worried about what your pup may do in someone else's home. And with good reason! Here are a few tricks of the trade to help things go well.

Here two well-behaved pups enjoy one of the Annual Family Dog Gatherings we host every July. What terrific pups!
SARAH WILSON

Yesterday we had a lovely outdoor lunch with friends. The table sat, spread with a summer feast, on a deck overlooking the Atlantic Ocean. The day was cool with the slightest breeze. In other words, it was perfect. Two of our dogs PJ and Wyatt joined us, lying quietly near the table after greeting everyone. A young, adorable Terrier pup also joined us. Wisely kept on lead, the pup did not stop moving the entire meal. He wound his lead around people's feet, grabbed sticks and leaves, played tug-of-war with napkins on our laps, and was generally a perfectly normal, slightly obnoxious puppy. The owners get huge kudos for bringing their pup out with them, but ask yourself, What good habits were being formed? Both owners admired our calm dogs, who lay quietly napping during the meal, listened to our soft commands, and were happily but politely social when invited. This luncheon didn't help those puppy people get closer to those goals, because they didn't know how to make it work for them. Here's how to start training manners early:

On Lead

This pup was on lead, so that was a good start. You do not know what someone has in their home—an heirloom figurine on a low table, a knitting project in a basket, a pound of chocolate on the coffee table (chocolate is toxic to dogs). Sarah let one of her pups off-lead once in her grandmother's house. Puppy promptly peed in the middle of a pale blue formal—and previously spotless—living room carpet. Lesson learned.

Foot on Lead

Before you go to visit, teach your pup to respond to lead pressure by lying down (see the "Guided Down" on page 92). Once learned, this is unbelievably useful. As one puppy class attendee said with a smile, "This was worth the price of the entire class!" In any new spot, when you want your pup to settle, put your foot on the lead. Give him maybe two feet of lead for a large breed pup and one foot for a smaller dog. Now wait. The pup will walk a bit, fuss a bit, and then settle. If he doesn't, shorten the lead a bit. Give him some time, shorten again. He'll settle. Remember, you get what you pet and you raise what you praise. So only pet and praise calm behavior.

Especially Good Chewy

When we travel, we always make sure to bring along puppy pacifiers such as a compressed rawhide, favorite hard nylon bone, or a new food-filled toy. When the puppy gets restless, one of these will keep him busy for a while longer.

It Won't Last for Long

Few young puppies can be calm for long. They either get restless or fall asleep. Right now, at five and a half months old, we expect a good toy to give us about twenty minutes of calm from Pip before she starts to roll, moan, chew the lead, try to get up, and generally fuss. Other pups fall apart sooner, some last longer. The only thing that matters is being responsive to your individual puppy. At that point we walk Pip before crating her for a nap. In an hour or so, we do another round. Nothing says you have to have the puppy out with you the whole time. Bring a crate if possible so you can tuck him away when it all gets to be too much.

What *Not* to Do

Put pup in backyard with resident dog

This is not a plan. Always supervise your puppy around any unknown or non-family adult dog. Make sure they meet off the adult dog's property, where he is likely to be more relaxed and less territorial. Even "nice" adult dogs don't always have endless patience for a strange puppy in their home. Unless these people are dog savvy and have a well-socialized dog, keep the dogs separated or keep your puppy crated.

Don't leave your puppy unsupervised. You don't know what he could get into or what experiences he could have.

Ignore wanted behavior

Get in the habit of praising and petting your puppy whenever she does something wonderful such as sitting quietly or doing nothing—even if you have to stop midsentence and midconversation. The conversation will be there when you get back, while the moment with your puppy might have passed. Grab the good when you spot it.

Come unprepared

Doing anything with a young puppy is all about the puppy; it's quite similar to traveling with a two-year-old. First you attend to the youngster, then you do what you hope to do. So we arrive with well-walked puppy on lead, a crate and a small bag of clean supplies in the car, carrying a small tote bag with poop bags for pickup, treats, chew toys, a long line, and a bowl for water. Can't go wrong!

This puppy person came to one of my lectures prepared: crate, blanket, toys, and her puppy on lead. Bravo!

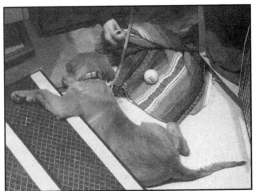

Pip and I are about to go into a store. Pip is looking at the auto-matic doors: What the heck are those? MELISSA FISCHER

OUT AND ABOUT: THE REST OF THE WORLD

Here's where things can get interesting. You never know what is around the corner, so you have to have a bag of tricks to pull from when the unexpected happens. Here's a start:

I'm Okay, You're Okay

Back to "act the way you want your puppy to act." When you are tense, worried, speaking fast, and/or breathing shallowly, your pup knows. He will not say, "Gee, my human is worried because I am worried." He's much more likely to think some canine version of "Human worried—this must really be scary!"

Support Confidence

Pet and praise confident behavior. You get what you pet; you raise what you praise. It is easy when your puppy has shy tendencies (or is in a sensitive period) to become attached to watching vigilantly for those signals. Don't. Be vigilant for normal behavior—after all, that's what you want to see more of, right?

Avoid Overwhelming

When we take a pup to a new busy place, we use the vehicle as the safe place. From there we do short forays out, ending up back at the car every few minutes. We might walk and treat, then crate in the car for a few minutes, then repeat. Inside the van it is rest time, not cuddle, stroking, sympathy time. All the good stuff happens *with you* outside, not inside the car.

People who love pups and rush toward yours squealing can scare the heck out of a puppy. We step forward in front of our pup blocking the person from him. If that doesn't slow them down—our hand goes up in a stop signal. Once the person is slowed down, enlist their help. Ask them to squat or bend down, and allow the pup to approach them. Do a little Check It Out as needed. You give the treats. If your pup does not come forward to greet, do not force him and do not allow the person to go to the pup. Pup has already said, "Nope, don't feel safe." Respect that.

I laugh and feed Pip a treat as a noisy shopping cart rumbles by. When carts equal treats, Pip will soon love carts. MELISSA FISCHER

WALKING THE WALK

Some puppies are sensitive to stepping on new surfaces, and others couldn't care less. Either way, play this game. Find different surfaces and things for your puppy to walk on, over, and through. Ideas include a flattened box, a metal grid, a plastic tarp, a low wall, a wobbly board, a bench, or a large rock. Be creative, have fun, make it happen. Like Check It Out, Walking the Walk is a game of approach and retreat. While it teaches your puppy to have confidence in you and the world around him, more importantly, it teaches you how to recognize stress in your puppy and to move him away from it before he becomes overwhelmed. The single biggest mistake people make with fearful puppies is to stay too long in a place that stresses them. The second biggest is sounding bored or, worse, worried. Make this a game, cheer your puppy on, have a playful attitude about it. Approach with enthusiasm, treat, then retreat. It is the fastest way to get your puppy to accept something new with confidence.

SCARED OF THE CITY

You live in the city so your pup has to adapt but your pup is scared on the street. What do you do?

Short Stretches

Keep things short and sweet at first. Better to do multiple short trips at first rather than one long one. Each short trip gives your puppy a chance to cope all over again, then return to a safe area. Good!

Check It Out with the Building as Safety

Get a pocketful of really good treats, have your puppy take a few steps out the door of your building, give a treat and praise, then return to the building. Pause there for a few seconds; say nothing to your puppy (because the good stuff happens away from the building, right?). Repeat. When your puppy lingers when you head back toward the building, give him another tiny treat or two before you both go back. That's your cue that he's ready to go a bit farther next time.

Give the Pup a Break

If your pup just had his shots or had a frightening experience, give him a day or two of his normal routine at home to recover before taking him out and about again. We know, in the city this is not always possible, just do the best you can. Often a short recess helps a pup cope better next time.

SARAH'S INBOX:

But She Won't Take Treats!

When I try to socialize my five-month-old rescue puppy, she just cowers and shakes. She won't even take her favorite treats. What can I do?

When a puppy is too frightened to eat, it means she is too frightened to learn. If she is frightened of you, try walking past her rather than up to her, tossing a yummy treat in her direction as you walk on by. Don't stop, don't look at her, don't speak to her—walk past, toss, and go. Your goal is for her to start *wanting* you to walk by. See "Sensitive/Shy: Help for Our Wallflowers" in Chapter 8. Mix it up in your home, playing Check It Out and Near Is Dear with objects and people. With these puppies focus on the Trust and Attention Games in Chapters 3 through 5.

DOG PARKS

Dog parks are often not a place for young pups to play any more than the middle of a high-school football game is a place for a nine-year-old child. If there is a smaller dog run, that can work, provided your puppy doesn't play too roughly with those little ones. Even when your dog is older, say ten months old, stand outside and observe the dogs there before entering. What sorts of games are they playing? Are their tails straight up (which means they are being pushy and are stimulated)? Do they take turns chasing each other or target one frightened dog? Standing outside also allows all dogs to meet and greet through the fence, helping to avoid some of the excited, intense gate greeting that can intimidate pups of any age.

Trust Your Gut!

Your obligation is to your puppy—not to anyone else. Most pups are not ready to play pell-mell with adolescent and adult dogs until they are of similar age. Getting rolled or run over by larger adults or sub adults can hurt your pup mentally and physically. If a dog is trying to hump your pup nonstop, then ask the owner to intervene. If he will not, leave. Sometimes two young dogs can take turns humping, though usually it is one dog asserting him- or herself over another in a persistent and obnoxious way. Any owner who says "Oh, he's just playing," totally does not get it. Take your dog and leave. Go for a brisk walk instead.

If someone's dog tears into the park or runs head, ears and tail up, and comes up stiffly as if walking on his tiptoes, leave. If someone starts throwing a ball around or near a group of dogs (some parks are bigger than others), leave, even if your dog isn't chasing the ball. A pack of dogs in pursuit of a toy care little for what's in their path—dog or human.

BRIAN'S INBOX:

Is My Puppy Aggressive?

I have been taking Willow to the local dog park. She has been doing very well for only thirteen weeks old. She allows all the dogs to come over and sniff her—if they are big or a bit rambunctious she flips over belly up. However, if they get too nosy with her for too long she bares her teeth and snaps. She doesn't make contact but she tells them to back off. I did not think that pups this age had aggression yet. Is this a sign that she will have aggression issues? Or do they know how to protect themselves at thirteen weeks old?

Puppies who have been with their litter for six weeks or longer do know how to interact with other dogs. Puppies, like people, vary in their social skills. The snapping she is showing is natural. My suggestion: Skip the dog park for now. Find older, sensible dogs for her to interact with or puppies about the same age to play with one or two at a time. While things have gone well at the dog park so far, if a young puppy panics then runs, other dogs can give chase. That can happen very fast and be quite scary for her and you. She could also be injured by just being in the way of adult dogs playing. Last, one of these days her "puppy pass" will expire, then things may change in a blink. We don't like most dog parks and runs for young puppies. Wait until your dog is the same age or older than most of the dogs there. Until then? Let her socialize through the fence. She can still greet and play bow but will be safe from being overwhelmed and won't have to practice defending herself.

DOGGY DAY CARE

Be careful here. Look for a place that uses crates, gives dogs rest periods throughout the day, has *experienced* staff in with the dogs, and breaks the dogs up into compatible groups. Too many doggy day cares have opened based on pure enthusiasm and "love" of dogs, but are short on experience. Big red flags: Dogs playing wearing slip, choke, or prong collars. If a dog's jaw gets caught in another dog's collar, both dogs panic and start to spin and roll. The collar tightens around one dog's neck and the other dog's jaws. To help them, you either need heavy-duty bolt cutters or a strong, dog-savvy person who can manhandle the dogs into untwisting. This is not the time for a teenager on a cell phone to learn the ropes. Or is the staff throwing toys for a large group of dogs? Doesn't that look like fun? It's about as much fun as an all-day rugby match. We know of several dogs injured and one smaller dog killed in that same situation. Pick a place that talks about safety, not one that is trying to sell you on how much "fun" the dogs are having. Your puppy is going to learn from these people and these dogs. What are they teaching?

EXERCISE AND THE GROWING PUPPY

Growing bodies need exercise. They need to romp, play, tumble, and chase. Puppies, normally raised with siblings, are used to interactive play—often the type that makes humans yelp. Whenever possible, find other similarly sized youngsters for your puppy to play with. Put up a note at your veterinarian's or see if a local trainer or day care has puppy play times.

Here are three general guidelines:

- No forced exercise
- Limit rough play
- Supply good footing

A good game of chase between well-matched puppies is great fun for everyone! SARAH WILSON

Activities like scootering with your dog are a blast, but have to wait until your puppy is all grown up to start. At eighteen months for most dogs, twenty-four or more for the giants.
SARAH WILSON

No Forced Exercise

No jogging or long on-lead hiking with growing puppies. Debbie Gross Saunders, canine physical therapist, suggests about ten to fifteen minutes walking per month old. So a two-month-old puppy would get two ten-minute walks a day, a five-month-old more like two thirty-minute walks or three twenty-minute walks. There is a limit to this math as most of us have lives to lead, but it is a good guideline to contemplate.

If you have not been doing this much walking, start slowly so your puppy has a chance to build up his muscles, maybe five or ten more minutes each walk for a week before adding the next level. Off-lead walking in areas where your pup can play safely is great but unfortunately not a reality for most of today's puppy owners. By the time your pup is giving out and lying down on lead you've already gone too far. Jogging and hiking start once your puppy has completely finished growing her bones. This is usually around eighteen to twenty-four months of age, depending on the size of your dog. The larger the dog, the longer growth takes to complete. Don't take a pup's enthusiasm for more as proof positive that it is a good idea. They don't know anything about it!

Now, about the weather. Every year heat kills dogs. The bigger bodied your dog or the shorter the nose, the harder heat is on him. In hot weather, exercise early, like "at dawn" early, and as dusk falls. Always have water on hand and learn the signs of overheating. A tip? When the tongue starts to turn bright red and widen out so it looks more like baloney than a normal tongue, stop immediately and seek shade, water, and rest.

Limit Rough Play

Some breeds really like rough play—Retrievers and Terriers are a good example. For many of them, play is an all-out, full-contact sport. But for any pup who is racing and slamming, spinning and tumbling, such play should be limited to about half an hour at a stretch, less if you're worried or have an at-risk puppy. "At risk" applies to pups, pure or mixed, who come from breeds where bad hips and/or elbows are common. Play does not *cause* bad hips, but it can make them worse. If your goal is to have a companion who is as sound as possible for as long as possible, limit rough play. Rough play between adult dogs and your puppy should be eliminated entirely. Quiet games are fine, but anything that is high impact or high speed is high risk.

Supply Good Footing

Slippery is risky—for anyone. A game of touch football on grass is a whole different game than if you're on linoleum wearing socks. Pups don't understand risk and most will play equally hard on a slippery hardwood or icy surface, risking injury in the process. It may be just a pulled muscle, but it could be something worse, like a torn ligament. The latter is more prevalent in heavy or big-bodied breeds, such as Rottweilers, Bulldogs, and some Labrador Retrievers

Dogs with fuzzy feet—Poodles, Cavalier King Charles Spaniels, Shih Tzus, Lhasa Apsos, Havaneses, Old English Sheepdogs—and breeds at particular risk of hip or elbow dysplasia—all the Retrievers, German Shepherd Dogs, Old English Sheepdogs, and many other large breed dogs—need extra-good footing. We purchase rubber-backed carpet runners when raising pups to give them safe passage over slick flooring. Pay particular attention to corners on tile near a back door or a spot where the carpet ends and slick floors begin. Whatever you pay to make these areas safe is less than the cost of surgery which could be a thousand plus (plus, plus) in many cases.

SAFETY FIRST

Sticks

Pups love to carry sticks, but just as a child shouldn't run with a sharp object in his mouth, a pup should not run with the end of the stick pointing down his throat. Pups carry sticks by the part you last touched. If you want him to carry it in the middle, rub the middle and offer that to your pup. Chances are he'll take it and march proudly (and more safely) along.

Carrying a stick by the end is dangerous!

Balls

Pups love balls. But as with toddlers, puppies should play only with toys that cannot be swallowed, meaning your pup should have to open his jaws a bit to fit in the ball. Cat toys are rarely safe for dogs, and handballs can be a bad choice for large-breed dogs. The good old-fashioned tennis ball is usually safe but if your pup is a disassembler, give them only when you are home. Be sure to throw them out when they start to come apart, or get a solid rubber or hard plastic dog ball to play with.

Rocks

We call a rock in your pup's mouth an eight-hundred-dollar rock because that's what it may cost you to get it out of your pup's belly if he swallows it. Carrying rocks also wears down teeth. Granted, some dogs carry rocks around their whole lives without a single problem. Feeling lucky? We don't think so.

WALKING AROUND SUBURBIA

Young puppies (under twelve weeks old) are not generally ready to stroll around the average suburban American neighborhood. If you have loose dogs in your area or dogs who rush their fence-line barking, try to find quieter, less frightening places to walk your little one. The goal at this age is to minimize scary events while still getting your puppy out and about. When she is older and wiser and you both are a more polished, connected team, you can take on this gauntlet.

Often, choosing a shopping district is a better bet. Encourage strangers to greet your puppy whenever they show an interest. Make play dates with friends who enjoy your newest addition. Show her the world, a little at a time. Keep things brief, go to different places, have fun.

How about a local puppy class? These can be wonderful ways to get your puppy off on the right foot with strange dogs and people. Most include handling, manners, and socialization, along with some basic puppy training. Even if you've had dogs all your life, getting to a puppy class just can't be beat.

Greeting Other Dogs

Do not allow your puppy to drag you toward a strange dog. Period. We know—he just wants to make friends, but running full bore at an adult dog is a good way to make enemies and get snarled at by the dog (or the owner or both). Don't tell us you can't stop him; you can. If he were dragging you into traffic, you

This young Jack Russell Terrier approaches PJ head up, ears up, tail up. PJ pricks her ears forward, gives the young one a hard look. Message received, he stops at a polite distance, ears back, tail low. PJ's ears are at ease, she sees that he has gotten the message to "respect his elders." SARAH WILSON

would stop him. If you cannot, then find a trainer, use a head halter, and get some control now, because this is only going to get worse as your puppy gets larger.

Greet a strange dog the way a child would greet a previously unknown adult human. Walk up politely. Stop, say "Hello," offer a hand to shake. Nowadays, parents know better than to assume that every adult human is safe for their child to meet. The same applies to strange adult dogs. Your puppy may be friendly, but the other dog may not be. Protect your puppy. Ask if your puppy can greet the dog. Go back and read the "Dog-to-Human Pictionary" (page 7) so you know a few of the warning signs should you see them. Then proceed. As the two dogs interact, laugh, praise, and sound happy. Set the stage for a good exchange. Dog owners everywhere will thank you.

Puppies will often bark at strange dogs at one point or another, usually more from fear than anything else. They may bark as they back up, bark from a hiding pace, or bark while looking bold, then turn tail with a yelp if the adult dog approaches.

Try not to be upset with your puppy. She is a baby and doesn't know what else to do. Correcting her can make her more fearful of the situation and more stressed. Instead, give her something else to do, move away from the dog, work Mine (page 82) using the other dog as the distraction then praise and treat her attention, or just hang out for a few minutes and let her watch what is going on. Getting her around social dogs is very helpful in teaching her to accept strange dogs. A puppy class is a great place to start.

SOCIALIZING WITH OTHER PEOPLE

Puppies are used to what they know. If they were raised by one gender, race, or age of person, variety can be shocking. Imagine that you rounded a corner only to see a tiny, bright blue man standing there smiling. What would you do? Stop dead in your tracks, walk by pretending you didn't see him, become frightened and tell him to come no closer, take it in stride, or run away? Now imagine that this bright blue man saw you, started to squeal and rush toward you, arms outstretched. Get the idea? This is what it's like when your puppy meets someone entirely different from anyone else he's ever met.

If your puppy is showing signs of stress, don't allow people to walk up to him, attempting to pet him. That can tip him into panic, which is an experience we'd like to avoid. Always allow your puppy to approach a person, not vice versa. If someone is coming in like a guided missile, step out in front of your puppy, put up your hand, smile and say, "Wait just a second; I think he's a little scared."

SOCIALIZING WITH YOUR CHILDREN

First rule from our book *Childproofing Your Dog:* Never allow your child to do to a puppy what you would not allow done to a younger child. This includes but is by no means limited to: lying on top of; holding down; chasing after; carrying around; hitting; smacking; kicking; waking up; bothering when eating; hopping at, after, or on; or in any way intentionally frightening, annoying, or harassing the puppy.

The second rule is to supervise. When you cannot supervise or there is too much going on, crate your puppy.

Even though your child is delighted with the puppy, the pup is not a baby-sitter or a toy for your children to do with what they want. If you abandon your puppy to your children, expect your puppy to start defending himself accordingly. How does your puppy say, "Enough"? By turning or moving away. If your puppy has taken himself under a table or into another room, insist that your child leave him alone. Every year, tens of thousands of children are seriously bitten, mostly by known dogs, mostly on the face and hands. This can often be avoided if you teach your children to respect your puppy's signals that enough is enough.

KEEPING KIDS BITE FREE

Too many children get injured by dogs every year, injuries that might have been avoided by following one simple rule: The dog always approaches the child, not the other way around. Put another way: If the dog stays away, your child stays away.

Teach your children always to "ask" a dog if the dog wants to play, say hello, or be friends by stopping four to six feet away, turning sideways, and speaking kindly. If the dog doesn't move toward your child, don't let your child move toward the dog. Period. Known dog, friend's dog, your own dog, strange dog—doesn't matter. If the animal says, "Not right now," that must be respected. Do not force a dog to "speak" more clearly. This applies whether the dog is sleeping, eating, or chewing. Avoid entirely dogs that are behind a fence, on a chain, or in a car.

A great way to get your child involved in safe habits is to enlist him or her as the puppy's protector. Explain that the puppy is younger and can't speak up, so he needs your child's help to feel safe. Most children take this sort of assignment seriously, doing a good job especially when friends are over. *Note for parents*: If your dog growls at or threatens children at any time for any reason, get help today!

SOCIALIZING WITH OTHER CHILDREN

First off, some puppies love children. Even if they've never met any before, they positively melt the first time they do. Their ears go back, their eyes soften as they wiggle and wag with glee. Everything about them says "Oooooo, kids!" Milo is such a dog. If you have one, count yourself lucky.

Children, who look, sound, move, and smell (hormonally) differently from adults, can cause much confusion and fear in puppies. Your puppy may fly backward, bark in alarm, hackle up, and otherwise make you want to crawl under a rock. But don't. Instead, act the way you want your puppy to act: relaxed and confident. Move him away from the child then do Guided Downs, Left Circle, Leave It, and Look At Me games, rewarding him with treats, praise, and slow petting with gentle massage down the back. Let him observe the children at a distance.

A little girl asks to greet Pip. I gently hook two fingers through Pip's collar so I can help her to resist the urge to jump. MELISSA FISCHER

Park your car or sit on a park bench on the outside of a playground, away from the front gate. Bring delicious treats, play some Near Is Dear (page 110). Make that spot a wonderful place to be. As your pup relaxes, spend more time there, feeding the treats less frequently as you relax together in the sun. Enjoy the moment.

Do not allow children to stampede up to your frightened puppy. Body block the child as you would your puppy in a Mine (page 82). Recently Sarah and Pip went into a pet-supply store. A young child entered, grabbed a squawking pheasant toy off the shelf, and ran at Pip, squeezing the toy repeatedly. Pip, frightened flew back to the end of the lead, struggling to get away. Sarah stepped in front, blocking the child. The child moved to cut around her, so Sarah blocked him more clearly. She was not letting that child get past. Better she be seen as rude than let Pip be frightened further. Not only does this keep the child safer, but it showed Pip that Sarah would do one of her jobs as her leader: protect her. Working with a puppy leery of children can be complicated. Get some hands-on coaching if you are not sure how to proceed.

When Pip first got home she decided she needed to bring my boots upstairs. Why? We have no idea. Once she accomplished this, she never attempted it again.
SARAH WILSON

CHAPTER 7

A CLEAN HOUSE: HOUSEBREAKING AND PAPER-TRAINING

Most puppies want to be clean. Given half a chance, they can be mistake free with our help at twelve to sixteen weeks and fully "I'll hold it!" housebroken by six to seven months old. Before that, mistakes can be kept to a minimum by keeping them in one or two rooms when not confined, watching them like a hawk, adhering to a routine, and feeding them a consistent diet. While most housebreaking goes smoothly, there can be bumps along the way. We've helped thousands through those bumps and we share what we've learned here.

HOUSEBREAKING: THE RULES

Rules of Supervision

Keep Your Puppy in Sight

"Just around the corner" is often "just making a mistake." Many pups don't care to urinate or defecate close to their people, so keeping a puppy on lead with you in the house can prevent many a puddle and alert you to the ones that are about to happen.

Go from Less Confinement to More

Whenever your puppy is out with you, progress from less confinement to more. Supervised in a room with you (the least indoor confinement) moves to on lead with you (a bit more confining) moves to crated (the most confining). Always move from less confinement to more. Each new level of confinement increasingly encourages your puppy to "hold it." It isn't magic, though; if your puppy really has to go, he will.

When You Go from More Confinement to Less, Walk Puppy

When you let your pup off the lead or out of her crate, she will want to pee, even if you just walked her half an hour ago. When you let the pup out of your apartment and into the hallway, she will want to pee. Anytime you go from a situation of more confinement to less, she will feel freer to go. So if you've had her on lead at your side for twenty minutes then you unclip her to play ball for a bit in the hall, guess what will happen? Give her a quick potty break first.

Go Out with Your Puppy

Pushing your puppy out the door in wet or cold weather is tempting, but not helpful. Your puppy may just sit on the step waiting for you or, if your puppy is like our Pip when she arrived, slam repeatedly into the door in an effort to get to you. We have to go out with her; it is December in New York—too bad for us. We need to be there to tell her to "hurry up" and "get busy," she needs praise and treats for doing so, and we're the ones to give her those things so out we go—day and night.

Neither rain, nor sleet, nor dark of night shall keep you from your housebreaking rounds. Here Pip does circles in the snow, while I wait quietly.
MELISSA FISCHER

Use Crates Wisely

Crates are wonderful tools. We can't imagine raising a puppy without a crate—for their safety and our sanity. But, like a car seat for a baby, they can be misused. Neither a crate nor a car seat are meant to take the place of good hands-on care. No puppy should be in a crate for twenty-two hours a day. How does twenty-two hours a day happen? Out for an hour in the morning, crated while the person is away at work, out for an hour in the evening during which the puppy annoys their owners to the point where the pup is crated, again. This is a recipe for an undersocialized, overly active, teeth-everywhere puppy. If you must leave a puppy for long hours, then you must arrange for midday care, get up earlier, and come home promptly ready to train and interact. You have to accommodate your puppy's needs, and what a puppy needs and craves is your time, attention, and teaching. There is no replacement for you.

FIRST FEW DAYS AT HOME? MISTAKES HAPPEN

It is common, normal, and rather expected for your puppy to have an accident or two the first few days. You're both learning about each other. Get him out as often as you can—every half hour or so when he is out of confinement. Go out with him—praising and rewarding him for going outside and he'll soon catch on. Baby puppies, under sixteen weeks, have little muscle control. They can't help when they go, so don't be angry. What is a disaster is allowing mistakes to happen routinely—daily—without adjusting your schedule to prevent them. That's setting the groundwork for a decade of wet rugs and frustrated family.

Gates and Ex-pens: How to Keep Puppies Where You Put Them

The key to using gates and exercise pens is to have the puppy stay wherever you put him. This may be obvious, but the implications probably aren't. You don't want your puppy climbing or pushing on the gate or pen? Then don't pet him or pick him up when his feet are on the gate or pen. The first thing to try is simply ignoring him. Just look away when he jumps. When he stops jumping, look back, smile, and scoop him up. If he starts jumping again before you can reach him, stand up, look away, and say nothing. He'll figure it out.

For more persistent puppies, we rattle the barrier whenever we see the puppy up on it. When we go to pet the puppy, we rattle the barrier until he gets off—then we pet. With bold puppies, ones likely to try climbing these barriers, we want to create a minor aversion to having their feet on these objects. Once a puppy learns to climb these, he won't unlearn it. This habit can be dangerous for toy-breed puppies, who can have squirrel-like climbing ability and end up teetering precariously three to four feet off the ground.

Other approaches are: install the gate with a slight inward tilt that makes it harder to climb. Also, working your Wait There (page 150 in Chapter 5) will get things on the right track.

We get what we pet, so what will we get more of here? If we want our pups to stay where we put them, we can't pet them for jumping on the gate. No matter how cute it is! SARAH WILSON

Rules of Scheduling

The basic rhythm of your pup's life until fully housebroken is:

Confine: Crated, Gated, or On Lead with You

For housebreaking and paper-training purposes, your puppy is either in a room with you, on lead with you, or in a crate. Gating in a room all alone rarely works. The exceptions: some giant breed pups for whom a small puppy-proofed bathroom is crate-like and anytime you must leave your puppy for longer than he can reasonably be expected to hold it. In that case, a small, puppy-proofed room with papers is the best option.

Walk: Straight Out

Stay quiet and don't excite the puppy. Get your shoes and coat on, find your keys *before* you open that crate door. From crate to outside needs to be a direct, nonstop flight. If you can carry him, carry him quietly. Speak to him and greet him *after* you're outside.

Exercise and Education

After your puppy goes in the spot you've chosen, then go for a longer walk. Young puppies can dawdle and explore, but keep them moving—this is exercise, not sight seeing. Now, if you slipped a minute or two of teaching into each walk, your puppy would be the best-trained dog in the neighborhood in no time! Mental stimulation is as important as physical and often more calming.

Supervision

Supervision isn't just shared space—it is awareness. The younger the puppy, the more awareness you need to have. If you can't really supervise, then have your pup on lead with you or crated. Give him something to chew on or you may quickly find yourself with half a shoelace or a damaged table leg.

Thinking of each interaction as a chance to teach integrates training seamlessly into your life. Pip rarely gets more than five minutes a day of formal training but many little lessons are taught a few seconds at a time whenever she comes out of her crate (Wait, Sit), waits at the door (Sit, Look At Me), sits for a toy to be given (Look At Me). It is a way of living with your puppy, not "school." It is quite like teaching a child manners. You don't sit down and have a "class," rather you teach the behavior every time it is needed, starting with gentle urging and praise, then moving to expecting the child to do it on their own.

Confine Again . . .

And the cycle begins again.

With a seven-week-old pup, this routine (confine, walk, exercise, supervise, confine again) repeats itself every two to three hours with relatively brief exercise and supervision periods. By the time your puppy is seven months old, the routine is on an every six- to eight-hour rhythm with longer exercise and hang out periods.

CHARTING YOUR PROGRESS

Keep a chart such as the one here by the back door or on top of the crate. Keeping records helps to get things on track (and enables you to see trends forming quickly).

Time	Urination/ Defecation	Where?
7:00 A.M.	U / D	Outside
8:30	U / D	By Back Door—Try Recrating at 8:15.
10:00	U / D	Outside, went on cue! YEAH!!!

Rules of Correction

Imagine this: You are an eight-year-old child. You reach to touch a doorknob (a completely normal thing to do in your world) and a family member runs up to you screaming. He takes your head and forces it toward the doorknob continuing to scold. He may smack you on your butt or give you a shake but at no time does he tell you what he wants from you.

Now since you *have* to touch a doorknob from time to time and you have no idea what the problem is, what do you start to do? How about wait for that person to be somewhere else before you touch the doorknob? Because clearly, *he* has a big problem with doorknob touching. So whenever he leaves the room, you use the doorknob. Now that person is probably calling you "sneaky," "stupid," "spiteful," and "stubborn." If they come into the room you may lower your head a bit or turn away. Now you'll be accused of "knowing what you did wrong."

This is a puppy's experience with housebreaking. If you yell at him, smack him, or rub his face in his mistake, it will teach him—that you are crazy around urine and feces. It will not teach your puppy to think: Gee, I need to go. I should probably ask my person to let me outside. It will teach your puppy to think, Gee, I need to go. Better get as far away from my person as possible. She has a weird aggression problem.

What can you do? Interrupt the behavior. If you catch your puppy in the act of squatting in the house, make *one* sudden, loud sound—slap a wall or table with the flat of your hand or make one loud clap—with the goal of startling him into stopping midstream. Then rush him outside, where he is praised for finishing the job. If you find a mistake after the fact? It's too late. Clean up and learn from it.

Rules of Walking

"Hurry, Hurry" and "Get Busy"

Teaching a puppy to go on "command" sure can make life easier when you're traveling or in a rush. And it's easy. When your puppy is peeing, say, "Hurry, hurry" quietly over and over. When he's done, praise and give a treat. When he starts to poop,  chant a quiet "Get busy." Follow with praise and a treat. Over time, your puppy will make the connection.

Be Boring

There is an art to getting a puppy to pee and/or poop, and it is the art of being really, really boring. When we take a puppy outside on lead, we go to the designated bathroom zone and walk in slow laps around the area. Think of walking around a bathtub—make your circle about that size. We do not look at the puppy. We do not speak to the puppy. We walk slowly. If the puppy stops to sniff, we pause a second to see if he might pee. If he does, "Hurry, hurry" then "Yeah!" If not, we keep walking while we squeeze/ pulse the lead to get him moving. Once walking, we give him slack. We look for sniffing, quick circling, or spinning on the lead, repeated sitting down, pulling off as if just over there is the perfect spot (it isn't—stay where you are). When the puppy starts to go we calmly say the cue words "Hurry up" or "Get busy." When the puppy is done, we celebrate! Treats, petting, praise, the works. Leave no doubt in your puppy's mind that you liked what he did!

Play or Walk After

Be sure you do something fun *after* the puppy goes. Why? Because some Smart Puppies learn to delay going if they know doing so means going right back into the house, ending the fun walk. So reward pottying with some play or exploration.

Male pup peeing. They stand still, tail raised a bit. A totally still pup is often a peeing pup.
SARAH WILSON

Female pup peeing. Females usually squat, tail raised a bit.
SARAH WILSON

Rules of Feeding and Watering

JACKSON YOUNG

Feed meals at regular times using regular foods in regular amounts. Free feeding is a bad idea both for housebreaking and for your puppy's health. Feed puppies under four months of age three meals a day; after that twice a day is usually fine. Feed a premium puppy food and don't mess around with it too much. The more regular the diet, the more regular your puppy.

Water needs to be available whenever your puppy is out of her crate. If you think she is drinking a lot, please see: "Drinks Too Much," page 286.

Crating

Used properly, a crate can make your and your puppy's life calmer, easier, and safer. Think of the crate as you would a car seat or playpen for a child; not for use forever but as a tool needed to keep your youngster safe.

MELISSA FISCHER

What Type?

If puppy is familiar with a certain type, use that type. Otherwise, we are fans of the plastic crates. Easier to clean in case of accidents, less prone to certain dangers (such as getting a toe stuck in the threshold of the door or a jaw getting caught in the bars), and they are nearly impossible to assemble incorrectly.

The soft-sided fabric crates were created for dog sport enthusiasts so they could contain their dogs easily without having to wrestle heavy, awkward, metal or plastic crates from show to show. Those dogs are supervised and crate-savvy dogs. Fabric crates were *not* made for puppies!

What Size?

For a puppy under twelve weeks of age plan on needing two crates. The first is for your young puppy and it should be a bit larger than half your pup's expected adult size. Meaning, if you expect your pup to grow to a forty-pound dog, get a crate for a twenty- to twenty-five-pound puppy. Not sure how big your puppy will be? Then buy a crate for a bit more than twice your pup's current weight. This will be small enough that your puppy shouldn't want to mess in it, but large enough for your puppy to have room to grow.

When your pup is entirely mistake free in this crate for several weeks or is outgrowing it, get the adult-sized crate. This crate can be more spacious, as your puppy is already in the habit of keeping it clean. For people who feel better leaving their companion in roomy accommodations (we're two of those people) go ahead and get a roomy crate.

If your puppy is older than twelve weeks, and still being housebroken, you can probably use an appropriately adult-sized crate. Meaning if you're guessing your pup will finish off at about forty pounds; get a crate for a forty-pound dog, no larger. Usually you can guesstimate the adult size of your puppy by doubling their weight between four and five months of age. Pip was seventeen to twenty pounds during that time, so we expect her to be thirty-four to forty pounds as an adult. When you bring that crate home, feed your pup kibble or treats off the bottom for the first couple of weeks to deter her from using it as a bathroom.

What to Put in It?

Not newspaper! Having newspaper in the crate will only encourage using it for a bathroom—exactly the opposite of our goal! Most pups shred any bedding you put in at first, so the plain crate floor is fine for them. Exceptions are tiny toy breeds and thin-coated breeds like sighthounds, Dobermans, or Weimaraners. They need some padding. We love artificial fleece because it is so lightweight, easy to clean but durable. You can often find yards on sale at fabric stores at reasonable prices.

Petra enjoys her crate, napping in it whenever it is open. Notice the blanket between the crate pan and the crate bottom. This keeps it from rattling as she steps in and out. MELISSA FISCHER

Where to Put It?

Put the crate where the action is in your house: the family room or the kitchen are the top two spots. You want your puppy to be exposed to your life without running freely through it all the time. Isolating a puppy in the basement or garage will lead to barking from loneliness and fear as well as missing out on critical socialization.

Many people crate their puppies in their bedroom at night (we do). This means you'll hear him if he fusses, allowing you to take him right out. Also, if you're away all day long, having him near you at night is a good idea.

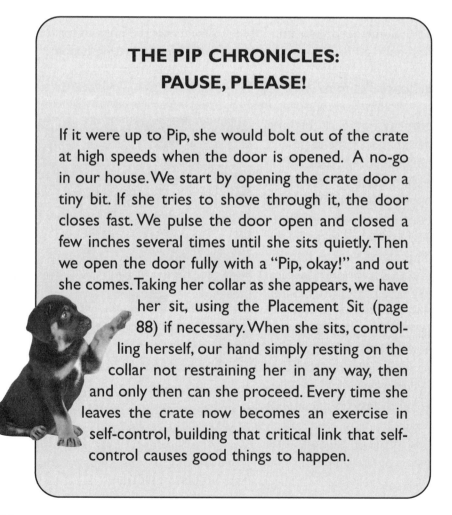

THE PIP CHRONICLES: PAUSE, PLEASE!

If it were up to Pip, she would bolt out of the crate at high speeds when the door is opened. A no-go in our house. We start by opening the crate door a tiny bit. If she tries to shove through it, the door closes fast. We pulse the door open and closed a few inches several times until she sits quietly. Then we open the door fully with a "Pip, okay!" and out she comes. Taking her collar as she appears, we have her sit, using the Placement Sit (page 88) if necessary. When she sits, controlling herself, our hand simply resting on the collar not restraining her in any way, then and only then can she proceed. Every time she leaves the crate now becomes an exercise in self-control, building that critical link that self-control causes good things to happen.

My Smart Puppy Person	Problem Puppy Owner
Is calm as puppy goes into and comes out of the crate. She knows she is helping her puppy stay relaxed and form good habits. She's proud of her calm puppy and confident that she is making her puppy's life less stressful.	Frantically praises the puppy as it comes out of the crate because she is "happy" to see it. She doesn't see that this is creating stress in her puppy. She is proud of the leaping and barking because it proves her puppy "loves" her.
Ignores the puppy in the crate (unless specifically and calmly rewarding him). She knows eye contact and talking will only create frustration.	Talks and looks at the crated puppy often. She wants the puppy to know that she loves him and takes the puppy's whining as proof of puppy's unhappiness, not of frustration she helped to create.
Uses a schedule. She knows that routine helps all young things, and that it is a gift she gives both her puppy and herself.	Plays it by ear. She labels the puppy's slow housebreaking, chewing, and demanding behavior as "stubborn" or "difficult," taking no responsibility for her role in all those things.

Introducing the Crate

Set yourself up for success. Since many pups will be frightened if the crate moves when they step in, put a towel or rug between the crate and the floor. If you have a metal crate, put a towel between the bottom pan and the bottom of the crate so the pan doesn't clink and shift. Once the crate is secure, then toss all toys and a few treats in the crate and leave the door open. Allow your pup to explore at his or her own speed.

Try reverse psychology. Put his dinner inside the crate and close the door. Wait a minute or so, then open the door and allow him to eat. This works like a charm for pups with a hearty appetite. Barking, digging, and general fussing are to be expected.

Collars and crates don't go together. We've never had a problem with a crate-trained dog being left in a plastic crate with a flat, plastic or metal clasp-type collar on, but we are very cautious with puppies. The best course? Collar free!

But then how do you get the collar on an excited, squirmy puppy? One way is to use a martingale-type collar for walking. This allows you to slide it over your pup's head and go. You can practice this part with your puppy by sliding the collar onto your own arm, then holding a treat in that hand. As your puppy sniffs at the treat, slide the collar off your arm onto your puppy. As you do that, give your puppy the treat. Presto! No-struggle collaring!

Oh, Ick! Cleanup Hints

Puppies can tell where their bathroom is by the smell, so it's critical that you remove all accident odor when housebreaking your puppy. Since your dog can smell one part urine in one million parts water, a simple water-and-vinegar solution will not adequately remove the urine smell. Never use ammonia, because ammonia is in urine. Purchase a specially produced odor neutralizer from a pet-supply outlet or your veterinarian. It is money well spent.

Here is our yard cleanup equipment. Keep your yard tidy.
SARAH WILSON

"Asking" to Go Out

Most dogs do show signs that they need to go, and we don't always pick up on those signs. Milo paces back and forth between me and the door. That one is obvious. PJ sits by the door, stoic. Other dogs we've had circle our chairs, put a paw on us and stretch, yawn in our faces. Whatever they do, we eagerly ask, "Do you need to go *outside?*" as we walk toward the door. Doing this quickly teaches the dog that we "get it," and their asking becomes stronger. Other common canine signals include whining, circling, circling while sniffing, restlessness, rushing out of the room, and lingering by the back door. It is your job to notice what happens before the puddle happens.

Note: The younger the puppy, the fewer signals she gives because the length of time between "Oh, look, I need to go" and going is about a blink. This will change as she matures, getting noticeably better around sixteen weeks of age for most pups.

Housebreaking: Problems and Solutions

There are many reasons for housebreaking mistakes; some of the most common are listed here. Many solutions suggest that changing foods may be worth a try. If you decide to do that, go slowly, adding a bit more new and a bit less old over the course of a week or so. The last thing you need is to cause a tummy upset during housebreaking.

After Spaying or Neutering

Every so often, neutering a pup triggers housebreaking mistakes, most commonly urinating in the house. Simply watch your pup more closely and add an extra walk or two for the first couple of weeks after surgery. Things should be back to normal quickly. No scolding, please!

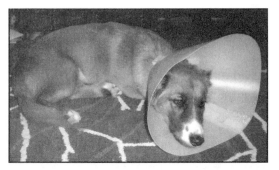

A spay is major surgery. Fudge needed extra rest and more walks for a week or so, then she felt all better. Jackson Young

Bedding Is Wet and So Is Puppy

Your dog wakes up from sleeping and the bed is wet, or the side of her body she was sleeping on is wet. The problem is often worse after hard exercise or very sound sleep. This can be caused by having too little of the chemical that signals the body to hold the urine in. In many cases, medication from the veterinarian works quickly and completely.

Can't Make It through the Night

If she is pooping in the middle of the night, try moving her dinnertime to 9:30 or so, with her last walk after 10:00 P.M. Sometimes that helps virtually overnight. If it doesn't, try feeding two-thirds of her daily amount in the morning, then one-third at night. Not quite there yet? Then consider a better-quality food that you can feed less of while still giving her the nutrition she needs.

Make sure you aren't chatting with her, petting her, or giving her treats on midnight walks or she may be waking you for the company. In the middle of the night, you are simply transportation in and out—nothing more. You're not angry, not happy, act what you are: sleepy.

Can't Hold It during the Day

Are you feeding the correct amount? More is not better when it comes to puppy food. If your puppy is defecating more than three or so times a day, he may be getting more food than his body can process (or a food his body doesn't process well). Consider trying a more concentrated food. It's worth paying a bit more for a higher quality diet that requires less food at each meal. Making a change to a higher-quality food alone can fix this issue. Now are things easier for your puppy? If not yet, then feed her one-third of her daily ration in the morning, and two-thirds in the evening.

Doesn't Poop First Thing in the Morning

If she's making it through the night fine, then move her dinner-time earlier thirty minutes or so every few days until you find the right schedule for your pup. Or feed her one-third of her daily ration in the morning, and two-thirds in the evening.

In the Crate

If your puppy urinates and/or defecates in his crate, there can be several reasons: a sudden change in diet, worm infestation, being crated for too long, a crate that is too large, or, more challenging, a puppy who has lost the desire to keep his sleeping area tidy. Most pups can be salvaged if you use the proper scheduling, supervision, and techniques.
What to do:

- Get him *out* of the crate. Since all housebreaking is based on the instinct to keep clean, you have to get that instinct built back up *before* crating again.
- Set him up in an exercise pen or a small, easy-to-clean room. Keep the door of his crate off or propped open toward the front of this small area and papers in the rear. Make sure the pup can't climb onto the crate and escape. This can be a mess and a real pain, but it is necessary. If he still dirties his crate even with the door open, then close the door, as the crate has become his bathroom.
- Feed him by dumping his kibble onto the bottom of a clean crate. This helps to transform his "bathroom" into the "kitchen."
- Feed your pup a high-quality food so that he does not have to eat a great deal to get the nutrition he needs. Be extra-vigilant about your feeding and watering schedules. Even minor variations in timing, quantity, or kind of food can cause major headaches.

- Consider changing crates. Many dogs are cleaner in a plastic crate with solid sides.
- Eliminate or limit bedding.
- Have a small dog? Try putting the crate up on a table or a bench. Sometimes being off the ground encourages puppies to be clean. Be sure the crate is someplace secure—we don't want anyone falling.
- After two weeks of being 100 percent clean, start to put him in the crate with the door closed after he has just urinated and defecated, for no more than two hours, when you are home and can watch him.
- When you are home and want to have your pup with you, walk him, then keep him on lead next to you. This way you can learn his signals and get him outside in time.
- Any frustration you show will either do no good or make things worse. Your pup can't help it, if he could, he would. He needs your help, not your emotional upset.
- If the mistakes start happening again, go back to the exercise pen or small room setup. You cannot rush this process. You must go the speed of the puppy. The majority of dogs, dirty or not, eventually get housebroken.
- Have a long-haired puppy? Consider a new do. Some puppies who don't mind slopping around when they have longer hair start to clean up their act in a crew cut.
- If you must leave a young puppy for long hours, arrange for a midday walker and don't crate at first. As the pup matures, making mistakes will take care of itself *if* it has not become a habit!
- Stick to the routine. Recently a client complained about her pup going in the crate. Turns out the owner had been out the night before and decided to walk her puppy at 11 A.M. instead of 7 A.M.! No matter if you are sick, tired, or late, you hold the keys to the bathroom. Get out of bed!
- Is your female puppy peeing frequently in her crate? Does she have a urinary tract infection? Best ask your veterinarian. Any female pup who squats multiple times on a walk should be checked.

Lifting His Leg Indoors

You walk your puppy, then when he comes home, he hikes his leg on the couch. What he is doing is marking your house as his territory. This little emperor needs a reality check. This is more an attitude problem than a housebreaking one. Less frequently, the leg lifter is an insecure dog in a new situation, such as a recent rescue. But either way, the treatment is essentially the same.

What to do?

- First, neuter him. Now's the time!
- Next, purchase a belly band. This is a wide piece of fabric that velcros around your puppy's waist and makes effective marking impossible. This way he can have some freedom and you can have a clean house!
- From here on, unless he is on lead with you (or supervised wearing a belly band), he should be crated during the retraining period. Part of the solution is simply to stop the behavior from happening.
- If your puppy lifts his leg through the bars of a wire crate, we recommend using a plastic crate.
- Demote him (see "Demoting Demanding or Difficult Dogs" in Chapter 8)! Since this behavior is usually based on confusion about whose home this is, you must change his attitude. Until then, attacking the behavior is useless.
- Feed him meals in his favorite (cleaned up) indoor marking spots.
- Have him Down and Stay in those cleaned spots.

Leg Lifting Outside: Endless Hiking while Hiking

As much as your male puppy may *want* to stop and urinate on everything, he does not *have* to. When you take him out, walk him back and forth in front of your home. If he knows what "Hurry up" means, encourage him to do so. Allow him to urinate two to four times, then go for your walk.

Once he goes, you *go*! Do not stop or slow if he attempts to sniff. Walk at a brisk pace, squeeze/pulse if he dawdles, which he will at first. He will soon learn to empty himself quickly and to keep up with you the rest of the time. Controlling this behavior is especially important for puppies with dog aggression potential. Dogs become much more aggressive within their territory and a dog considers anywhere he marks to be "his" territory. The less he marks, the less he claims, the easier he will be to control. Of course, neutering your dog would help with all of the above, and we highly recommend it.

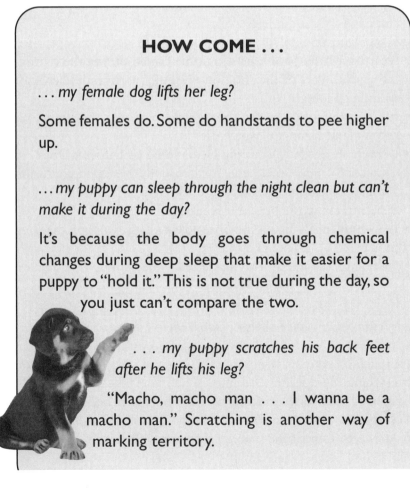

HOW COME . . .

. . . my female dog lifts her leg?

Some females do. Some do handstands to pee higher up.

. . . my puppy can sleep through the night clean but can't make it during the day?

It's because the body goes through chemical changes during deep sleep that make it easier for a puppy to "hold it." This is not true during the day, so you just can't compare the two.

. . . my puppy scratches his back feet after he lifts his leg?

"Macho, macho man . . . I wanna be a macho man." Scratching is another way of marking territory.

> *. . . my female puppy licks herself a lot, especially right after she pees.*
>
> First, fluffy pups with a lot of fur around their vulva end up urine soaked, which can lead to skin irritation. That skin stings when fresh urine hits it. Second, your pup may have a urinary tract infection of some kind. In both cases, a trip to your veterinarian is in order.

On Your Down Comforter

There is something about feathers—and something really annoying when you get a brand-new expensive comforter, only to have your usually squeaky-clean dog hop up on the bed and squat. So be warned. Keep your pup out of the bedroom for a few days while you spend some time reading or lounging on the new cover. Usually, when your scent is on it and it becomes part of home, pups leave it be.

On Your Bed

The first and by far the most common cause of a dog peeing on an owner's bed is that this dog thinks that he or she rules your roost. He is marking your bed as his, so you need to change his thinking. Next reason? Stress. If a dog is frightened or upset, he may run to your bed and let loose. Or it could be a disease (Lyme disease can cause housebreaking errors), an infection ("Peeing Small Amounts Frequently" page 238), or a chemical imbalance ("Bedding Is Wet and So Is Puppy" page 230).

- For the retraining period, he is in your sight or in his crate. He gets no access to the bedroom unless on lead and supervised.
- Demote your dog ("Demoting Demanding or Difficult Dogs" in Chapter 8).
- Keep the bedroom door closed.

- Throw a plastic drop cloth over the bed, this will deter many dogs and prevent urine from soaking into the mattress.
- If this behavior started suddenly due to change or stress and if your veterinarian has found your dog healthy, then increasing supervision and confinement while adding Space and Touch Games (see Chapters 2 through 5) will all help him over this behavioral bump.

Out of Sight

This can be caused by too much freedom, too long between walks, missing signals, or harsh scolding of the puppy (harsh in the puppy's opinion).

- Since your pup doesn't like going to the bathroom near you, use that to your advantage by keeping him close. Closing doors so he stays in the room with you, using gates for the same purpose, closing off all the rest of the house, and/or keeping him on lead next to you should all inhibit him from making a mistake.
- When you see him getting restless and ready to go, scoot him outside quickly. Be sure to praise him warmly and give plenty of treats when he goes outside, so he learns that you aren't upset at seeing him go out there.
- Remember: Scolding or swatting may have gotten you into this mess, so focus on rewarding the good behavior and preventing the problem.
- Correcting after the fact is a common, but not helpful, human habit. Once the deed is done it is too late to prevent it or teach your puppy another choice. If you're really in the mood to scold, scold yourself. Weren't you supposed to be watching this puppy?
- Spend time in mistake areas. Once they are all clean, feed your

pup in those spots. Often puppies pick places that aren't used much, like a guest room, under a formal dining room table, or behind a large plant. Make those places part of his daily routine and he'll keep them cleaner.

Peeing When Excited or Anxious

Submissive urination, as it's called, is a polite canine gesture of respect. Many pups will do this and, if you don't react to it, most will outgrow it. Unfortunately, it is all too often interpreted by us humans to mean "I know exactly what I'm doing and I'm doing it to tick you off." Consequently, the owner punishes the puppy, causing the puppy to think the owner did not understand his clear signal of submission. Next time he tries harder to communicate by urinating sooner and more profusely. The owner, seeing "defiance," punishes the dog more intensely—and on and on we go.

What to do:

- If you know your dog's trigger situations, then ignore your dog when you are in them. And we do mean ignore—no eye contact, no speaking to, no touching.
- If your dog is a doorway piddler, instruct guests to ignore your dog for the first ten minutes or so they are at your house. Then allow the dog to approach, while your guest is sitting, turned, and looking away from your dog. If your guest bends over to pet or reach toward your puppy, the floodgates will open. Best bet? Ignore the puppy or have guests greet your puppy outside.
- If your puppy piddles when just let out of the crate, put a heavy towel in front of the crate door. Then open the door without looking at or speaking to your puppy, hand

Mistakes happen. This Boxer pup got caught short during a photo shoot...oh well. Pass the paper towels. TAD DENSON

her a good treat to distract her as you're putting on her lead, then head to the door. Use another treat to lure her quickly outside. Feed her and greet her there.

- Find training that uses praise and enthusiasm to build canine confidence. If your puppy knows exactly what you want, exactly how to please you, and exactly what wonderful things will happen when he does, he will have no doubts. A happy puppy with no doubt about what a human will do is often a drier dog.

Peeing Small Amounts Frequently

If your female puppy squats many times each walk—get to the vet!
SARAH WILSON

Your female pup stops and squats and squats and squats. Little comes out. This is a "get to vet" situation. Often pups with a urinary tract infection (which is probably what is going on, but ask your vet) will urinate in the house. Please don't be angry—she is sick, hurting, and can't help it.

A male dog (or cat, for that matter) who strains and strains and nothing comes out is a "*drop this book and run to your vet*" situation. When males do this (rare in dogs, more common in cats) they are "blocked"—urine can't get out. Emergency!

Suddenly Peeing Large Amounts in the House

If your puppy has been clean for weeks and is suddenly flooding your home, something has changed. Is a heat wave, or a hot, dry house leading to more drinking? Is it a change in food that causes her to drink more? Is she sick? Anytime your puppy develops a sudden change in behavior, please consult your veterinarian. Lyme disease can, in our experience, cause such problems, so before you blame your dog make sure she isn't ill.

Peeing When Left Alone

This can simply be a case of too much freedom too quickly. If your puppy is less than eighteen months old (or a Retriever or sled dog less than two years old), crating is probably still needed when you leave. Feel free to get a large crate if you wish, as a bored puppy with free time on his hands and free access to your home is not a good thing.

This can also be a result of leaving a puppy too long. Puppies try to stay clean but they have their limits. A twelve-week-old puppy left for eight hours will go. It can't be helped. Not the puppy's fault! Or, it could be stress from being left alone. If it is your leaving that triggers it, he will make a mistake within minutes of your leaving. *Note:* If you scold him when you come back in, he will be *more* stressed next time you leave, make a mistake sooner, get corrected again, and become even more stressed. This will not get you to good.

Mistakes When on Medication

Your normally tidy puppy is urinating in the house and he's on some new medication. Could that be the problem? In short, yes. For various reasons, some medications can cause some dogs to drink a lot more (which they should be allowed to do), which inevitably leads to more peeing. More walks and more careful supervision are usually all that is needed. This resolves itself promptly when the medications stop. You should give your veterinarian a call anyway to make sure this is an expected result.

Won't Go Outside

After being quarantined in a city apartment for weeks or months waiting for their final vaccination, many an urban puppy becomes a bit too well paper-trained. When you can finally take

him outside, you walk and walk and walk your puppy but he won't go. When you give up and come back inside, the puppy races to his papers, and goes. He will not go outside.

These earnest little ones have been trained to use papers, and use them they will, holding their urine and bowels responsibly until they can race back inside to their former spot. While this frustrates their human, it is an excellent sign. Your puppy is really trying hard to get it right. Once these dogs know that outside is the new plan, they will be just as serious about that. We remind our clients: Just how long would you have to walk on a city street before it occurred to you to squat on it? Your puppy is the same way.

- Get him outside first thing in the morning. Walk briskly with him, since movement stimulates the body to go. If you can, run him around, play, let him play with a buddy or chase a ball a bit. Standard time it takes: about forty-five minutes the first few times, then twenty, then ten, then right away. We feel your pain; we've done this many, many times!
- Tank him up! Early on a morning when the weather is good and you have time, warm up a few cups of chicken broth and let him drink and drink and drink. Then take a good book, some excellent puppy treats, and outside you go. And outside you stay. Walk your pup, rest, walk, meet a friend, and walk some more. Eventually, your pup will have to urinate and when he does, praise him! Pet him! Give treats! Leave no doubt in his mind that peeing outside is *just* what you want.
- One piddle isn't going to get all that liquid out after tanking up. Expect a few more long walks. Usually, once a pup has been praised a few times for relieving himself outside, he will be happy to do so in the future.
- Start using the crate more and more as he starts going outside.

Until he is going outside consistently, you can crate only for short, supervised times so you can shuttle him out if he needs to go. If he isn't going outside easily yet, we don't want to leave him in a crate with a full bladder for long and risk forcing an "in crate" mistake to happen. Better to use the papers he is used to than to cause a "going in the crate" problem.

- If you must leave him, please confine him on his papers until such time as he is urinating outside three or more times a day and defecating at least twice a day for several days in a row. Otherwise you can start him dirtying in his crate—not what we (or you) want!
- When your pup urinates and defecates outside, then supervised playtime is in order. This is a stressful few days for both of you, so keep things as upbeat as you can. He *will* get this and it *will* be over with soon. It'll be a dim memory in a few months—hang in there.
- Don't get angry at the puppy for holding it outside. You taught him to go inside, so don't be angry now that he learned it so well. He has no way of knowing that you've changed your mind. Be patient—he'll catch on!
- If a pup has been punished for making mistakes in the house, he may now be inhibited about relieving himself near you—period. For this situation, walking him on a retractable lead while not staring at him may give your pup the distance he needs to feel comfortable.
- Some people try bringing soiled papers outside to encourage the puppy. We haven't had much luck with it but it's easy to do, so give it a try!
- Once your pup is going outside regularly, then pick up his papers, clean underneath them, and put the crate over that spot or feed him there. That should help prevent future errors in that area.

PAPER-TRAINING: THE RULES

A properly paper-trained (or litterbox-trained) small dog is a real convenience. This is especially true for long-haired breeds and

An exercise pen (ex-pen) set up with bedding, toys, and water up front and papers toward the back. Notice how we run the edges of the blanket and the papers under the ex-pen. That limits things shifting. SARAH WILSON

Tie the center panels close so that area becomes a narrow hallway between two larger areas. Vio, a young Papillon, likes this arrangement. SARAH WILSON

city-living white toy dogs like Maltese, as they can get astonishing grubby walking around in the rain. Once they're paper-trained, you can walk them outside anytime you want, but you do not have to. Getting your puppy paper-trained is similar to housebreaking with a few minor changes. Here are a few guidelines for success:

At first, set up a room (if it is long and narrow, so much the better) or ex-pen. Put the crate with its door propped open near the front, but far enough to make it impossible for your little monkey to climb the crate and then hop to freedom. If the door of the crate is removable, take it off. Place a nice blanket inside the crate. His food and water go up front as well, but not in a place where he will knock them over when he jumps with glee at seeing you.

Next, put papers (or the litterbox) toward the back. You can discourage your pup from climbing the gate by not picking him up when he jumps against it. More hints on this can be found at "Gates and Ex-pens: How to Keep Puppies Where You Put Them" on page 218 and "Wait There" on page 150. When you have to leave your pup for hours on end, this is where you leave him.

When you are home, use a crating schedule just like the housebreaking one. The difference is that instead of taking him for a walk outside, you take him to his papers. As soon as he goes, he gets a treat, praise, and supervised freedom. A week or so of this and he will relieve himself promptly.

Paper-training: Problems and Solutions

Doesn't Go in Pen Area

With some puppies, if you confine them to their pen they start treating it like their crate, and try hard to keep it clean. Then, when let out to play, they go. Leading frustrated people to groan and lament, "But he was just in the pen for *hours*!" This can be avoided by crate training your puppy. Keep on the same sort of schedule as any dog that is being housebroken: crated, walked (in this case taken to papers), supervised play, food and water when appropriate, then on lead or in the crate. If you reward going on the paper with immediate release from the pen, your puppy will soon get quite speedy. *Note:* Tiny pups need access to food all the time to avoid hypoglycemia. Be sure to discuss

any feeding changes with your veterinarian and breeder when you have a tiny, toy puppy.

Doesn't Run Back to Papers

To teach your puppy how to run back to his papers on his own, set him down a few feet from the papers when you take him out of the crate. Then walk him back to his papers, saying, "Papers. Let's go to your papers!" When he arrives, praise him and give a treat. If he knows what "Hurry up" means, instruct him to do so. When he is finished, give him a treat, praise, and reward him with freedom in the room with you. If he doesn't go, close up the pen and keep an eye on him so you can quickly reward the right choice. If he doesn't go in five or ten minutes, then recrate him and try again in twenty to thirty minutes.

Once your puppy understands this game, you can set him down all over the house and hustle with him back to his papers. A month or so of this and he'll race back to his papers on his own. During this process, it is best to spend most of his free time in the room with the papers, with easy access to them. When he has two mistake-free weeks, try adding another room to the area, still with easy access back to his papers. Please don't put papers in every room; that doesn't teach him how to run back to that one area and hit the mark.

Goes in Center or Front of Area

If you're using an ex-pen, pull in the center panels to form an hour-glass shape. Tie it so there is just enough room for your puppy to walk through. This stops some puppies immediately. Covering the top of the front half can also deter some pups from using it. Use less bedding if your puppy is squatting on his blankets.

Goes Half Off Papers

If your dog is sometimes half on and half off the paper, put the papers in a low pan. A litterbox works well for some small dogs. Clean under the papers every couple of days with an odor neutralizer. Otherwise, when the urine runs to the edge of the paper it can start attracting him to the edges, where he will then miss the target. Don't punish him for going with only his front feet on the paper—that could confuse him, making him leery of the papers. Instead use a pan, or practice "Papers!" and luring him all the way on, or dab a urine wet paper in the center of the clean ones, or put plastic underneath the papers. There's lots you can do!

Lifts Leg on Wall

If he isn't already neutered, then neuter him! Put a wad of newspaper in the center of the papers so he has a good place to lift that leg. Taping plastic on the wall behind then running it underneath the papers will prevent damage to your floors.

Housebreaking is one of those things every puppy owner goes through. Keep to a schedule that includes confinement, supervision, and regular walks. If your puppy is making mistakes, walk her more, watch her more closely, or confine her a bit sooner. This too shall pass and when it does, you and your puppy will be one more big step down the road of a long happy life together.

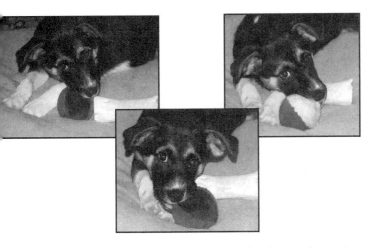

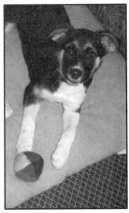

Okay, okay, there is no particular lesson here, but wasn't Pip an adorable puppy? SARAH WILSON

CHAPTER 8

COMMON PROBLEMS, EASY SOLUTIONS

The two foundation causes of problems between people and their puppies are either too much of a good thing or too little of the right thing. "Too much" means constant focus when you are home, constant stimulation by a distracting environment, freedom your puppy is not developmentally or behaviorally ready for, or endless understanding of problems rather than a commitment to finding solutions. The most damaging of these for the puppy? The epidemic of too much attention: virtual nonstop touching, talking, and looking at your puppy. Every effort is made by the caring owner never to upset or stress the puppy. They want their little one to be "happy." Sadly, what that creates is not a grateful companion who appreciates his puppyhood but a pushy, demanding, out-of-control puppy who has been raised to do what he wants when he wants. The human? Relevant when something is needed, and then only fleetingly.

The flipside of too much is too little. Too little teaching, too few boundaries, too little exercise, too few expectations, all with not enough understanding of what any of this actually does to the puppy. Both of these problems can largely be fixed by meeting in the middle. Give your puppy lots of attention, but give it when he shows self-control, compliance, and cooperation. Give brief moments of sincere praise, then do something else. Leave your puppy hungry for more from you, then give him ways to earn it. Doing this will give him the boundaries and rules he needs to develop into a wonderful, problem-free canine companion and will give you the interaction you crave from your new buddy. It's a win-win situation.

TEN KEYS TO PERFECT PUPPY PROBLEM SOLVING

1. Pretrain What You Want

You want a speedy Come off-lead? Better pretrain in the house on-lead. If on-lead isn't near perfect, off-lead will be a disaster. Want your puppy to Down without hesitation? Better pretrain his Guided Down. Pretraining is like homework, and life is the test. If your puppy is getting straight A's on his homework, chances are good the test will go well. If he is confused when tested, don't keep testing and testing—stop, regroup, do some more homework, try again. Pretrain! You'll be delighted with the results!

2. You Do Not Get to Choose What Your Puppy Needs

Your choice is whether or not you do what is needed. If your puppy needs treats to be able to focus and you don't like using treats, too bad. If your puppy needs hands-on work to learn how to calm himself and you'd rather be all clicker, oh well. Puppy training isn't about what you want, it is about what your puppy needs. Think of all training in those terms and you'll be well ahead in the game.

3. Beware of the 4 S's: "Sneaky," "Stubborn," "Spiteful," "Stupid"

If you find yourself thinking your puppy is "sneaky," "stubborn," "spiteful," or "stupid" replace those words with "confused." "Confused" will put you in a compassionate, problem-solving frame of mind, where the 4 S's are blaming words. Watch your thoughts, because such words often accompany frustration and, if allowed to grow they can lead to supporting anger or violence directed at your puppy. We humans normally have to make the "other" (be it person or puppy) "bad" in order to allow our own badness to be unleashed. Labeling your puppy as "confused" allows you to evaluate your actions rather than blame him, and then brainstorm for success. For example:

I left the house for ten minutes and he peed on the bed; he is so spiteful! Instead: My young puppy panicked when left alone, ran to his safe place (my bed) and urinated from fear. I never knew that phrase "to scare the p*** out of someone" was true. Next time I will tuck him into his crate. He's just not ready to be loose in the whole house by himself.

I say sit, sit, sit and he doesn't sit, he is SO stubborn! Instead: My puppy learns exactly what I teach him—nothing more and nothing less. If I say "Sit, sit, sit," how is he supposed to know when to actually sit? If my goal is for him to listen to my first command, then I need to get clear and consistent about it.

I call my puppy but he never comes; he is so stupid! In the past, I've sometimes gotten frustrated when my puppy didn't come and then scolded him when I finally caught him. I guess maybe he's learned that coming makes me mad. Also, everyone in the house is using different commands and I haven't really practiced much—geez, no wonder he's confused!

4. Get to Good!

Your job, quite simply, is to get to "Good!" In any situation with your puppy, focus on *What do I want and how can we get there?* Look for the shortcuts to "Good puppy!" Think of training as having a 10-to-1 ratio of reward to correction. If you want to learn about getting to good quickly, pick up a clicker. It's a very educational training tool—for trainers! Have fun, look for the good. My Smart Puppy people focus on solutions, not problems. Here are some examples:

	Average Puppy Person	**My Smart Puppy Person**
Puppy leaps against door before walk.	Puppy leaps against door, person opens door. *Lesson: Leaping makes good things happen.*	Puppy leaps against door, you ask for a Simple Sit (page153) or Mine (page 82). When puppy sits, you open the door. *Lesson: Sitting makes good things happen.*
Puppy barks at you for attention.	Person tosses a toy to quiet the puppy. *Lesson: Barking makes good things happen.*	Person stands up and shuffles into puppy's space. No eye contact. Puppy backs up and quiets. Then toy is tossed. *Lesson: Quieting down makes good things happen.*
Puppy jumps up for attention.	Person looks at puppy and speaks to puppy while he is jumping. *Lesson: Jumping makes good things happen.*	Person steps into puppy's space and signals Off. No direct eye contact. When puppy stops, person smiles, looks at the puppy, praises warmly. *Lesson: Jumping doesn't work but four on the floor makes good things happen.*

5. Accept the Process

With your help, your puppy can get better every day, but he will still be a puppy. He can't be an adult dog no matter how hard he tries. So be patient with him. Understand that his attention span is short, his experience is lacking, and he doesn't have any options yet. He will mouth you from time to time, he will chew things, he will bark, he will probably dig. That's a puppy!

6. Plan B—C—D

Never in the history of humans and dogs have there been so many great training options and tools. Just because you've done everything you know how to do doesn't mean you've tried everything there is to do. If something isn't working: *stop*. Try something else or apply the technique or tool differently. Dogs aren't stupid and neither are you—try something new! There is almost always a Plan B. And a Plan C, and a Plan D!

7. Become Relevant

Put yourself in the picture. Feeding your puppy? Have him Sit, then you put down the bowl. At the door teach him to look up at you, then the door opens. Make it so all good things come through you, and you are exactly what your puppy will pay close attention to. Use opportunities, create opportunities, and then your puppy being attentive to you will become a life habit.

8. Refuse to Confuse

When you teach your puppy a command, you are making a pact, a pact your puppy believes in 100 percent. He believes every single thing you teach him without question—without even the mental capacity *to* question. If you pet him for climbing onto your lap in the evening without an invitation and then scold him for climbing up when you are dressed up, he becomes confused. When that is the case, your puppy will jump until you stop him instead of learning not to jump on you at all. If you want your puppy to be 100 percent consistent, you must be 100 percent consistent in what you say, expect, and do. Never expect more from your puppy than you can deliver as the teacher. If you love him, refuse to confuse him!

9. Consequence Is a Gift

Somewhere along the way, sensible consequences for actions became, in some circles, synonymous with abuse. That is a real loss for the dogs and for people. The most uncontrollable, assertive, and dangerous adult dogs we see are, universally, the ones who were raised "all positive," without any consequences ever given, any boundaries ever set, or ever made to do anything they don't *feel* like doing. It's such a shame since the people were trying so hard to do it "just right."

Self-control is like a muscle: When it is worked, it grows stronger. Teaching a puppy that she only need to do things she *feels* like doing creates flabby self-control. Self-control could save your dog's life. Have fun when you train, but train—train for immediate response and excellent self-control. Be willing to apply calm, clear, sensible consequences, then allow your dog to figure out what you want. Your pup will. Dogs are smart.

10. Think Fun, Fair, Firm!

These three words, in this order, first made famous by Brian's mentor Barbara Woodhouse, sum up our approach nicely.

Fun!

Joy, connection, play! All of that is fun! If your puppy has fun, he will try harder to play these new "games" with you. If you have fun, you will want to train more often. So fun is your first

Fun is foremost, and isn't Hazel is having a great time playing with Brian! She doesn't know this is "work" and he's sure not going to tell her.
SARAH WILSON

goal. Think of training as a game you play *with* your puppy rather than something you do *to* your puppy.

Fair!

You've taken the time to teach your puppy what you want, you do not blame a puppy for your failings, you carefully use the same words in the same order with the same expectations. You honor your puppy's belief in you by being as consistent as you can be. In this way you are fair.

Firm!

Calm, clear, and unemotional equals firm. Upset, unclear, and emotional equals angry. Angry is not firm. When you say what you mean and you mean what you say, you are being firm. Firm means you always follow through, your expectations are clear and unvarying. You have a clear picture in your mind of exactly what you want from your puppy and you go for it. Being firm takes the guesswork out of things for your puppy, and that is a huge gift. Once people embrace this concept, training usually progresses more easily for all concerned.

YOU'RE IT!

You're your puppy's leader, whether you want to be or not. You can try to avoid it, but that just means you're dumping the job on his small lap. Since a puppy cannot imagine a world without a leader—literally cannot imagine it—in the absence of one he'll pick up the slack. It will stress him to do so, but in his world a leader is a must so if it's him, he'll do his best. Often such puppies are said to have "problems" but what the puppy really has is a people problem—he's just doing the best he can. He has no choice. But you do. You can decide to step up and do what the puppy needs or you can decide not to. Your choice.

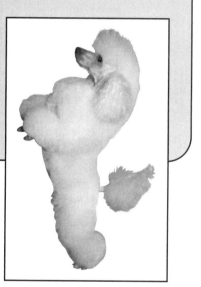

DEMOTING DEMANDING OR DIFFICULT DOGS

The testosterone levels of social creatures, including ourselves, rise and fall depending on perceived social status. When men are promoted in the military, their testosterone levels rise. When recruits hit boot camp, theirs plummets. Both men and women experience testosterone shifts. And, it turns out, not only do

*If you have a
strong puppy,
make sure she
plays with dogs
she cannot bully.
PJ and Milo will
make sure
Phyllis plays
nicely.*
SARAH WILSON

the players on a team experience a rise in testosterone before, during, and after, a win, but so do their loyal fans. Simply observing a successful competition that you care about can shift your body chemistry. So we're thinking that maybe this can happen in dogs and that, if it does, it goes a long way to explaining why the most assertive, aggressive, pushy, mouthy, demanding, don't-touch-me dogs we see universally come from "all treat" lifestyles. All they do is win. Win, win, win, win every day, every class, every interaction, and their hormone levels shift upward accordingly. This would explain why programs like this one work so well. They demote the dogs, and lowering of status apparently lowers hormonal levels just as it does in other animals. If you want to have a nicer, easier, sweeter, more attentive puppy? Demote!

Recipe for Demotion

Put Away the Treats

Work with your Space and Touch Games until you can get equally good response from your puppy with or without treats. When you no longer "have" to use them, you can use them again. But if your puppy is more responsive to a treat than to your touch or verbal praise, change things now. With treats away, you need to focus on your praise, both in amount and in quality. You must get that puppy tail wagging. Volume isn't as important as warmth and sincerity. Put a small tape recorder in your shirt pocket then listen to yourself. Do you sound confident, enthusiastic, happy? After you've checked your voice, check what your hands are doing as you praise. Review "Petting 101" in Chapter 2 to make sure your puppy is actually enjoying the touch you are giving.

More Work

You know that old saying "Idle hands are the devil's workshop"? That goes for paws as well. Puppies are active, smart, interactive little beings. Pups from hardworking breeds are even more so. In their canine minds, life without work cannot happen. Period. So either you work them or they work you. Many, many puppy/people problems from barking for attention to growling over a toy, are all part of the "puppy working people" scenario. A puppy cannot change his behavior on his own—it's all up to you. So give him something good to do!

Less Attention

Looking at, facing, speaking to, and touching all fall under the umbrella of "attention." With us social beasties, she or he who gets looked at the most is the most important and powerful. If you spend your time facing and looking at your puppy, he cannot help but think he is more important or powerful than you. Ever notice how many dogs give the least attention to the people who give them the most, and vice versa? They worship the person who barely acknowledges them. Welcome to the world of dogs. So, to demote your dog, get another hobby. Move the dog bed so it isn't in line with the television, turn away from your pushy puppy frequently. You'll see his attitude change. He may be pushy, but he doesn't want to be excluded!

Down and Down Again!

Body position matters, and, in our society, relative height matters. This is why kings and queens sit raised up on thrones and people kneel or bow before powerful people. Doing several Downs in a row calms most puppies. (See Guided Down, page

92.) When your pup starts to get out of control, Down him. Then step away, have him follow and Down him again. Have a relaxed, matter-of-fact attitude. You're thinking something along the lines of, Oh, you must be confused—let me help you. On the last Down, leave the lead slightly slack so it will tighten if the pup stands up. If he does, wait. Let him figure it out and lie back down. He will. Let your puppy park there for a minute until he calms himself.

Loss of Privileges

Beings who break social rules lose privileges. "Privilege" means something earned, not something automatically granted. In this case, your puppy has forfeited the right to be on your level. He must be below you at all times and not touching you without a direct invitation to do so. No couch for him, no floor for you. Dogs understand the value of the sleeping spot. We've watched pushy dogs get behind their owners and shove them slowly off the chair. We've seen dogs leap up, taking their human's seat the moment that human rises then growl when the human returns (human inevitably sits elsewhere with a comment like "Oh, that's his spot"). The dogs aren't kidding around. They know exactly what all this means. Until your puppy calms down, he stays down. Where does your dog sleep? The floor or his crate. Not your bed!

Respect My Space

This is so key that we made our first set of the START exercises Space Games (page 82). If you do nothing else but change your puppy's opinion of your personal space, you will make great strides in changing other behaviors. If you allow him to enter that space at will, block you, push you, shove you, and otherwise "walk all over you," then you will never have the relationship you want with this animal! If your puppy nudges you for attention or tries to drape across you, the answer is Off (page 86) or Go (148). A flying leap onto or over your person is a Go, out of the room, or a Down or a trip to the crate. Lying in your path is a Move as you shuffle on through. With some sweet, easygoing dogs, space really doesn't matter much, but if you're reading this section it does. Make the change today!

Have Some Fun

To stay positively focused, make sure to have plenty of fun. Teach your dog tricks that make you laugh. Go for a romp with friends. Look for everything he is doing right, instead of everything he's doing wrong. Try this: For three days you're only allowed to praise him for what he does correctly. Period. If he has to be redirected, do it silently with your body or lead. Then praise! Get to good fast and often!

MELISSA FISCHER

SARAH'S INBOX:

The Queen's Throne

My puppy has her own chair. If anyone else sits in it, she whines and nudges them until they move. If she's on it, she will growl at us if we try to make her move. We think this is pretty cute. After all, it is her chair. But our friends think this is a big problem. Will you be the tie breaker?

Did your puppy buy the chair with her own credit card? Unless she did, it is your chair. What would you think if your child was sitting in that chair and when you approached, she told you to go to hell. Would that be "cute"? Remember: The one who makes others move and the one who possesses the best sleeping spots is the one who is in charge. Your puppy is in charge. If you allow her to gain confidence by threatening and controlling humans, you are well on your way to loving your dog to death.

Barking: At People

Whether it is in your home or out and about, your puppy erupting into barking can be embarrassing for you, stressful for your puppy, and alarming to others.

- Play the Space Games in earnest, especially Wait (page 116) and Left Circles (page 119).
- Demote to clear up any confusion (see preceding section).
- Read Chapter 6 on socialization.
- Distance is your friend. If you can, moving away from what your puppy is barking at can make it easier for you both to concentrate.
- Reward any *hint* of attention. Don't ask for perfection. Praise any attempt, any glance in your direction. Don't wait for it to happen—get busy and make it happen.
- Take a group class. Working in a well-run group class can give you and your dog needed successful mileage around strangers.
- Act the way you want your puppy to act, so stay calm. Laugh, be relaxed.
- Redirect the puppy's attention. Puppies can't do two things at once, so work that little brain. The less focused your puppy is, the more direct and demanding you need to be. Message to your puppy: Never mind that person, pay attention to me! Your praise and treats must match the situation—use both generously for a job well done!
- Barking at guests? Prevent the event by crating your puppy away as they enter. Then when they are settled, bring your puppy out on lead, with treats he enjoys, and do some Near Is Dear, Check It Out, and Say Hello.
- If he is terrified, trying to run away from the guest, refusing to walk, or shaking, don't try to bring him into the room. Instead, reward him at a distance. Forcing a fearful pup to be touched in the hopes of making him "like it" will often just make him hate it more. Keep him at a distance and reward him for any calm or focus he can offer. Over time, he should gain confi-

dence. *Hint:* Switch jackets with your guest. Your puppy will accept his scent on you and like him better when he has on your scent.

- If your puppy acts aggressively—barking, growling, hair up on his back—keep him at a distance from others. Consider using a head halter on him so you can more easily control any barking or lunging he might do. If your puppy doesn't improve a great deal quickly, please seek hands-on help, as this is not how you want your puppy to grow up!

Barking: In the Crate

There are many reasons for this from normal initial adjustment to rewarded behavior, to boredom to stress around separation. You may need to mix and match the suggestions below to get the results you're looking for.

- Exercise. Have the last few days been busy? How much time has your puppy actually spent in his or her crate? How much time playing with you or another dog? Too little exercise makes for a restless pup.
- Accidents. If a puppy who normally crates quietly barks and fusses or refuses to enter the crate, check the crate. Did she have an accident or vomit in there? If yes, clean everything thoroughly.
- Routine. Keep your normal crating times on your days off, otherwise it creates too much of a contrast between when you are home and when you leave. Shorten the crate periods if you like, but start them at the same time.
- Cover the crate. This can lessen barking instantly.
- Reward quiet by giving a treat as you walk past. Don't excite your pup; this is just a driveby kibbling. Or praise him calmly from a distance. Do what works for you.
- Play Wait There, Stay: Basics, and Go games (pages 150, 105, and 148 respectively).

BRIAN'S INBOX:

Midnight Barker

My seven-month-old pup has suddenly started barking in the middle of the night. It's making me crazy! I have tried walking him, talking to him, giving him a biscuit, everything—but he's still doing it. I don't want to crate him but he's trying to drive me crazy!

Assume the puppy is doing this for a good reason. When a healthy dog develops a new behavior, it is usually because either something is physically wrong or it is working for him. Ask yourself: What does he get out of it? What happens when he barks? In this case, he gets both company and food. Since you raise what you praise and most certainly what you feed, you're getting more barking. Step 1: Stop rewarding barking. Step 2: Crate him. Seven months of age is way too young to be left to roam a house at night. Crating him in the bedroom may resolve the problem.

Barking: Out the Window

Standing vigil at a window overlooking the street or front door waiting to erupt in barking can be a major (and annoying) pastime for many dogs.

- Prevent access. Remove the viewing platform or make it unusable. You could put a couple of chairs upside down on a couch or place a plastic carpet runner on it nubby side up. If you can't keep the puppy away from the window, then keep him away from the area. Use a gate or open exercise pen to prevent access.
- Redirect. "No" gets you nowhere. Try Leave It, Come then make sure it happens. That gets you to good! Use pulse/squeezing on the lead as you back up—no dragging or yanking. Your goal is to engage the brain, not be a pain.
- Practice what you prefer. Call him to you when nothing is distracting him. Make that a *highlight* of his day. Give him a favorite toy, or a special treat, or take off! Having him chase you can be a fun reward for many pups.
- Bark equals squirt. Try a plant sprayer set on stream. Barking starts, spray puppy. Be quick and quiet. The *instant* he stops, you stop. Then praise him: Good puppy!
- Find another hobby. Give him other interesting things to do besides lingering at the window. A bored puppy is a creative puppy, so keep that little canine mind occupied. Feed him from toys (page 189), rotate chew toys, teach him tricks, play your Space Games but keep that mind occupied.
- Do homework. Leave It (page132), Look At Me (page 95), and Come: Basics (page 102), will make him more capable of listening when distracted.

REFLECTING ON REFLECTIONS

As far as we can tell, puppies cannot recognize themselves. That can be hard to imagine with our brains, but what we can see is that dogs don't appear to have any sense of "I." They look at the world as an infant does—through emotion and direct experience without the ability to ponder questions like "Who am I?" Therefore, when they look in the mirror, what they see must be quite like a ghost: a body-less image with no smell or sound. Your puppy may bark at her reflection the first few times, shy away, or try to look behind the mirror for her new friend. Or she may approach it with a wagging tail or stalk it with hackles raised. But soon she'll simply ignore the reflection as it becomes one more thing that makes no real sense.

Barking: In the Backyard

This is the bane of dog owners and neighbors everywhere.

- Bring him inside. That is a surefire cure.
- Go out with him. That way you can call him away if he's getting started.
- Bored dogs bark. What exactly does he have to do out there? Barking at strangers he sees can be a deeply ingrained "preprogrammed" behavior, so your puppy enjoys doing it. He won't stop unless you teach him how.
- Block the view. When you can, shift things around so he can't see whatever he's barking at.

Most dogs enjoy barking so they will never stop on their own. If you want it stopped, you have to stop it.

- Near Is Dear (page 110) and Check It Out (page 139) can help him calm himself.
- Leave It (page 132), Come (page 102), Look At Me (page 95) are key.
- Do Door Chores (page 129) to prevent bolting into the backyard in full cry!

Barking: In the Car

Oh! This is a headache in the making, especially if your puppy barks when you're driving.

- Crate. This can be the quickest solution. Crate your puppy, then cover the crate. Many pups quiet down immediately when this is done. Crating is also the safest way for your puppy to travel in your car. We like the plastic crates for barkers. Set one upside down so the windows are at the bottom. If he can't look out, it can mean less barking. *Note:* In hot climates, a wire crate may be cooler.

- Guided Down (page 92). Once your puppy learns the Guided Down, you can run a long line under the passenger seat and up to the backseat, where your puppy is. If she barks, your assistant gives steady pressure upward on the long line, which creates the downward collar cue. When your puppy lies down, you praise calmly and treat as you release the pressure. Repeat as needed. Don't say "Down"—it's simply cause and effect. Barking causes Down.
- Consider using a head halter. This snugs the mouth closed when it is tightened and can allow an assistant (or you, if the assistant drives) to quiet your puppy. Be sure to loosen the lead quickly once your puppy is quiet.
- Ultrasonics. For some dogs, usually sensitive ones, a handheld ultrasonic device used with "Quiet" can work wonders. A quick button push as you say the word can effectively stop some dogs. Then praise calmly.
- Safety first. Please do not turn around and wrestle with your puppy. Keep your eyes on the road! Better to arrive at your destination annoyed than not at all.

Begging

Dogs hassle people for food because they are either pushy puppies or puppies trained to push (or both). Pushy puppies think they should always be fed before humans. They kick up a fuss on principle. Puppies trained to push have been fed from the table by someone.

- Stop feeding him from the table! If you want to share meals, put the food in his dish after you're done. Make sure you do Sit for Your Supper (see box). Stick to plain meats and vegetables—no rich or spicy sauces. Also skip fried foods, and bones, and be careful with the onions. With a growing puppy, we recommend sticking with a premium puppy diet.

You get what you pet so what is this woman going to get more of?

- Mine (page 82) and Off (page 86) are also key so your dog understand your space and the off hand signal.
- Play Go (page 148) so you can back him up if he begs. When begging equals leaving the room, he'll stop begging quickly.
- Teach Stay: Basic. Work on that away from meals until his Stay skills are strong then use it to resolve begging.
- Distant Down. Tethering can teach him to stay calm at a distance.
- If none of this works, crate and cover him while you do more homework away from meals. More successful practice is what gets him passing the test.

SIT FOR YOUR SUPPER

Want to see how smart your puppy is? Play this game: Make your puppy's meal. Hold it by your waist (a bit higher for giant-breed puppies) and have him sit. When he sits, start to lower the bowl straight down (about two feet in front of your puppy). If he stays seated, good puppy! Tell him "Okay" and put the bowl down under his nose. He can eat.

If he stands up (and he probably will), simply lift up the bowl without comment. Most puppies will immediately sit again, and you immediately lower the bowl again if he does. Very quickly your puppy will learn that sitting causes the bowl to be lowered and standing up causes it to disappear. It's an easy choice for most puppies!

Bites at Feet or Grabs at Lead

These common puppy problems may have different targets but share similar solutions.

- Refuse to confuse. Don't play tug-of-war as a game unless you want tug-of-war on the lead. You can play this game if you can stop it and start it instantly but you can't yet, so skip it. Play other ways until you've helped your puppy develop more self-control.
- Make the lead unattractive. No, we don't mean give it a bad haircut, we mean spray it down with some icky anti-chew product daily. That deters some dogs.
- Make it boring. When the lead goes in your pup's mouth, calmly and silently reach down, take hold of her collar, and hold that collar cup against your leg. (Never grab a slip or chain collar

Yoshi is getting tired and fussy. Look familiar?
SARAH WILSON

but we don't like those on pups anyway.) Say nothing, look elsewhere, wait. When the lead drops out of your pup's mouth, instantly praise (calmly—use words, not touching—as touching here may restimulate that mouth to grab) and release your hold and go on. No big deal. Repeat. Expect this to take ten or so times to really sink it.

- Make it impossible. Give your pup a special toy to carry. Use it only for walks. Make it a big deal! Praise her to the heavens for carrying it. What a *Smart* Puppy! Present it to her with awe and wonder, sell her on the idea this is a *great* thing to do! Praise her verbally while she carries. When she drops it, become quiet. Pick it up, tease her a moment or two with it, then give it while telling her how great she is! Touching her can cause her to drop it at this stage. *Hint:* Do not use a toy that rolls or you'll be chasing after it every time your pup drops it.

- Become a skunk. Using your handy-dandy canister of breath spray, calmly give your release command. Ours is "Out." Then spray down at where your puppy is mouthing. If his nose is gone by the time the spray arrives, so much the better. Don't try to spray your puppy's nose or threaten him with the canister—simply speak, spray, then put it away. Calmly praise when the puppy releases.

Biting

Biting—aggressively grabbing your body to protest something you are doing—is not "mouthing." Biting usually happens over something a puppy wants—a sleeping spot, a toy, food—or something the puppy doesn't want—to be restrained or handled. Most puppies will growl, bare their teeth, or freeze before they bite. A puppy who seriously bites humans needs help ASAP. There are so many reasons for biting, from people teasing puppies to unstable tempera-

ment, from hurting a puppy unintentionally (such as picking up the puppy incorrectly) to biting off more than you can chew (so to speak) during puppy selection. There is no universal answer for this problem.

- Get professional help. Aggression can be a life-or-death matter for your puppy. Getting competent hands-on coaching is critical. Few pet owners have the knowledge to handle aggression on their own, and you need to find out if a pro thinks this is a fixable blip or a big problem with long-term ramifications. Try to find someone with over a decade of dealing with problem dogs and who can give you a range of methods to select from. Beware the extremes, both the heavy-handed and the "all positive." Neither can give you the well-rounded program you need for success.
- Memorize this definition of insanity: doing the same thing over and over and expecting different results. If your puppy bites when he has a rawhide, expect him to do the same thing tomorrow and the day after tomorrow until you teach him another option. Do not give him a rawhide to "see" what happens. We know what will happen, right? He will bite.
- Talk to your veterinarian. Consider having a full thyroid panel pulled. Low thyroid issues can be at the root of many an aggression problem. Even healthy-looking dogs can have low thyroid levels. Also discuss tick-borne illness, as aggression can be a symptom of some of those widespread diseases.
- Demote your puppy. Demotion (page 254) is a lifestyle. You can't quit doing the program just because the puppy seems better. The puppy seems better *because* of the program. If you ease back on it, expect a full return of the problem.
- Pretrain for success. Out, out, and more out (pages 136).
- See "The Daily Dozens: An Anti-Bite Protocol" (page 272)
- Touch, Space, and Requirement Games. Start at Level I and keep going!
- Consider the entire family. Your puppy is important to you (or you would not be reading this), but he is no more important than any other family member. If your child(ren) or another pet is at risk or is severely stressed or frightened by this puppy (with good cause), that has to be carefully considered.

- Don't ignore this! Avoiding the problem doesn't mean the problem is gone or getting better. If a puppy bites you for trying to get him off the couch so you stop trying to get him off the couch, things are not better. You are not safer and, in fact, your puppy learned that aggression works. Get help! In the meantime, train, leave a lead on your puppy when he is out and about with you, look for good behaviors to reward with hawk-like vigilance.

CAN A CUTE LITTLE PUPPY REALLY BE DANGEROUS?

Yes.

Does it happen often? No.

Many people fear they may have a dangerous puppy when they are living with a normal, mouthy, untrained puppy. A puppy is potentially "dangerous" if he shows quick, extreme aggression with little to no warning when faced with normal daily events. Example: Your puppy has a toy. You attempt to take it and he lunges forward with a snarl, biting you hard, leaving several punctures or, worse, bites multiple times or, worse yet, bites hard and holds on.

Can we find reasons for the behavior? Sure, he didn't "like" his toy taken.

Does that excuse an attack from a puppy? No.

Is there lots of training that can be done? Yes.

Will that guarantee you a safe, nonviolent companion. Sadly, no.

If biting is his hard-wired, inborn response to a

small life stress, we have a major problem. He had plenty of other options. He could have walked away, growled, or turned his head but he chose direct, immediate, intense aggression. To put it in our terms, imagine asking a six-year-old for his crayons and, without comment, he pulls a knife, stabs you deeply, then continues to color.

Some dangerous dogs are made, not born, through neglect, isolation and mishandling or, these days, through indulgence and failure to teach self-control. But dangerous dogs can also be born, and when they are born there is little you can do to change who and what they are. What normally happens is people try hard, the pup appears "better" because the triggers are avoided, then life happens, a trigger is hit—and someone is hurt.

If your puppy gives you little or no warning before he bites, breaks skin (on people or other dogs), bites multiple times within seconds, or bites and holds on in response to normal everyday events, please get professional help immediately.

The Daily Dozens: An Anti-Bite Protocol

A Dozen Rewards

Notice and reward a dozen things each day. Rewards can be verbal praise, petting, treats, play, opening a door, or in any other way granting your puppy something he enjoys. Since you interact with your puppy dozens of times a day, this one is a no-brainer. Why? Because we want you to notice everything good your puppy does.

A Dozen Downs

Park your puppy at your feet when you eat, watch TV, or work on the computer. Grab a few kibbles before meals and lure him into four or five Downs. Once he understands the Guided Down, use it before you unclip the lead after a walk or as a part of the walk. Be creative, work them in, and you'll have a puppy who Downs immediately and without hesitation. Why? Because Down is a great canine emergency brake. If you see a problem about to happen: Down! This tends to change your dog's mental focus as well as his body position.

A Dozen Directions

Tell your pup what to do *at least* a dozen times a day (besides the Downs). Between sitting for petting, meals and toys, this one is a breeze. Why? Because giving directions needs to be a habit for you and taking direction from you a habit for him.

A Dozen Minor Restraints

When putting his lead on, taking it off, or when petting him, do a brief restraint, asking the pup to calm himself before you release. We want this habit of relaxing to become second

Working on this a little every day makes your puppy safer with everyone.
JACKSON YOUNG

nature. Why? So when a person does something he is not expecting, he won't panic.

A Dozen Blocks

Get in your puppy's way. Play Mine with his toys, at doorways, around the cat—and *anytime* your puppy tells you to "get out of my way!" Why? Because we want his response to you becoming pushy to be to back away, not to push back.

Total extra time spent: About five minutes.
Total value of time spent: Priceless!

Body Slamming: Get Out of In My Way!

Your puppy slams into you, shoves you out of the way, pushes, leaps, tackles, and otherwise assaults you. This is no mistake and can really hurt you. Act!

- Step forward. If we see a puppy careening our way, we wait until he is ten feet or so away. Then we take a couple of sudden steps toward him, clapping our hands in front of us and saying something forceful, like "Hey!" Usually this startles a puppy enough to stop him from hitting you. The moment he turns away, stop all sound and forward movement. That's his "Good dog." No treats or praise for avoiding—we don't want to encourage him racing at you. *Hint:* Keep your knees slightly bent around groups of dogs or a full-contact puppy so if you do get hit, you knees will bend the way they are meant to.
- Work all the Space Games (Chapters 2 through 5). Getting really good at those can fix this problem quickly.
- Off—really. No kidding around. Puppy must learn to stay Off (page 86). If he won't stay off you in the kitchen, he won't avoid you in the park, either.

MOVE!

Whenever your puppy is in your way, shuffle on through him. Shuffling means feet on the floor at all times. Do not—we repeat do *not*—step over or around him. This is doubly true for herding breeds, who love to make anything change directions, and toy breeds, whose safety depends on staying out of your way. Keep your knees bent, your feet on or close to the ground, and close together. Have a clear intention: I *am* going through! If your puppy isn't moving, try upping the tempo of the shuffling rather than shuffling harder. Focus on something across the room, not on your puppy. If he is confused, start by tossing a treat off to the side as you shuffle through. This will help him get up out of your way.

Car Sickness: Help for the Queasy Rider

Most pups grow out of car sickness with exposure and age. Some cases seem to be an inner-ear issue related to the rapid growth large breed pups can go through, which resolves as their growth slows around nine to ten months of age. Some pups, like some people, are just sensitive to motion.

- Practice. If the weather is cool, sit in the car with your crated pup. If you can, feed him in the crate then let him rest. This will help build a positive association with being in the car.
- Hold the kibble. Avoiding meals close to a car ride can at least give you less to clean up.

- Cover the crate. This helps some pups, as watching the world whiz by incomprehensibly seems to make them more nauseous than being in the dark. Doesn't help them all, but worth a shot.
- Take short drives, very short at first. Begin by just turning on the car and idling for a few minutes (garage door open, please!). When your puppy can handle that, back down your driveway, then come home. When that's okay, go a little farther. Try to quit while you're both ahead. If the ride is heave free, you're doing it perfectly!
- Talk to your veterinarian. Get his or her recommendation for medication that might help.

Chasing: The Cat

Most puppies chase cats from curiosity, though sometimes it can be more serious. You can and should stop it, as this could become dangerous for your cat and disruptive for you as your puppy gets bigger.

- On lead. When you don't have mental control, you must have physical control. If he starts to harass the cat, then use it to call him back to you.
- Work Mine (page 82), Look At Me (page 95), Simple Sit (page 153), Wait (page 116) and Guided Down(page 92). Play Near Is Dear (page 109).
- Give your cat a way to escape. Use baby gates or tall cat climbers or access to the tops of the bookshelves to keep cat safely separated from your puppy.
- Teach your puppy how to look away (see "The Pip Chronicles" below).
- Try a spray of water. Puppy focuses on cat, puppy feels a stream of water. Puppy looks away from your cat, you praise. When this works, it works well. When it doesn't, oh well. Don't use a sound-based correction as that will probably stress your cat, who is already having a bad day.

THE PIP CHRONICLES: LEARNING TO LOOK AWAY

Today, Pip was—yet again—intensely sniffing our wonderful cat, Ben. Now Pip doesn't know she *can* leave the cat, since neither side of her herding/terrier family have "just walk away" in their heritage. We must show her that it is both possible and fun! Seeing a golden opportunity to teach, Sarah grabbed a few bits of kibble. She went over to Pip, put the kibble under her nose, and, when she saw she had Pip's interest (Pip loves food), Sarah backed up and said her name. Praising warmly, Sarah fed her when she responded. Then Sarah walked Pip back over to Ben (who cooperated nicely) and repeated this game. By the third approach, Pip stayed focused on Sarah, ignoring a thankful Ben. Perfect! Smart Puppy! Lots of treats and praise!

Chasing: The Kids

The sad news is that it is a rare puppy who can be calm when kids are running around. Most give chase. That is normal, but not acceptable. Prevent your puppy from chasing first, then retrain.

- On lead. Put the puppy on lead so he cannot chase.
- Practice attention. Play Look At Me (see page 95) and Come: Basics (see page 102) around the kids.

- Build Distance Downs (see page 128). Once mastered, these will give you control of your puppy if he starts to chase.
- Use Mine body blocking to get him to focus on you and stop chasing.
- Help your kids practice Mine (page 82), Wait (page 116), and Off (page 86). When your puppy responds to them, he will be less likely to nip or jump on them.
- Leave It (page 132) is key!

Chasing: Cars, Bicycles, Joggers

Dogs chase things that move. This is a self-rewarding behavior, meaning that puppies love doing it, so it isn't going away on its own.

- Distance is your friend. When possible, stay well away from the movement so your puppy can focus on you, at least a little. Reward him well for listening. As he gets better, move a little closer next session.
- Feed around speed. The moment *you* notice a fast-moving temptation coming your way, start feeding your puppy. Give treat after treat (be sure to adjust his meals accordingly, so you don't end up overfeeding). When the distraction moves past, stop feeding. Soon movement will equal look at you for treats. That's a great start!
- Head halters. This can give you better control. Keep your lead short so your puppy can't hit the end of a long lead hard.
- Sit Is It! If your puppy is sitting, he can't be chasing. Bring out really good treats, and use those to reward sitting. Make sitting around moving things extra special. Praise warmly, smile, make it a big deal.
- Use Follow the Leader. A puppy cannot do two things at once—get going! Move, turn, pulse that lead—insist that he focus on you and when he does, "Good puppy" and treats!
- Leave It (page 132), Look At Me (page 95), and Simple Sits (page 153) are great tools to have in your toolbox.
- Now add all your Come Games, as you want to be able to get him back if he is in hot pursuit headed for trouble.

Chewing

All puppies chew, and some take it to an art form. If you have an oral, teething, bored, or athletic puppy, expect chewing. Don't just accept it, expect it. It's up to you to prevent bad habits from developing and damage from occurring, but chances are pretty good something will get chewed at some point. One year when we still had a large flock of sheep here at the farm, Sarah ran to the barn for a quick check on the ewes. On her way out, she left the door to our storage area ajar. We walked back to what looked like a blizzard had hit our living room full force. In the center

This doll will never be the same. Prevention is key to surviving the chewing stage of puppyhood.

was a delighted ten-month-old PJ, mouth wide open in a classic Terrier grin, eyes dancing with delight, the remnants of the plastic cover of a twenty-four-pack of toilet paper at her feet. Oh well. We laughed then and we laugh now. No harm done. Was that "separation anxiety"? Not in the least. It was puppy fun, pure and simple.

- Prevent the event. Keep the pup in sight, encourage him to play with his own toys (try rubbing them between your hands before you hand them to him), and confine him when you cannot supervise.
- Exercise. Has it been snowy or rainy? Have you been busy? Any of those can lessen exercise, and less exercise means more energy with fewer outlets. Walk that puppy! Work up to ten to fifteen minutes a day per month of age, and see if that doesn't help.

- Is he stressed? If there is fighting or tension in your home, if people are visiting (especially if you're not all that fond of them), if it is crunch time at work, if you are going through a divorce or a family illness, your puppy can absorb all that tension like a sponge, then mirror it back to you in his behavior.
- Rotate toys. Give her one or two at a time. This tends to keep the toy "fresh" and interesting to your puppy. Right now Pip has a spotted rooster she adores. Anytime we give it to her she spends her time making it crowcrowcrowcrow—nonstop. When we can stand no more, we remove it with a smile and hand her something else. After ten minutes or so of romping around, we give her either a food-filled toy or a chewie. The older dogs are out of the room for this, so we have no competition or arguments. She usually lies down for a good chew. Perfect!
- Supervision. When Pip is out, we are on. She is almost five months old at this moment, deep into teething and full of energy. We keep our eyes on her. Anything that happens out of our sight would be our fault.
- Confinement. And by confinement we mean in the room with you, on lead with you, in a pen or behind a gate, or crated in the house. Confinement doesn't (and shouldn't) mean isolation.
- Work your Touch and Space Games in Chapters 3 and 4.
- Pretrain a nice release; work on Out (page 136).

Countertop Cruising

Grabbing stuff of the counter? What a hassle! Nip this problem in the bud!

- Use counter intelligence. There is no reason for any puppy to have his front paws up on or near the counter or table. No good can come from that. Paws are up? Try a flat-handed whomp on the counter, table, or nearby wall. That startles many puppies to the floor.
- Body block. Move as if you're playing Mine (page 82). You can do that while facing the counter if you wish, just shuffle into

him and through him. Message: Counter is mine—get out of my way.

- Make paws up a one-way ticket out of the kitchen using body blocking. Read Go for instructions.
- Paws on counter means puppy in crate. When you see paws on the counter, pick up your puppy and take her to the crate. No comment, no petting, no treats.
- Close the door or install a gate to keep your puppy out of the kitchen.
- Use an indoor fence unit. These come in citronella (a spray) or electronic (a shock) and can be set so that they beep only if the dog's head is up near the countertop. Both beep first, then deliver a spray or small shock so puppy can avoid the correction by moving away. Sometimes for older, professional food hounds this is the only thing that really works.
- Reward sitting. Whenever Sarah prepares the dogs' meals, she gives a kibble to any who are sitting quietly. Result: they all sit quietly. If a puppy is sitting, there is no jumping problem. Do one of these things, do a combination, but do something! If your puppy never gets a foot or nose on the counter, you won't have to live with the dreaded "counter cruising" food thief.

Demanding Dog: It's All About Me!

If your pup *must* be touching you, pawing you, interacting with you every moment, you are raising a "you" addict. While that may fulfill some of your own needs, it can create dependent, neurotic, fearful dogs with separation issues. If your heart shrinks at the idea of sitting in the same room with your pup but not touching, talking to, kissing, stroking, hugging, or looking at your "baby," please sort this out with a good friend or counselor before you hopelessly confuse your puppy.

- Stop the rewards. Be sure you aren't rewarding him for being a nudge. If you've tossed him a cookie or a toy to quiet or calm him, if you've looked at him, spoken to him, or if you've reached down your hand to stroke him, then you rewarded him. To stop this behavior, you must stop all rewards for the behavior.

- Leave a lead on. When demanding starts, do not look at or speak to him. Calmly pick up the lead and use your toe to do the Guided Down cue. When he Downs, then look and smile at him briefly.

ROXANNE FRANKLIN

- Back off. Or when the demanding behaviors start up again (you're holding the lead, right?), without looking at or speaking to him, shuffle into him, forcing him to back up a few steps. Then go back up to your spot and sit back down. This should be sudden without being violent in any way. When he's quiet for a few seconds, look at him, smile, and invite him over for a brief petting. Quiet, polite puppies get your attention.
- Go! He gets pushy, he leaves the room. It's a simple equation any dog can figure out.
- Work all your Touch and Requirement Games. Your pup is clearly both smart and bored, so do something about both.

Digging

Digging is one of the few canine pastimes. Dogs dig for fun, to hunt, to make a cool spot under a bush. Why they dig determines what you do to control it.

JACKSON YOUNG

- Give puppy a cool spot. If this is August and your puppy has "suddenly" started to dig under the porch or a bush, he is probably looking for a cool spot. Bring him inside where it is cooler or give him a cool area where he can dig to control this. Supply plenty of clean water!

- Backfill. Many puppies have a natural aversion to feces. If yours is one of those, then, when you scoop your yard, fill each hole with feces then cover with dirt. That prevents them from going back to that one spot.
- Pretend you don't have a yard for a while. Walk your puppy, take him to play with another dog, play games with him.
- Get some new toys. Play with those in the yard with him. He needs a new hobby, one you have to supply.

Don't Pick Me Up!

Your puppy growls or snaps when you pick her up. The most common cause: picking up incorrectly. If you pick up your puppy under her "armpits" as you might a child, you are probably hurting your puppy. Do this repeatedly and she may start telling you to stop. If you do not know you're hurting her, you may ignore or miss her signals and eventually she starts to growl when you reach down to pick her up. Typically these are sweet puppies who show aggression nowhere else in their lives. Now, there are rare puppies who are both confident and assertive who may "correct" you for attempting to lift them. These puppies are normally assertive in other areas as well. If you have this type of puppy, get hands-on help yesterday. You'll need guidance.

Safe and secure, well supported at both ends, this Cavalier is quite comfortable.

- Learn the proper pickup. For a small or midsized pup, start by sliding one hand over her body and under her chest. This allows you to support her while your arm holds her against your body securely. With a squirmy puppy, reach up between her front legs and hook a finger through the collar. Your other hand is free to open doors, stroke her, or get your keys from your pocket. Another way is to scoop your puppy up. Put one hand on her chest, and the other behind her rear legs so you can lift her securely and easily. This is usually for larger puppies.

- Treat, then retreat. If your puppy associates being picked up with pain, you have to teach her otherwise. Get a handful of treats. Put a treat in one hand, with your other reach under your puppy as if to lift her up, and give the treat then retreat by standing up. Reach under, treat, retreat. Praise her warmly while doing this. As she relaxes, you can begin to lift her a little bit. Reach under, lift a few inches, treat, put her back down then retreat. Do this right and your puppy will enjoy being scooped up by you in no time!
- Don't worry, be happy. You must set a happy and relaxed tone here. If you are tense, your puppy will stay tense.
- Make haste slowly. There is no rush. Stay at the level you both are comfortable at. When you are confident, go to the next step.
- All Touch Games. Do one a day until this is resolved.

Don't Touch My Collar, Head, Ears

Your puppy stiffens, growls, pulls away and generally resists handling.

- Are his ears infected? Have they been in the past? If yes, your puppy may not look forward to human hands near tender ears. A quick head swing can be a signal of pain, the canine version of "Hey, watch it!" If it happens in the same place consistently, please speak to your vet about what might be going on. It could be many things: soreness from a big romp, an illness like Lyme disease, growing pains, or the first sign of an infection brewing.
- Play Face It (page 155) and all your Touch and Space Games daily.
- Resistance could also be a threat from a confident puppy. This type of puppy will watch your hand come over his head and threaten as it moves closer. He may mouth your hand if you take his collar or flop on his back to kick with all legs while he spins and mouths. He won't get easier to deal with when he's

twice the size, so don't ignore it or hope he'll "grow out of it." As Brian likes to say, "He might grow into it!" If this is what's up, please find a qualified dog behavior professional to help you. Do not delay.

TRAIN THE PUPPY YOU HAVE AT THIS MOMENT

You can only train the puppy looking back at you right this second. The shy, quiet, hide-behind-me puppy you had a moment ago is gone. You now have a barking, bouncing, let-me-chase-that-squirrel puppy who needs a whole different level of energy,  intention, praise, and direction. Shifting to match the various moods of your companion is one of the challenges of puppy training. Think of it as driving a car that is sluggish at ten miles an hour one moment, then becomes responsive and goes from zero to sixty in 2.6 seconds the next. It's exciting, it's interesting, but it isn't always easy. Just keep saying: The only puppy I can train is the one I have on the lead right now.

Drinks Too Much

Does your puppy regularly drink and drink and drink until his belly is distended?

- Since overdrinking can be a sign of ill health (most often it isn't in puppies, but it is worth checking)—please discuss it with your veterinarian.
- Change foods to a premium food. Inexpensive foods can cause a lot of drinking.
- Presoaking your puppy's meals can lessen drinking considerably. If your puppy drinks a lot, try soaking.
- Puppies that consume rawhide or other edible chew toys can also drink heavily. Change what they play with for a few days and see if your puppy eases up on the water.
- Excessive drinking can also happen if you've been limiting her water intake too much. She may have learned to drink everything she wants and more whenever she can. In that case, you have to find an easy, pleasant day off. Put down a bowl you refill as needed, then take your puppy out a lot—every thirty to forty-five minutes for the next two to three hours after the last major drink. Once she realizes the water is now available as often and as much as she wants, she should slow to a normal drinking rate,

Eats Cat Food

Put it out of reach. How long would you last around a plate of a favorite food? Why we expect more from our puppies than we do from ourselves is a bit of a mystery. Give them a break. Put the cat food out of reach and call it a day. Most of the time, for all of us, removal of the temptation is a more reliable fix than counting on willpower.

Eats Own or Other Dogs' Poop

Okay, everyone together now: "Yuck!" Scolding your puppy will stress him without teaching him, so your puppy will just eat it faster at a distance.

- Practice success. Work your Look At Me (page 95), Leave It (page 132), Out (page 136), and Come: Basics (page 102) so you have a way to "discuss" it with him that gets to good. Your puppy must have a way to win.
- On lead. Leave him on lead so you can help him succeed (and prevent him from getting into ick).
- Is he healthy? Make sure he is parasite free and eating a premium-brand puppy food. If he is targeting a specific dog's stools, have that dog checked by the veterinarian as well.
- Deterrent products, like Forbid, are worth trying.

Eats Too Fast

"Too fast" is a relative term. Canines are "grab and gulp" by design. If you're concerned, speak to your veterinarian. If everything is okay, then here are a few things to try.

- Crate as plate. Eating from the clean crate bottom can prevent too much gulping. A side benefit: Your puppy will soon love his crate!
- Soak it. Puppies can't gulp mush as fast as kibble. So soaking kibble in equal parts water can help slow your binger.
- Prize inside. A Busy Buddy can be packed with his dry food while a Kong requires the food to be soaked before packing, but either way, both slow him down.

Fence Running

We all are what we practice. If your puppy practices racing at or along the fence line while barking aggressively, he or she may well become increasingly assertive and potentially aggressive around the target of that behavior: passing bicycles, walkers, other dogs.

Dogs enjoy this so it won't go away on its own.

- If your dog runs the fence, stop that. Until retrained, go out with your puppy as if your yard weren't fenced at all.
- Leave a long line on your puppy if you need to, and practice calling your puppy back to you, at first randomly, then from along the fence, and then when barking. Remember to make it really clear when your puppy makes the right choice. Good puppy!
- Changing the fence system can help as well. Moving your puppy back from the road or sidewalk can help. Sometimes this can be done simply, sometimes not. But if you can, do it.

Finicky Eating

Pups vary in the amount they eat. If fed more than they want and need, they may leave food. This is usually nothing to fret about if your pup is a good weight, having normal bowel movements, and your veterinarian says your puppy is healthy. Finicky is when a puppy consistently walks away from a full food bowl. What to do?

- Puppy suddenly refuses food. This may be something as simple as teething or it might be something more serious. Please consult your veterinarian for guidance. A puppy who is lethargic, vomiting, has diarrhea or no bowel movements at all or is refusing food is an EMERGENCY!
- Stop rewarding finicky behavior. If you pick up the bowl and add something yummy when he doesn't eat, you just rewarded it. Imagine if your mother quickly added cookies to your plate when you skipped your lunch. What message would that send?

- Implement mealtimes. Food goes down for twenty minutes, then is put away until the next meal. Use few if any treats in training for this period. Many dogs will fast for a day or more, then will start eating with gusto. *Note:* Toy breed puppies *must eat* to avoid hypoglycemia. Always have food down for them, letting them graze as they wish. If they don't eat, contact your veterinarian quickly. What is no big deal for a larger puppy can be critical for a toy.

Food Bowl Issues: Mealtime Menace

Your puppy tenses up, growls, and/or lunges at you if you come near his food bowl while he is eating. As with all aggression, please get immediate hands-on help from a professional.

- Feed a good diet in the right amount. How much do you feed your puppy, what brand of food do you feed, and is this a new problem? One twenty-week-old Golden Retriever puppy was growling around his food bowl because he was being fed what he had been fed when he arrived in the home at seven weeks old. He was, literally, starving. Once the puppy was on an appropriate amount of food, his growling ceased.
- Good nutrition. If you are feeding a cheap brand of food or if your puppy carries a parasite load, he may not be getting all the nutrition he needs to thrive. This is especially true for large- and giant-breed puppies. Investing in a premium brand of puppy food can help these puppies relax.
- Divide and conquer. Next mealtime, pick up your puppy's food bowl. Spoon about a quarter of his meal (doesn't have to be exact) into the food bowl and set it down. Step away from the bowl and let your puppy eat. When your puppy has finished, smile and say nice things as you pick up the bowl, put more food in it, and repeat the process. Do this until all food is fed. Goal: For your puppy to want you to approach his bowl.
- It's raining treats. Feed all the food at once, ideally plain dry kibble. Walk up, drop in something extra delicious from a foot or so above your puppy, then walk away. Do not linger, do not touch. Be sure to stay relaxed; smile and praise as you do this.

If you are not confident your puppy won't lunge, please don't do this.

- Interlopers. A puppy who growls at other animals while he is eating aren't usually "problems." Keep other pets away or feed your puppy in his crate, where he can eat in peace.
- Practice Sit for Your Supper, Mine, and really all games through all levels.

Garbage Hounds: Indoors and Out

Oh, the bane of puppy people everywhere. The puppy nose constantly finding the most disgusting thing in the vicinity, honing in on it with superhero-like precision to grab it up with the goal of swallowing before you can get it out. There are many ways to deal with this.

- Head Halters. A simple yet effective fix. They give you better ability to close the mouth quickly. Get control over that nose, and you control what the dog grabs. These can be especially helpful for the short-legged breeds like Bassets, Corgis, and Dachshunds, who are so temptingly close to those delicious icky bits.
- Look At Me! Bring treats. Anytime you catch your puppy looking up at you, smile, praise, and treat. Move closer to temptation so he sees it, then pause. Use his name calmly and squeeze/pulse the lead until he looks up—when he does praise, back up, treat and repeat.
- Practice Leave It (page 132) in hopes of keeping him out of trouble and Out (pages 136) for those moments when he gets into it.

Growls When on Couch

Any puppy, but especially comfort-seeking puppies, can claim the couch or sofa for their own. Any growl or threat is unacceptable. Start resolving this today!

- Prevent the event. Keep the puppy off the couch. Gate him out of that room or use an upside-down clear plastic carpet runner, nubs up, to discourage the habit. Leave a lead on your puppy when you are home and he is loose so you can control him without grabbing him.
- Avoid a confrontation. If he won't Off and you aren't prepared or can't reach the lead safely, go ring the doorbell or get ready for a walk. He'll hop off to join you—then praise him! Good puppy! Now, go put that carpet runner back on. (These do not work for heavily coated puppies; blocking those pups out of the room can be the best bet.)

Yoshi is what Debbie describes as "floppy" or hyperflexible. Note her rear legs. This improved as she matured. SARAH WILSON

- Make Off good. Use really good treats, put him up on the couch, ask him to get off, pulse the lead, and back up until he does then praise and reward. Repeat until he jumps off instantly. Perfect!
- Is your puppy "floppy"? Deborah Gross Saunders, animal physical therapist, reports that such puppies can need more sleep and can be "grumpy" when awoken. Let them bed down in their crates for naps on comfy blankets. Make sure they get the sleep they need.
- Go allows you to send her from the room.
- Get help! You need experienced, hands-on help for any growling puppy.

Growls When Someone Comes Near You

If your puppy growls at or blocks someone when they approach you, he is being possessive of you. Don't be flattered. It's as "cute" as a family member threatening to hit your friends when they come toward you.

- Careful! Don't deal with this behavior by picking the puppy up or stroking him to "calm him down." Since you get what you pet, you get more growling.
- No lap! Your lap is a place of puppy power, so no more lap time for him!
- Demote him (page 254).
- Work your Daily Dozens (page 272).
- Build a really solid distance Down.
- Use Go (page 148). Point toward the nearest exit and shuffle into your puppy. Block him physically until he turns around and leaves the room. Be direct—no smiling. When he has moved off, invite the person he growled at to come sit next to you. If your puppy rushes back, take him by the collar (do not pick him up) and march him to his crate.
- Get help! You need experienced, hands-on help for any growling puppy.

Growls When Woken Up

Some puppies wake up cranky. Let's see if we can change that!

- Pretrain what you want. Start when your puppy has *just* curled up but isn't in a deep sleep. Walk over, drop a treat in front of his nose, praise warmly as you walk away. That's it. Do this three to five times a week, no more. Otherwise you risk annoying him instead of relaxing him. Our goal is for him to start thinking: Oh, a human is approaching, great!
- It must rain treats. Dropping the treat in front of his nose is key—do *not* hand him the treat from your hand. Why? Because we want him waking up and sniffing around in front of him, not whipping his head toward the nearest hand.
- Move away. Walking away is important, as we don't want to

pressure him or annoy him. In general, it is best to leave sleeping dogs alone, but this game ensures that if someone errs, your puppy won't mind at all.

- Demote him! If your puppy is pushy in other areas of his life, demote him right away (see page 254).
- Get help! You need experienced, hands-on help for any growling puppy.

OVERTIRED?

Like some toddlers, some puppies get cranky when they are tired. If your angel puppy starts getting grabby, mouthy, or wild, try a nap. In active households, naps may need to be regularly enforced with a crate—otherwise he'll go until he is overtired, then head right toward brattiness. Puppy in crate means kids leave puppy alone. Use a plastic crate to minimize fingers through the sides. Overtired puppies can absolutely wake up growly. Step one is have your puppy nap in his or her crate and let the nap go as long as the puppy needs. The crate is off limits to the kids. Put a plastic crate in a corner of the kitchen or family room to minimize sleep interruptions.

Pip gets tired and starts to fuss during a long lecture. I am explaining this to the audience before crating my little one for a nap. Fussy pups happen to us all.
Melissa Fischer

Haranguing during Hugging

When you hug your sweetheart or your mom, does your not-so-little-anymore puppy leap up barking or push between you? Pushy, pushy, pushy! Sometimes dogs do this because they are unsure and are being protective and at other times they are trying to insert themselves between the two of you. Either way, it isn't his business.

- Body block. Do a Mine (page 82). Just keep your back to the pup and block him off you and your partner. If you've been playing this game regularly, your dog should understand this immediately.
- Ignore. Turn your back to him when he does this. Do not look at, speak to, or touch him for this. When he grows puzzled and stops, praise him warmly (use words, not touch—touch may be too exciting).
- On lead. Step on the lead before you hug. Keep the knee of the leg on the lead bent and lean your weight on it. When he jumps, he will self-correct. Ignore the jumping, praise the stopping.
- Down him. Use the Guided Down if you need it. Pretrain it first. If he starts to hassle you, down him calmly.
- Tether him. Then reward calm behavior and ignore noise or upset.
- Send him away. Use Go and body block him out of the room.

Hyperactive

Your puppy seems crazy! He races around, jumps nonstop, barks at everything and generally works himself up into a frenzy. Help!

- What is his breed or mix? Some breeds are more active and/or sensitive than others. What seems like "crazy" may be a normal activity level for a Miniature Pinscher, Irish Setter/Jack Russell cross, or a field-bred Labrador.
- Isolation? How much time does your puppy spend alone? The more your puppy is crated, the wilder he will tend to be for the

first half hour or more after he is let out. Letting him burn off some steam by playing outside or going on a brisk walk can help.

- Exercise? Three ten-minute walks on lead a day isn't enough for an active six-month-old puppy. She'll need at least double that or, better yet, some playtime with a suitable buddy, some swimming, or some other way to really let her cut loose safely.

- What are you rewarding? If you get what you pet and you raise what you praise then what are you petting and praising? If you ignore the calm (because you are just so grateful to have a minute to do something else) and attend to the wildness, you'll get more of that.

- Is she kept active? In some households with children, the puppy is being constantly woken up and revved up. Multi-dog households can teach the same thing if one (or more) of your older dogs is constantly urging your puppy to play. The puppy soon learns to stay up at that high activity level all the time.

- Check her diet. A premium brand can make a big difference, and some puppies are helped by feeding one sort of diet or another. Make any changes slowly.

- Be careful with your hands. Buffing or rubbing your puppy's face or head revs most pups up, setting off a flurry of activity. If you want calm, be calm. If you want her to slow down, slow down your hands and your voice.

- Time to START. Focus on the Space and Touch Games first as building self-control is your training pursuit for now. Pick a calm place to teach, and keep relaxing yourself by breathing in through your nose and out through your mouth. Do short sessions.

- Demote her! Generally, the more boundaries and well understood rules these puppies have, the better they become.

- Be patient. This is usually worst between four and seven months of age with a peak of "OHMIGAWD what have I done?" in the fifth month. This will pass and give you many good stories to tell.

Introducing Puppy to Resident Dog

Many people worry how to do this well, so we'll share some hints here.

- One at a time! Before you bring in your new puppy, put away your other dogs. After you've allowed the puppy to explore a bit, scoop him up for another walk. If you have a helper, have him go let your resident dog(s) into the house to explore the new scent while you walk your puppy. If you don't have assistance, crate your puppy after the potty break so your older pets can explore.

This is fun, not fierce. You can tell by Rowan's lips. He is not baring his teeth.
Melissa Fischer

- Away from home. It's best to have your puppy and older dog meet off your property if at all possible. You'll need someone you trust to handle your puppy while you handle your adult dog. Allow them to see each other. If your adult dog is calm and nonaggressive, then proceed to let them sniff. Praise and laugh in a relaxed way to signal that this is all okay. If you tense up, holding your breath, you may convince your older dog that this puppy makes you anxious. If your older dog seems tense or aggressive, this is not the time for a nose-to-nose introduction.

Here a tolerant Wyatt accepts young Niko's licking. In a minute, Wyatt will calmly tell him to stop with a brief freeze of motion and a light growl. Niko will stop. SARAH WILSON

- Separate. If an outside greeting isn't possible (or doesn't go too well), then after the walk, crate your puppy. Use a baby gate, exercise pen, or some well-placed chairs to keep the adult dog away from the puppy's crate at first. Allow them to get used to each other at a distance for a day or two, then progress without the barrier but still crated for a few more days, or until your adult dog doesn't much care. There is no reason to rush the introduction.

- Reaction is normal. Expect your resident dog to have a reaction to an unexpected and unrequested addition to his life. Adult dogs may growl or bark at first. Redirect them to Sit or Down, then pet and praise all calm, happy behavior. And as always, act the way you want your pet to act. So remember to breathe, laugh, and have a good time.

- Exception? If you have a delightfully social, friendly, puppy-loving dog who has greeted dogs in her home many times, then you probably have no worries.

- Near Is Dear. If your adult dog is none too sure about this new addition, play Near Is Dear (page 110). Message: Being near this puppy makes good things happen. When your dog is happy with that, start working him on his basic commands—sit, down, come, back up—this prepares him to listen in the presence of this new, wonderful distraction.

- Puppy equals praise. Or . . . ignore your resident dog totally for the next few days except when he happens to be near the puppy's crate. Then praise him warmly.

- Common scents. Rub each down with a towel. Give the towel with the puppy's scent on it to your adult dog to nap on and the one with your adult dog's scent to the puppy.
- Get help. In the rare event that your adult dog is persistently aggressive toward the puppy—standing tail up, staring at him growling, barking hysterically or standing with his head low, and tail stiff, and motionless (how he looks when he sees a squirrel)—please get some hands-on coaching on how to manage the introduction from an experienced dog professional.
- *Warning:* Toy breed puppies need special consideration. They must be protected from a larger dog's responses. Greeting through baby gates, keeping the puppy on your lap, putting your older dog on lead, taking things slow, and interrupting vigorous play are all ways of keeping your tiny toy safer.

IS THIS OKAY?
TYPICAL INTERACTIONS BETWEEN PUPPIES AND ADULT DOGS

Puppy jumps onto older dog with paws or whole body.

Typical response: Older dog spins and roars in pup's face. The older dog may or may not bump or hold down the puppy with a paw. The puppy may squeal in surprise and/or run off. If the puppy comes back harder, jumping back up into the adult's face, your older dog may need to make his point more firmly. All normal exchanges are brief and to the point. A very tolerant older dog may walk away the first few times but then may lose patience. This is also normal. Worrisome responses include chasing after your puppy and any reaction that lasts more than a few seconds or draws blood.

Puppy comes too close to adult dog chewing a toy.

The adult dog may freeze, silently lift a lip, growl, then snap. This is an expected warning sequence that the pup will soon learn to respect. Some dogs may leap up and go a step or two toward the puppy (especially toy breeds with larger-breed pups). This may cause the puppy to squeal, run away, cower, grovel back to the adult or stay well clear. All are normal.

The rare older dog allows the puppy to take the toy. This may mean your adult dog is extremely tolerant or the puppy extremely powerful. Either way, it is not the expected response. Some adults will be very tolerant of pups under four months of age, but that may (and should) change as the pup grows up. The adult dog's role is to teach your pup safe dog behavior, and that is better learned at home.

Puppy gets in dog's face over and over and over.

Intervene! Stop the puppy or let him learn about being a dog, if you trust the adult dog to teach him. If the puppy misses subtle signals, that can force the adult dog to "speak" more clearly. Our personal dogs have raised many a puppy. Any youngster who races up slamming into any of our adults will be corrected for this wildly impolite behavior. If the pup is under four months these corrections will happen quickly and quietly; if he's over four months, they'll probably happen more loudly with more forward body motion into the puppy (but still safely). Please do not yell at or scold your older dog for setting reasonable, clear canine boundaries. He's probably doing you and your pup a favor.

Puppy leaps onto sleeping adult.

Expected responses range from doing nothing to roaring, snapping, standing up and snapping, putting his mouth on the pup's head or neck (without injury), or putting his paw on top of the pup to hold him down. What you get depends on the size, breed or mix, and age of both your puppy and your adult dog as well as the energy of the contact.

Older dog does harm to the youngster.

Be concerned anytime your adult dog follows your puppy around with a stiff tail and low head, which is stalking behavior or if one dog is deeply frightened of the other. Learning to read canine body language and intention is tricky. If the harm requires veterinary treatment, separate the two dogs while you seek competent professional assistance. If you aren't sure, ask for help from an experienced dog professional.

YOUR PUPPY PASS EXPIRED!

Most adult dogs give young puppies a lot of leeway in their behavior, much as we humans do with toddlers. But as the puppy matures, this "puppy pass" generally expires. When it does, frequently around four to six months of age, your adult dog will (sometimes quite suddenly) get down to the serious business of teaching your puppy how to behave in the world of canines. As long as these lessons are taught with restraint and are brief, with no one getting hurt, it is usually safe to let them happen.

Introducing Puppy to Your Cat

If you want this to go smoothly, go slowly. Do not carry your cat in to meet your puppy. You're likely to end up with scratch marks, a frightened cat, and an excited puppy.

- Limit access. Use gates and ex-pens to keep your puppy in a limited area.
- Keep necessities near. Make sure the cat's food, water, and litterbox are not in the puppy's area and don't require your cat to cross through it to get to what he needs.
- Near Is Dear. Practice this game with your puppy around the cat.
- The cat is mine. We use Mine whenever new dogs enter our home. It both establishes our great cat, Ben, as ours and tells us just how interested a puppy is. If a puppy pushes and pushes

Pip's constant attention annoys Ben. Pip surrenders but not in a language Ben can understand. They work it out.
Sarah Wison

to cut around us then we know we have to (a) block more clearly and (b) watch this puppy around Ben as the pup is intensely interested.

- Come: Basics (page 102) is critical, as are Leave It (page 132), Move (page 159), Look At Me (page 95), and Follow the Leader (page 159). The good news is you have a fabulous distraction to work with. Once you get your puppy to focus on you around your cat, you're well on your way to having excellent attention no matter what.

- Expect a reaction. Cats will often freeze, hiss, and retreat. Some will stalk the puppy in the crate. Have a spray bottle of water ready to spritz your cat silently should he appear aggressive. A few confident and dog-friendly cats will stroll up to the crate for a curious sniff—that is lovely.

Jumping on People

There are many types of jumping, from the gentle paw placements of a sensitive or fearful puppy experimenting with making friends to the full-body-contact slam of an assertive or bold puppy. Being the social creatures they are, dogs are savvy about how hard they are hitting you.

- Refuse to confuse. Don't reward your puppy with attention or touch if he doesn't have four on the floor. This includes when you first get home, opening a door when he's jumping, putting down a food bowl or tossing a toy when he's in the air, or petting him when he's draped across your lap. See any room for improvement at your end?
- Practice Off (page 86) so you can clearly communicate what you want.
- With Sensitive/Shy puppies, gently guide them off into a Sit, then scratch their chests to keep them from flopping over. Every few seconds, back up a couple of steps, which allows your puppy to come to you, then repeat. This will keep his

stress from building and raise his confidence level.
- Build his Sits. Don't throw the toy for your puppy, set his food bowl down or open a door if he is jumping. Sit Is It!
- Solidify Space Games. Practice the level you are at while working toward the next level. Space Games make controlling this annoying habit much easier.
- Use Simple Sit. Once your puppy learns this cue, you can use it to modify jumping. See "How to Control Jumping Using the Simple Sit" (page 155).

JUMP-UP INJURIES: YOURS!

Sarah's front tooth was broken in half by a dog who leaped happily up into her face (now she has a hand in the collar of bouncy dogs she meets). Other injuries we know of include: a broken cheekbone, a tooth through the lip, the badly bitten tongue when a Labrador's skull smacked upward into the human jaw, black eyes—the list goes on. Discourage leaping toward your face from the start. One hand on the flat collar is an easy way to protect yourself, control your puppy, and set the stage for success. Space Games will help with this.

Mouthing

Mouthing is what almost all puppies do. Teething, which occurs from around sixteen weeks to twenty-four weeks of age, can make mouthing worse. You can and you should teach pups not to mouth people. Does one method work for all puppies? Nope, so don't feel frustrated if the thing your friend or another book said would "work like magic" doesn't.

- Stop making this worse. No pushing on his face in "play," no teasing him with your hands, no using fast back-and-forth "buffing" actions around his head, no continuing to pet or play when his mouth is on you.
- Give outlets. If he's teething, make sure he has many compressed raw-hides, sterilized bones, and other good gnaw objects. Some people give ice cubes when the puppy seems especially uncomfortable.
- Play your Touch Games? Calm = Release can be key to managing mouthing effectively. It changes your puppy's view of you. Play it daily for best results.
- The moment puppy teeth touch human flesh, startle dramatically (your whole body jumps a bit, as if someone said "Boo!") and give a meaningful "Ouch." Then take your hands and attention away from your puppy. Try not to use a high tone of voice, as your pup may mistake that for play. Some pups will respond to this, some will not, but it is worth a try.
- Give the cold shoulder. All social mammals use withdrawal to display displeasure. And be dramatic—go from fun play to immediate, silent, haughty withdrawal. You need to really act it out so the pup can't miss it. The more of a contrast you make between smiling, attentive play and gone, the better.
- Down. Once your puppy understands the Guided Down (page 92), use that. Apply pressure to the lead to prevent further problems. Once your puppy settles, hand him a good chew toy and let

him work on that. After a few minutes, quietly remove your toe from the lead and go about your day. Repeat as needed.

- Confine. If your puppy is still fussy and mouthy, crate him up. Don't be angry. He just needs a break and chances are you do too. Crate him calmly but without comment or praise. This is a good choice for puppies who get mouthy when they get over-tired. There's no point in trying to change their behavior when they are cranky. After the puppy naps and you take a breather, you'll both be in a better place to start again.
- If your puppy enjoys mouthing, none of these things may make much of a dent in the behavior. For those pups, we use breath spray. These are small metal canisters that are easy to tuck into your pocket. When your puppy begins to mouth, calmly say, "No bite," then spritz down at the place where his mouth is on your body. Don't spray up his nose or at his face; spray straight down at your own body. If his nose happens to be there too, that would be his problem. Try to be quick and don't threaten him with the canister. It's "No bite"spritzgoodpuppy!

Poles: Tired of Tangles?

If you're tired of finding yourself literally on the opposite side of the pole from your pup, don't fret. This is easy enough to fix.

- Stop doing his homework for him! If you thoughtfully reach around and untangle the lead, then you've done his work for him. What chance did he have to learn anything but sit there and my human will untangle me?
- Let him learn! Give a little pulsing in the direction of fastest disentanglement, then cheer as he comes around. He will soon learn that when faced with a pole, parking meter, or sign, he needs to stick close to you. This is much more convenient.

Here Niko tangles. I step to the left and pulse the lead as I encourage him around, he's got it now! SARAH WILSON

Possessiveness: Finders Keepers

If your puppy runs off with food or a toy, hiding under a table or turning away from you, he's playing Finders Keepers. Pups who come from large litters or have gone without food can arrive in your home with an attitude. Other strong pups are simply born with this opinion. Telling him "No" or scolding him isn't going to enlighten him. Since your job as the coach is to create reward-able behavior, what would you prefer your pup to do? How about staying nice and relaxed when you take an item from him?

• When you stroll past your puppy, drop a treat as you go by. Do not look at or speak to or pause by your puppy. Just walk

past, drop the treat, and keep going. Stay at whatever distance your puppy can tolerate without moving away from you. Whatever that distance is, that is where you start.

- Puppy relaxed? Then stop, smile, drop a few kibbles, stroke her once, drop a few more kibbles and walk away. Still relaxed? Good job!
- Touch and Space Games. Work these so she sees you as an understandable, consistent leader. Focus on Calm = Release (page 122) every day.

Pip has a cow trachea (Moo Tube). It's not bringing out her best self. We reserve those for in the crate.
ELI ORLING

- Practice Out (page 136).
- No body parts. Some puppies get aggressive over chewies that are animal body parts (sorry, that is gross but true). These include rawhide, pigs' ears, hooves, bones, and "bully" sticks. Don't give these to puppies who run off with them when you come near.
- Head halter. If your puppy grabs things off the ground on walks, then use a head halter so you can easily control where that nose and mouth are. Few puppies love these at first, but they get used to them in time.
- Lead on. Leave a lead on your puppy when you are home so you can literally "get a handle" on the situation.

- Praise party! No matter what your puppy spits out of his mouth, you must—must—praise him for doing so. Once the item is in his mouth all you can do is build an excellent release. So if he spits out your wallet, the remote, your favorite shoe—too bad. He *did* spit it out, so reward that.
- When you can, let your puppy have the item. Not clothing or dishtowels but if she grabbed a bit of lettuce from the floor and you get it from her, praise her and hand it back. There's nothing dangerous about a bit of lettuce.

THE PIP CHRONICLES: MINE, MINE AND THAT'S MINE TOO!

On her first day home with us, we noticed that Pip grabbed toys with her whole mouth and then tried to grab more again. If we walked near, she ran away with her prize. We did everything described in "Finders Keepers," which helped stop the running away, but Pip wasn't bringing us her toys yet. To work on that, Sarah played fetch in a narrow hall so she could block any escape route. Rolling the tennis ball down the hall, Pip had to come past Sarah to exit. When she did, Sarah gently reached out her arm, snagging her, praising all the way, then stroking her and laughing! What a Smart Puppy! Sarah stayed relaxed and completely *not* focused on the toy. The goal was to have Pip love coming to her. After a few minutes, Pip was racing to Sarah and flinging herself to the ground, tail wagging, paws playing, asking for a tummy tickle. Excellent! We're heading in the right direction!

Pip relaxes with a stuffed toy, no longer worried about running away with it.
SARAH WILSON

Possessiveness: Guarding

This is the more dangerous and worrisome next level up from "Finders Keepers." This puppy doesn't run away with an item; this puppy locks eyes, growls, and tells you "I dare you to try to take this from me!" Put another way, the finders keepers' T-shirt would read "He who grabs then runs away lives to grab another day." The guarding puppy's reads "The best defense is a strong offense."

- Remove the problem. If a certain toy/chewie brings this out in your puppy, get rid of that thing. Really: put down the book, toss that thing out and then read the rest. Yes, yes, we know—that doesn't teach your puppy anything. Right, but it does prevent him from learning more about using aggression to intimidate humans. Once you've done that, call around to get referrals for a good trainer. You want a professional assessment on this ASAP.
- Demote your dog. Start the demoting process on page 254 as you apply everything outlined in the above section on possessiveness.
- Daily Dozens. Do your Daily Dozens: An Anti-Bite Protocol (page 272).
- Stay happy. Go back to acting the way you want your puppy to act. If you get tense and "attack" your puppy he may have decided *you* have the guarding problem!
- No more trading. If you were taught to deal with this situation with a trade, stop. That may well have helped get you here in the first place. Too often, in an attempt to get the puppy to release, people present food treats *after* the puppy is latched on in full resistance. While a few puppies may spit the thing out to take the treat, some make the connection that it was the guarding that caused the food to appear. Uh-oh.
- Use trickery. How do you get something away from a puppy

who has no intention of releasing it. Number one choice? Trickery. Try going to your front door and knocking. Greet your imaginary guest warmly. Chances are your puppy will come running to see what's up. Good! Praise him warmly (assuming he has dropped the item) as you reach down and pick up the lead. Other trickery might be offering a car ride or starting to make his meal.

- Work him. Pick up the lead and start to work your puppy on Sit, Down, Catch My Drift. Many will drop what they are holding in a few minutes if you are clear, quick, and demanding.
- Ignore him. If the item isn't dangerous (or valuable), sometimes just ignoring him will cause him to lose interest.

ARE YOU "GUARDY"?

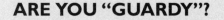

Sarah just had a lovely conversation with a puppy owner. Her young retriever had a great "out" for toys and a terrible one with items he stole himself. He was reluctant to drop items, and he had put his mouth on her a couple times in protest. The owner was puzzled. How come he was so easy with toys and so hard with other things? When asked if she responded differently when he had one or the other, she gave a knowing *"Oooohhh."* Turns out yes, with toys she had him release playfully for much praise. When he stole something, she got upset, rushed to him scolding, then pried open his mouth. "Do you think your puppy might think you have an aggression problem around certain things?" Sarah inquired. The owner laughed—she got it in an instant. "Maybe," she replied, "maybe he does." When she started to give him a way to win, they started having success. Well done!

Running Away: From You

Puppies can play Catch Me if You Can when around the house, get out the front door and take off, or scale your fence to freedom. Regardless of the root cause, the result is that you cannot catch your puppy. Now what do you do?

This puppy is wisely dragging his lead. Until you have verbal control, make sure you have physical control. Use a lead.

Brian squats down, claps his hands, and, sounds happy. The pup comes running! SARAH WILSON

- Run with fun. If your pup is safe, you can try an age-old dog catching technique. Run away from the pup, clapping your hands and whooping it up. Sound like you are having the *best* time without him. Keep running! Remember your pup likes to chase moving things, so *you* be the moving thing.

- Run parallel. Do the same thing, only run parallel to your pup, not at him. Running at him will drive him away; running parallel to him will attract him to you. When he arrives, praise warmly, stay light and happy, squat down, and reach up under his chin to take his collar. No scolding or spanking. That only teaches him not to get caught.
- Act interested. Sarah once lured over a large stray Rottweiler in Prospect Park in Brooklyn by doing this game. She squatted and got fascinated with something on the ground. Slowly this skeptical dog inched closer until she could just reach up to his collar and clip on the lead.
- "Wanna go for a ride?" Use your car. Many a running dog has been tempted back to safety by an open car door.
- Got him back? Good, get to work on your Attention and Requirement Games tonight! Focus on Door Chores—do many, do them often, do them well.

Scratching at Screens and Doors

Your puppy digs noisily at doors to get to the other side.

- Sit Is It (page 91). This game builds his automatic Sit whenever he wants something.
- Practice those Space Games so you can communicate with your puppy through a glass door without having to be dramatic.
- Do Door Chores (page 129) to teach him to wait patiently instead of getting pushy.
- Notice quiet. Let him in when he is quiet, as he may be good for a few moments before he starts scratching.
- Play Wait There (page 150). Treat him if he has four on the floor and turn away or use your "Off" signal to get his paws onto the floor.

JACKSON YOUNG

Separation Issues

Being alone, away from her family, is a completely unnatural situation for a young puppy. In her world, a puppy alone is a puppy in danger, but you can help her learn to be comfortable alone. Those first days of howling and familial sleep deprivation? Transient with help, but perfectly normal.

- Is your pup a "you" addict? Make sure it isn't all about you. If your puppy is on your lap, in your arms, constantly being tickled and petted and talked to and carried and loved, loved, loved, you are creating this problem.
- Make meals last longer. Forget the five-seconds-and-I'm-done food bowl. Buy a few Kong toys, soak kibble, and stuff the Kong as you would a Thanksgiving turkey. Freeze it. Let your puppy work on that. For dry kibble, we like the Busy Buddy Squirrel Dude and Twist 'n Treat toys best. For fun, smear the inside of a sterilized bone with cream cheese, peanut butter, or wet food. He'll love that!

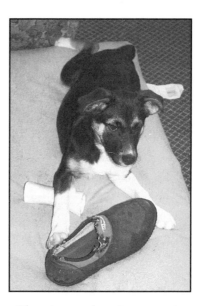

Chewing a shoe is not a sign of separation anxiety, it's a sign of being a puppy.
SARAH WILSON

- Stay calm. Greet and leave your pup the way you greet and leave your partner, spouse, or parent. Mostly it's "Hey, I'm home." You want your pup to be calm, so act the way you want him to act. If you get excited, he'll get more excited, and that excitement can easily turn to stress if you're not careful.
- Be realistic. Puppies can't wait forever. Young puppies need to be walked every few hours, and all puppies can benefit from a midday walk. If you cannot walk them when they need it, please do not crate them. That will only force them to dirty

Our favorite food holding toys: Planet Dog Orbo, the Busy Buddy Squirrel Dude, the Kong and, in front and opened, the Busy Buddy Twist 'n Treat. The Twist 'n Treat is easy to open and clean. All are dishwasher safe. SARAH WILSON

their crates, causing you both unhappiness. Instead leave him set up with papers in a puppy-proofed room or an exercise pen. It'll be a mess but will cause fewer long-term problems than messing in his crate.

- What is separation anxiety? True separation anxiety (SA), a label widely used these days, is fairly uncommon. Most "home alone" problems are about boredom, age, or opportunity rather than "anxiety." Your Chesapeake Bay Retriever puppy rips the Sunday paper into confetti when you run to the store? He probably wasn't anxious. He probably had a grand time! Actual SA is when your puppy panics when you leave him. Not the normal barking and howling almost all puppies do, but he *panics*. This pup urinates or defecates in fear, then "finger paints" the crate as he spins in place, salivates, rips his crate apart or tries to, bloodies his paws or mouth trying to escape, rips at doorjambs and windowsills, and/or chews/rips everything within reach. If this is your puppy do the following:
- Play all games with a goal of getting up to Stay II, Go, and Wait There.
- Demote your dog (page 254). I know you feel for your puppy, but more attention and "love" from you is only going to make this worse. If you want something new *from* him, you have to do something new *with* him. So more work, less attention is the right place to start.
- Less touching. He's a "you" addict and it's time for you both to go cold turkey. Reward and encourage him to be farther away from you.
- Up his exercise and check his diet. Feed him the premium puppy food.
- Get help from a qualified local dog professional. This can be turned around, but most people need hands-on help to make headway.

Sensitive/Shy: Help for Our Wallflowers

"Shy" or "sensitive" dogs react to whatever they are frightened of by retreat (flight) or locking up (freezing). Regardless of what is making your puppy react this way, your goal is to give him other choices, while developing a predictable routine for handling those moments.

- Play those Trust Games. Learn how to do Near Is Dear and Check It Out with your puppy. Practice at home with things she is confident with, so you both understand the games. Set the tone for her. Keep things upbeat. If her tail wags when you start to play, you're doing it right!
- That is you; this is me. Separate your emotions from your dog's. What she is and isn't frightened of is not under your immediate control. What you *can* control is how you handle the situation. If you get embarrassed or upset at her fear, you will not be able to help her effectively.

Pip is unsure about the plastic Christmas stockings so I squat down near them, leave the lead loose, encourage Pip with praise and a treat. Pip decides to risk it and comes forward. She's still a little nervous but coping. Good girl, Pip! MELISSA FISCHER

- Act the way you want her to act. You can pet your puppy if you are confident and relaxed when you do so. If you are fearful and hesitant, then hands off! She doesn't need you participating in her stress with her. That is no help.
- Practice. If you avoid what frightens her, she cannot learn to get past her fear. When Pip showed concern about noisy toys, we bought the most obnoxious toys we could find. Now she is over it. When a puppy shows fear, it is real fear. She isn't faking it. We would never leave an animal we loved in that state if we could help it. Make the world her oyster, a little at a time. She would thank you for it if she could.

FIVE WAYS OF HANDLING STRESS

There are five general ways that dogs of any age handle stress: fight, flight, freeze, faint, and foolishness. Fight, which becomes assertiveness and aggression, is one choice. Flight, running away, is the shy or sensitive dog's first pick. Freeze, becoming motionless with the mouth closed, head a little down, and tail tucked, is another choice of the overwhelmed dog. Sensitive dogs often freeze when they cannot run away. Then there is the rare faint, where the dog becomes so stressed he passes out. Last, is the rollicking foolishness. When stressed, these dogs become goofy. Many a sporting breed dog falls into this zone and so does our Beagle, Milo. At low levels of stress, he dances, spins, flirts, and is generally a complete goof. A bit more stress and he runs, but his first reaction is acting the fool.

Sneak Attack from the Rear

Insecure puppies, adolescent dogs with dreams of glory, and some herding breeds will grab a person's ankle, often as they go to leave. Such puppies are often not all that fond of strangers being slow to warm up and fast to bark.

- Space Games. These help your puppy learn to respect human space.
- Prevent the event. In this case, put the pup on lead, behind a gate, or in a crate when it is time for your guests to leave. Prevention at least stops practice.
- Lead on. That will allow you to reward him for sitting calmly without risking another sneak attack.
- Replace the unwanted with the wanted. Start giving your pup treats when your helper heads to the door, stop when she exits. Repeat. Another easy solution can be tossing a handful of treats in the opposite direction from the door so the pup is busy doing something pleasant when guests exit. For some dogs, this is all that is needed.
- Stay back. Teach your puppy to stay back away from the door. Giving him a bed in view of the door but well away from it, teaching him to stay on that bed when people come in and, more importantly, when they leave can prevent this behavior entirely.
- Throw it in reverse. If Space Games have gone well, sometimes having your friend shuffle backward quickly as he claps his hands loudly can take a puppy by surprise. Dogs don't plan on a human noisily going in reverse. The moment the pup backs off, the sound and movement stops.
- Make noise. Having your guest throw his keys down by his own feet (at the floor, not at your puppy) as your puppy rushes in. This can teach a puppy to stay back. Now call your pup back to you away from your guest and praise your pup for coming. Do not make it a big deal. If you have a tiny toy breed and your friend has a big set of keys or if your puppy is frightened of strange sounds, use another method. For those pups, a spray from a bottle of water can do the trick.

Whining

Some breeds and mixes tend to whine, any individual can be a whiner, and many pups will whine in some situations. Whining is usually caused by habit or stress. It can also be due to excitement or pain. Habit happens when dogs whine and we look at, pet, or speak to them about it. Since we raise what we praise, you're raising a whiner. Or whining can show up when a puppy would like to be doing one thing but must be doing something else. For instance, he may whine when sitting next to you watching other dogs romp. What to do?

- Keep him busy. Give him something else to do. Most dogs can't whine and be focused on you at the same time. So work that puppy!
- Develop self-control. Focus on Leave It (page 132), Wait There (page 150), and Stay: Basics (page 105). Those should all help him develop some patience. Work on getting that lead loose so your puppy is controlling himself. If he's fighting you, he'll whine more.
- Reward silence. Be calm when you praise, but catch him being quiet. That's a good puppy.

Won't Come Back Inside

Your puppy is smart. He may have learned that coming inside in the morning leads to the crate and then you leaving. Sensible puppy solution? Do not come back inside. This can be really annoying.

- Make coming inside fun. Take away all squeaky toys except one that you keep by the door. Stand sideways in the doorway, then call him: "Name, come!" Immediately squeak for all you're worth. When your puppy rushes to you, praise him as you toss the toy into the kitchen. Close the door and play with your puppy for a minute or two. It is time well spent.

- Make him want to come in. On a weekend or a day off, play hard inside by the door for ten seconds, then put your puppy outside mid-game. Wait a few seconds, open, call, and play. In other words, practice success when you are likely to have success.
- Toss in treats. Open the door, show your puppy that you have treats, now toss a treat out the back door, then call her back in with another. When she comes in, give the treat then let her go back out. Laugh. Have fun! And now look what you've done? You have created a puppy who loves to come back inside.

And here we are at the end of our journey together. Downstairs I can hear Pip, now nine months old, yawning loudly in her crate. This is her polite way of saying "I need some of your time," and she is right. It is time to stop writing this puppy book and go play with our puppy. We hope you have found this book helpful and that you and your puppy have a great time learning together. If you'd like to talk training, come to our message boards at www.MySmartPuppy.com. We'd love to chat with you!

We close by sharing some of our favorite training phrases. Enjoy!

WORDS WE TRAIN BY

Act the Way You Want Your Puppy to Act

Corrections Create Opportunity
   to Reward

Distance Is Your Friend

Effective Is as Gentle as You Can Be, as
   Firm as You Must Be

Get to Good

Homework First, Then Test!

It's Not about What You Want but What the Puppy Needs

It's Not the Lead That Connects but the Connection That Leads

Minor Moments Matter

Never Optional, Always Pleasant

"No" Gets You Nowhere

Pretrain What You Want

Prevent the Event

Proceed When You Succeed

Refuse to Confuse

Stay Positively Focused

To Change How They Feel, Change What They Do

You Get What You Pet

You Raise What You Praise

What Is Your Intention?

SARAH WILSON

ELI ORLING

RESOURCES

We have an ever-growing, always-welcoming message board community, as well as an extensive library of articles for you to enjoy. Our books are available, signed for you, and the My Smart Puppy DVD. Come visit us!

Contact us at: MySmartPuppy@aol.com

Web site: www.MySmartPuppy.com

OTHER BRIAN AND SARAH BOOKS

Metrodog: A Guide to Raising Your Dog in the City
Brian Kilcommons and Sarah Wilson
New York: Warner Books, 2001

Childproofing Your Dog
Brian Kilcommons and Sarah Wilson
New York: Warner Books, 1994

Good Owners, Great Dogs
Brian Kilcommons and Sarah Wilson
New York: Warner Books, 1992

Tails from the Barkside
Brian Kilcommons and Sarah Wilson
New York: Warner Books, 1997

Paws to Consider
Brian Kilcommons and Sarah Wilson
New York: Warner Books, 1999

Good Owners, Great Cats
Brian Kilcommons and Sarah Wilson
New York: Warner Books, 1995

VETERINARY INFORMATION

Dog Owner's Home Veterinary Handbook
Delbert G. Carlson, D.V.M, and James M. Griffin, M.D.
New York: Howell Reference Books, 1999
   This has been and remains our favorite home veterinary guide. Comprehensive, easy-to-use and understand, this book does the job. It doesn't replace your veterinarian (nor should any book), but it gives you the information you need when you need it.

ALTERNATIVE MEDICAL CARE

While we value and rely on our traditional veterinary practitioners, we have had wonderful experiences using alternative treatments to help our animals. If your companion is having a persistent problem, a second opinion is always a good idea—and a second opinion from a different perspective can sometimes be especially helpful.
   To find alternative veterinary care, go to: www.altvetmed.com.

ANIMAL PHYSICAL THERAPY

Wizard of Paws Physical Rehabilitation for Animals
Debbie Gross Saunders
www.wizardofpaws.net
   If you have a puppy with orthopedic problems (or you'd like to do what you can to prevent them), a trained animal physical therapist can help.

Understanding Ourselves

Your dog gets all of you—good, bad, and in between. Knowing yourself allows you to make choices about how you react to things rather than being locked into lifelong habits.

Wellesley Centers for Women
www.wellesley.edu/wcw/scssub.html
Here is a treasure trove of information on how women form relationships and function within them. Since our companion animals form close, unique bonds offering us a quality of connection that cannot be found among people, understanding how we connect and what we look for in that connection helps us be aware and thus better dog people. Articles, books, and audiotapes are usually quite reasonably priced.

Dealing with Anger

The Anger Management Sourcebook
Glenn R. Schiraldi and Melissa Hallmark Kerr
New York: McGraw Hill, 2002
Get a solid overview and much insight into what your anger pattern is and then how to make different choices about dealing with it.

The Dance of Anger: A Woman's Guide to Changing the Patterns of Intimate Relationships
Harriet Lerner, Ph.D.
New York: Harper, 1997
Women in particular can have a muddied, shame- and fear-based relationship with their anger. And since you cannot be a caretaker of anything or anyone without anger coming into play, we need to understand, appreciate, and then handle our anger in ways we feel proud of. A *New York Times* bestseller, this is a readable book on a complicated subject. Dr. Lerner's *Dance of Intimacy* is also a great read.

Understanding Trauma and Abuse

What is this section doing in a book on puppy training? It's here to help. With some one in four girls and one in seven boys the victim sexual abuse, and many more children experiencing verbal, physical, or emotional abuse—not to mention countless others who cope with life trauma such as the death of a parent—a great many of us have a lot to sort through.

Trauma and Recovery: The Aftermath of Violence—from Domestic Abuse to Political Terror
Judith Herman, M.D.
New York: Basic Books, 1997
   As you would imagine, this is not an easy read. It is well worth it, though, as the human mind behaves in predictable ways even when faced with the unavoidable and the unthinkable. If you are just starting or deep into recovery from trauma, then you need to know you are not alone. You are reacting normally, and you have already done the hardest part: lived through it. You will live through coping with it as well.

Stop It Now! The Campaign to Prevent Child Abuse
www.stopitnow.com

National Clearinghouse on Child Abuse and Neglect
   Information
Gateways to Information: Protecting Children and
Strengthening Families
www.nccanch.acf.hhs.gov

Learned Optimism: How to Change Your Mind and Your Life
Martin E. P. Seligman, Ph.D.
New York: Alfred A. Knopf, 1990
   An oldie but a goodie. Why mention it here? Because people recovering from trauma generally have some unwanted and unhelpful mental habits that would be nice to change. This book gives you insights into how to do just that. Well worth a read.

Horse Training

Some of the most interesting thinking about dog training is going on in the horse world. The dog people can go way down the road of theory-based, I-do-this-because-it-makes-me-feel-good-not-because-it-actually-works. Horse people are clear: They need things that work and that are safe for trainer and trainee. Enjoy!

Beyond the Mirrors: The Study of the Mental and Spiritual Aspects of Horsemanship
Jill K Hassler-Scoop
Montana: Goals Unlimited, 1988

Pat and Linda Parelli
www.parelli.com
This dynamic duo has put more careful thought into breaking training down into bite-sized pieces and then delivering that information than anyone in the training world, dog or horse. They will make you think, and you will be a better trainer/teacher for it.

John and Josh Lyons
www.JohnLyons.com
John is a master of breaking things down into the smallest possible pieces, to make sure the animal understands exactly what is being asked. Clearly, his goal is to have a calm, thinking horse, and he achieves that. His emphasis on safety of person and horse is excellent.

Chris Irwin
http://chrisirwin.com
Chris demands of the human. Don't try to go animal-blaming here: If your animal student has a problem, then look to the *teacher*. His book *Dancing with Your Dark Horse* is part autobiography and part zen exercise. It will get you reflecting on yourself as a teacher of another species, and that's our goal.

Dogs

There are a myriad of dog books out these days, more all the time, so we don't want to give you names and titles. For those, stop by our message boards, cited earlier: We have an ever-changing, growing list there. Here we confine ourselves to general guidelines for finding competent dog training help, be it hands-on or written.

Lives with Multiple Dogs in the House
Find experts who have owned multiple breeds of dogs—*in their home,* with them—for *at least* a decade. You may be surprised

just how many "experts" do not own a dog or have one dog in the house.

Experienced
Listen to professionals who have trained professionally for more than ten years and who have worked with a wide variety of breeds, mixes, clients, and problems. Generally we find that a trainer is ready to leave the beginner professional level after their first hundred dogs trained.

Pro in What You Need to Know
Being an expert in training dog agility, police work, or herding doesn't make you an expert in pet dog behavior any more than being pet dog training experts qualifies us to teach agility, police K9 training, or herding.

Hands On
If you go to seminars, insist on seeing this person handle a few untrained, unfamiliar dogs. If they cannot make their methods work for them in front of you, there is little hope those methods will be useful for you. Anyone who lectures using only video-taped examples is hiding major flaws in their methodology and skill level.

Helpful
If you cannot accomplish something they are suggesting, they should easily demonstrate with your dog in a way that makes your dog enjoy their company. If they suggest a piece of equipment, they should be able to introduce it to the dog with clear explanations to you about what to look for and expect from this tool.

Beware the people who spout opinion loudly and in the narrowest of ways. They often fail the above in more than one area. Real professionals know there is no one answer, no one tool, no one way. There is just a goal: a happy, relaxed, responsive dog with a confident, knowledgeable handler. Armed with these guidelines, you will easily be able to sort the "talks a good game" and find a trainer who can actually be helpful.

Reading Dogs

Canine Body Language: Interpreting the Native Language of the Domestic Dog
Brenda Aloff
Washington: Dogwise, 2005
This book represents a massive effort on the author's part and a big step forward for the dog-loving community. This book is pricey but if you want to understand what your dog is "saying," it is well worth the investment.

TOOLS OF THE TRADE

Planet Dog Orbo
www.planetdog.com

Busy Buddy Twist 'n Treat
http://www.busybuddytoys.com

Kong
http://www.kongcompany.com

Leads, Long Lines, Martingale Collars
http://www.amerapet.com
The best-quality leather leads at the best prices. Also excellent long lines (we use ten-footers) and Martingale collars.

Triple Crown Collar
www.aboutdogtraining.com
A plastic prong device, currently our favorite training collar. A bit hard to operate at first, but you'll figure it out. Always use a backup collar with any prong or head halter.

Head Halters
http://www.coastalpet.com
Manufacturer of our favorite head halter, the Halti, which comes with its own backup attachment. More readily accepted by more dogs than other head halters, it effectively closes a dog's mouth if the dog lunges, barks, or "Dumpster dives" on walks.

Grief Resources

You are not alone. Losing a pet is devastating to those of us who love our animals. The relationship we have with our dogs is unique and unlike what we have with other humans, so it hits us hard and deep when a dog dies. Get support from others who understand.

http://www.vetmed.ucdavis.edu/ccab/petloss.html
A clearinghouse for books, groups, Internet sites, and more.

INDEX

A

Adopted dog, 46
  older puppy from limited environ-
    ment, 28–29
Ages and stages, 23–49
  birth to 3 months, 24–31
  FRAP behavior, 32
  human equivalent to dog's age,
    24
  nine to twelve months, 46–49
  six to nine months, 40–46
  three to six months, 32–39
Anger, yours, dealing with, 35, 253
Annual Family Dog Gatherings, 192
Anthropomorphizing, 73–74
Attention Games, 57–58
  Beat the Clock, 54, 161–63
  Catch My Drift, 54, 99–101
  Door Chores, 54, 129–31
  Follow the Leader, 54, 159–61
  Leave It, 54, 132–33
  Look At Me, 54, 95–98
Australian Shepherd, 9, 27–28, 30

B

Ball, 207. *See also* Toys
  safety issues, 201
Barking
  as aggression, 261

in the backyard, 265
begging and, 266–67
in the car, 265–66
Check It Out, 265
Come: Basics, 262, 265
in the crate, 261
crating and, 262
Door Chores, 265
effective and ineffective responses
  to stopping, 61
fence running and, 287–88
Go Games, 261
at guests, 260
Leave It, 262, 265
Look At Me, 265
midnight barker, 262
Near Is Dear, 265
out the window, 263
at people, 260–61
puppy barks for your attention,
  250
at reflections, 264
Space Games to correct, 260
squeeze/pulse, 262
Stay: Basics, 261
terriers, 2
ultrasonic device for, 266
Wait There, 261
Basset Hounds, 290
Beat the Clock, 54, 161–63
  common problems, 162–63

Begging, how to stop, 266–67
  Distance Downs, 267
  Go Games, 267
  Mine, 267
  Off, 267
  Sit for Your Supper, 266, 267–68
  Stay: Basics, 267
Behavioral trial balloons
  freezes or glares when eating or
    chewing, 42
  getting on the counter, 42
  growling or baring teeth, 42
  lunging at things on lead, 42
  not giving up sleeping spots, 42
  not moving out of your way, 41
  slamming past you in doorways,
    41
  struggling, mouthing when han-
    dled, 42
  taking your seat when you get up,
    42
  whining to get you to move,
    42
Belly Up, 188–89
Birth to 3 months: the age of attraction, 24–31
  instinct to follow, 25
  sensitive/fear period, 26–27
  special circumstances, delayed
    development, 31
  special circumstances, older
    puppy from limited environ-
    ment, 28–29
  special circumstances, separated
    too early or orphaned, 30–31
  special circumstances, sick puppy,
    28
  special circumstances, singleton
    puppy, 27–28
  special circumstances, special
    needs puppy, 29
Bites at feet, 268–69
Biting, 269–74
  building biting inhibition, 48–49
  children and prevention, 210
  children and prevention, guide-
    lines, 211
  Daily Dozens: Anti-Bite Protocol,
    272–74
  dangerous dogs, 272

  demoting demanding or difficult
    dogs, 270
  human lack of understanding
    dog's language and, 8–9
  medical issues and, 270
  preventing with Mine exercise,
    60
  professional help, 270, 271
  puppy bites, 271–72
  reaction to frustration, 31
  sneak attack from rear, 318
  warning signs, 269
Border Collies, 2
Boredom, 263. See also Home alone
  barking and, 265
Bow trick, 188
Boxers, 29, 30, 56
Bracing, 113
Breath spray (for correction), 121,
  268, 269, 306
Bringing puppy home
  introducing to a cat, 301–2
  introducing to a resident dog,
    296–301
Bulldogs, 205
Bull Terriers, 30

C

Calm=Release, 54
  common problems, 123–24
  treats with, 124
Car rides
  barking during, 265–66
  car sickness, 275–76
  crating during, 265–66
  Guided Down during, 266
  halters for, 266
  safety issues, 177, 266
  socialization and, 176–77
Car sickness: help for the queasy
  rider, 275–76
Cats and puppies, problems and
  solutions
  chasing cats, 276
  Come: Basics, 302
  introducing puppy to, 301–2
  Leave It, 302
  Mine, 301–2
  Near Is Dear, 301

Catch My Drift, 54, 99–101
  common problems, 100–101
Cavalier King Charles Spaniels,
  205
Chasing behaviors
  cars, bicycles, joggers, 278
  the cat, 276
  Come: Basics, 277
  Come Games, 278
  Distance Downs, 277
  feed around speed, 278
  Follow the Leader, 278
  Guided Down, 276
  head halter, 278
  the kids, 277–78
  learning to look away, 277
  Leave It, 278
  Look At Me, 276, 277, 278
  Mine, 276, 278
  Near Is Dear, 276
  Off, 278
  Simple Sit, 276
  Sit Is It, 278
  Wait, 276
  water sprayer, 276
Check It Out, 54, 139–43
  common problems, 142
Chewing problems, 279–80
  confinement, 280
  exercise, 279
  Out, 280
  prevention, 279
  stress and, 280
  supervision to prevent, 280
  toy rotation for, 280
Childproofing Your Dog
    (Kilcommons and Wilson),
    210
Clicker, 67–68
Collars
  crating and, 228
  flat, 66
  getting it on a squirming puppy,
    228
  introducing pup's first collar,
    74–75
  martingale, 66, 228
  metal prongs, 67
  slip, 68
  triple crown plastic prong, 67

Come: Basics, 54, 102–5, 263
  common problems, 103–4, 249
  missed obedience, 47
  Two-Treat Game, 105
Come: Making It Work, 54,
    134–36
  common problems, 135–36
Commands, five types, 64
  sensation, 64
  signals, 64
  situational, 64
  spatial, 64
  spoken, 64
Communication (dog behaviors as)
  aggression, 300
  bold and confident stance, 17
  cowering, 10
  dog parks, watching before enter-
    ing, 200–201
  dominance over another dog, 8,
    9, 200–201
  fearful, anxious, or submissive,
    8
  flattened body, whites of eyes
    showing, 28
  frightened/worried, 8
  greeting other dogs, 208–9
  hackles raised, 10
  laughing, 8
  "play bow," 8
  possessive of object, 8
  "reading" a dog using
    T.E.E.T.H., 8
  showing teeth, 9–10
  stress behaviors, 317
  stretching behavior, 8
  tail down, ears back, over-
    whelmed pup, 21
  wagging tail, 9
Congruency, 152
Corgis, 290
Corrections
  breath spray for, 121, 268, 269,
    306
  plant sprayer for, 263, 276
  rules of, 221
  types to use, 62–63
  urination when anxious or
    excited, 237–38
  what is abuse, 63

Couch, claiming, 42
  avoid a confrontation, 290
  gating to prevent, 290
  Go, 290
  Off, 290
  professional help, 290
Countertop cruising, 280–81
  Go, 281
  Mine, 280
  Move, 280–81
Cowering, 10. *See also* Fear
Crating
  barking and, 261, 262
  blanket tip, 225, 227
  car rides and, 265–66
  collar removal, 228
  feeding on floor of, 287
  housebreaking/paper training, 3,
    216–17, 240–41
  hyperactivity after, 295
  introducing the crate, 227–28
  naps and, 293
  pausing before exiting, 226
  Placement Sit and, 226
  smart puppy person vs. problem
    owner, 227
  sporting breeds, 42
  urinates or defecates in the crate,
    231–32
  what size, 224–25
  what to put in it, 225
  what type, 224
  when you are out of the house, 42
  where to put it, 226

D

Dachshunds, 290
Daily Dozens: Anti-Bite Protocol,
    272–74
  dozen blocks, 274
  dozen directions, 273
  dozen downs, 273
  dozen minor restraints, 273–74
  dozen rewards, 272–73
Dalmatians, 9, 30, 37
Deaf puppies, 29, 30
Demanding dog, 281–82. *See also*
    Demoting demanding or diffi-
    cult dogs

Go, 282
Guided Down, 282
leave a lead one, 282
Move, 282
stop treats, 281
Touch and Requirement Games,
    282
Demoting demanding or difficult
    dogs, 254–58
  biting and, 270
  downs and, 256–57
  have some fun, 258
  less attention, 256
  loss of privileges, 257
  more work, 256
  possessive of you and, 291
  put away the treats, 255–56, 281
  respect my Space, 257–58
  testosterone levels and, 254–55
Diet. *See* Feeding
Digging problems, 282–83
Doberman Pinschers, 9
Doggy day care, 202–3
Dog parks, 200–202
Don't touch my collar, head, ears
    problem, 284–85
  Face It, 284
  medical issues and, 284
  professional help, 285
  Touch and Space Games
    daily, 284
Door Chores, 54
  common problems, 130–31
  leaps on door before walk, 250
  Stair Safety and, 131
Downs. *See* Distance Downs; Guided
    Down

E

Ears
  don't touch my collar, head, ears
    problem, 284–85
  infected, 284
Equipment, 65–70. *See also*
    Corrections; Crating
  belly band, 233
  clicker, 67–68
  crates, 224–25
  flat collar, 66

front clip harnesses, 68
harness, under forelegs, 68
head halter, 66, 261, 266, 278, 290, 308
leather leads, 70
martingale collar, 66
metal prongs, 67
retractable leads, 45, 69
slip collar, 68
triple crown plastic prong, 67
Exercise and the growing puppy, 203–7, 279
amount needed, 295
no forced exercise (jogging, on-lead hiking), 204–5
rough play, limiting, 205
supply good footing, 205–6
time of day, 205
weather warning, 205
Exercise pen. See Gates and exercise pens

F

Face It, 54, 155–58
common problems, 157–58
no-struggle nail trimming with, 158
Fainting, 317
Family or home environment, impact of, 10–15
abandonment/loss/divorce, 15
busy parents and/or many siblings, 12
emotionless/depressed house, 14
physical abuse/threat of abuse, 13
yelling/verbal intimidation, 12
Fear and fear behaviors
car rides, 176
Check It Out and, 199, 200
don't baby, 176
fainting, 317
give the pup a break, 199
Near Is Dear and, 200
of people, barking and, 260–61
protecting your pup, 212
pup scared of the city, 198–99
rescue puppy, cowers and shakes, 199–200
sensitive/shy pups, 316–17

separation anxiety, 315
short stretches to overcome, 199
signs of, 180–81
Trust and Attention games for, 200
urination when anxious or excited, 237–38
what can frighten your pup, 182–83
Feeding
appropriate amount, 289
Busy Buddy or Kong inside, 287, 314
cat food, puppy eats, 286
eats too fast, 287
finicky eating, 288–89
food bowl aggression, 289–90
growling at other dogs and, 290
housebreaking/paper training problems and, 230–32
longer meals, 314
Mine, 290
people food to avoid giving, 266
quality dog food and, 230, 286, 289, 315
raining treats, 289
refusing food and illness, 288, 289
rules, 223–24
Sit for Your Supper, 266–67, 290
small dogs and hypoglycemia, 243–44, 289
soaking food, 286, 287
Feet. See also Exercise and the growing puppy
fuzzy, slip danger, 205–6
handling/touching your pup, 185–86
no-struggle nail trimming, 158
supply good footing for play and exercise, 205–6
Fence running, 287–88
"Floppy" puppies, 290
Follow the Leader, 54, 159–61
advanced, 161
common problems, 160–61
Food bowl aggression, 289–90, 307–8
Forbid, deterrent product, 287
FRAP (frenetic random activity period), 32

Frustration, yours, dealing with, 32,
33–35

G

Garbage hounds, 290
  head halters for, 290
  Leave It, 290
  Look at Me!, 290
  Out, 290
Gates and exercise pens, 218,
  242–43
  don't pet puppy jumping on gate,
  218
  keeping puppy off the furniture
  and, 290
  litterbox in, 244
  paper training in, 243–44
  Wait There with, 218
German Shepherd Dogs, 38, 48,
  205
Go, 54, 148–50
  common problems, 149–50
Go Games, 148–50, 261
Greyhounds, 10
Growling or baring teeth, 139
  children and, 211
  claiming the couch and, 290
  food bowl aggression, 289–90
  medical issues and, 284
  picking up your pup and, 283–84
  possessive of you and, 291
  touching collar, head, or ears and,
  284–85
  waking up cranky and, 291–92
Growth
  coat, type of, predicting, 36–37
  color change, 37–38
  ears, standing up or not, 37
  feet size and, 36
  giant-breed pups, 36, 59
  how big will your puppy be, 36
  large breeds, weight gain, 5
Guided Down, 54, 92–95, 124–29
  common problems, 94–95,
  127–28
  Daily Dozens: Anti-Bite Protocol
  and, 273
  demoting demanding or difficult
  dogs and, 256–57
  Distance Downs, 128–29
  Place with, 166–67
Guided Down II, 54

H

Hackles raised, 10
Haranguing during hugging, 294
Harnesses, 68
Havaneses, 205
Head halters, 66, 261, 266, 278,
  290, 308
Heat danger
  digging as sign of, 282
  warning signs, 205
Home alone. See also Crating
  arranging for a midday walker,
  232
  hyperactivity and, 294–95
  peeing and, 239
  separation anxiety, 315
  separation problems, 314–15
Housebreaking/paper training,
  215–45
  age, 217, 220, 229, 239
  asking to go out, 228–29
  can't hold it during the day,
  230–31, 234, 239
  can't make it through the night,
  230
  charting your progress, 220
  cleanup hints, 228
  confinement, 219, 220
  crating, 3, 216–17, 224–28,
  240–41
  doesn't poop in the morning, 231
  exercise and education, 219
  gates and exercise pens, 218
  go out with your puppy, 216, 217
  "hurry, hurry" and "get busy,"
  222
  introducing the crate, 227–28
  lifting his leg indoors, 233
  mistakes, 217
  older puppy from limited environment, 28–29
  paper training: the rules, 241–43
  play or walk after going, 223, 241
  problems and solutions, 229–41
  rules of correction, 221

rules of feeding and watering, 223–24, 230–31
rules of scheduling, 219–20, 227
rules of supervision, 215–17, 219–20
rules of walking, 222–23
spaying or neutering and, 229
urinates or defecates in the crate, 231–32
urinating during the night, 3
urination, interrupting, 221
urination, more confinement to less as signal for, 216
urination on down comforter, 235
urination on your bed, 235
urination our of your sight, 236–37
urination when anxious or excited, 237–38
walking your puppy, 219
wet bedding, 230
won't go outside (goes on paper), 239–41
Human equivalent to dog's age, 24
Hyperactivity, 294–96
breeds and, 294
causes, 294–95
children and, 295
corrections, 295
demoting demanding or difficult dogs, 295
FRAP (frenetic random activity period), 32
modeling desired behavior, 295
rewarding (negative attention), 295
START games and, 295
worst months for, 295

I

Illness, serious, signs of, 288
Indoor fence, 281
Instinctive behaviors, 2
Irish Setter/Jack Russell cross, 294

J

Jumping up, 303
for attention, 250

body block to stop, 294
collar holding, 212
crating, 183
don't reward, 303
Guided Down, 294
ignoring the pup, 294
injuries, yours, 304
leaps on door before walk, 250
Off, 303
Off to control, 250
protecting yourself, 304
Say Hello, 169–71
send him away, 294
Simple Sit to control, 155, 303
Space Games, 303
step on the lead, 294
tethering, 183, 294
while hugging or embracing someone, 294

K

Kerry Blue Terriers, 37

L

Labradors, 2, 37, 205
field-bred, 294
Leadership, 254. *See also* Space Games
attention and, 57–58
confident, 113
consistency, 251–52
demoting demanding or difficult dogs, 254–58
Mine, 274
modeling desired behavior, 26–27, 196, 209, 284, 310, 311, 314, 317
Off My Plate, 88
protecting your pup, 212
puppy slams into you, responding, 274–75
puppy steps in front, stopping, 3–4
qualities of a good leader, 7
sleeping spot and, 258
small interactions and, 3–4
smart puppy person vs. problem owner, 227
support confidence, 196–97

Leads/leashes
  clip size, 70, 71
  introducing, 75–76
  leather, 70
  poles and tangles, 306–7
  pulling and choking on, 56
  puppy grabs, 121, 268–69
  puppy puts paw over lead, 77
  retractable, 45, 69
  squeeze/pulse, 96, 262
  tie-to-your-waist, 69
  using breath spray on, 121, 268,
    269
  walking on, 76–77
Leaps on door before walk, 250
Leave It, 54, 132–33, 263
  Advanced Games: Two Fist
    Game, 133
  common problems, 133
Left Circles, 54, 119–21
  common problems, 121
Lhasa Apsos, 205
Look At Me, 54, 95–98, 263
  common problems, 97–98
  how to squeeze/pulse, 96
  when to practice, 220
Loving your puppy, 3
  filling missing parts of yourself by,
    10–15
Lyme disease, 235, 239, 270, 284

M

Maltese, 242
Medication, giving
  Face It for, 155–58
Minature Pinscher, 294
Mine, 54, 82–85
  common problems, 83–85
  opening the door and, 250
  tether your puppy, 83, 84, 85
Mouthing, 284, 305–6
  vs. biting, 269
  breath spray for correction, 306
  Calm=Release, 305
  confinement, 306
  Guided Down, 305
  as normal behavior, 4
  teething and, 305
  touch on rear and, 57

Move, 257, 275
MySmartPuppy.com, 8

N

Nail trimming, 158
  Near Is Dear, 54, 110–11
Nine to twelve month-old dog: living
    with your pupteen, 46–49
  activities for, 48
  disobedience or missed obedience,
    47
  handling daily, 48–49
No Eye Can, 54, 167–68
  common problems, 168

O

Off, 54, 86–88
  common problems, 87
Off My Plate, 88
Old English Sheepdogs, 205
Older dog, introducing puppy to res-
    ident, 296–301
  common scents solution, 298
  manners taught to pup by older
    dog, 299–300
  Near Is Dear, 297
  normal reactions, 297, 298–300
  professional help, 298, 300
  puppy equals praise, 297
  "puppy pass" expires, 301
  separating the dogs, 297
  toy breeds warning, 298
Out, 54, 136–39
  common problems, 138–39
Overtired pup, 5–6, 293

P

Panting, 180–81
Paper training. See also
    Housebreaking/paper training
  common problems, 243–45
  the rules, 241–43
Parasites. See Worm infestation

Personality of pups
	appropriate/social, 19–20
	assertive/pushy, 16–18, 201–2,
		266–67, 284–85, 293
	avoidant/fearful, 22–23, 31,
		199–200
	each puppy is different, 2
	independent/aloof, 18–19, 38
	puppy profiles, 16–23
	reactive/energetic, 20–21, 25, 38
	sensitive/shy, 21–22, 25, 303,
		316–17
Petit Basset Griffon Vendeen, 19
Petting, 56
	guidelines, 57
Picking up your pup, 283–84
	proper way, 283–84
	Touch Games for, 284
	treats for, 284
Place, 166–67
Plate poaching, 41
Play. See also Exercise and the grow-
		ing puppy; Hyperactivity; Toys
	after peeing or pooping, 223, 241
	Beat the Clock, 190–91
	belly up trick, 188–89
	bow trick, 188
	cardboard box for, 187
	ending, Guided Down, 191
	ending, Simple Sits, 191
	guidelines, 190–91
	No Eye Can used with, 191
	rough, limiting, 205
	safety issues, 206–7
	shake trick, 188
	Sit Is It used with, 191
	socialization and, 187–91
	sticks, 206
	supply good footing, 205–6
	toys with food inside, 189, 287,
		314
	training as, 252–53
	Wait used with, 191
	what not to do, 189–90
Pleasing you, puppy's desire for,
		4–5
Poodles, 205
Poop, eating of, 286–87
Possessiveness
	Daily Dozens to control, 310

	demoting demanding or difficult
		dogs, 310
	finders keepers, 307–9
	guarding, 310–11
	head halters, using, 308
	ignoring the pup, 311
	modeling desired behavior, 310,
		311
	no trading, 310
	Out, 308
	professional help, 310
	Touch and Space Games, 308
	trickery, 310–11
	work him, 311
Possessive of you, 291, 294
	Daily Dozens and, 291
	demoting demanding or difficult
		dogs, 291
	Distance Downs, 291
	Go, 291
	professional help, 291
Puppy class, 208
	barking, correction and, 260

R

Requirement Games, 58
	Come: Basics, 54, 102–5
	Come: Making It Work, 54,
		134–36
	No Eye Can, 54, 167–68
	Out, 54, 136–39
	Stay: Basics, 54, 105–9
	Stay II: Working the 4 D's, 54,
		164–67
Rewards, 60–61
	demoting dogs and removing
		treats, 255–56
	food dependency, 147–48
	how to use food effectively, 71–73
	praise, focusing on, 255–56
	praise, showering your puppy
		with, 81, 195
	puppy grabs at treats, correction
		of, 73
	raining treats, 289–90, 292
	reward to correction ratio, 249
	for sitting, 281
	treats preferred, 72
	treats to support confidence, 197
	types of, list, 60–61

Risks to your puppy, 4
Rocks, 207
Rottweilers, 205
Running away from you, 312–13
   corrections after catching, 313

S

Saunders, Deborah Gross, 290
Say Hello, 54, 169–71
   common problems, 170–71
Schnauzer, 17, 21
Scratching at screens and doors, 313
   Door Chores, 313
   Off, 313
   Sit It Is, 313
   Space Games, 313
   Wait There, 313
Self-control, 226, 252
   tug game to improve, 49–50
Separation problems, 314–15
   demoting demanding or difficult
     dogs, 315
   exercise and diet, 315
   professional help, 315
Separation anxiety, 315
Stay II: Working the 4 D's, 315
   Wait There to solve, 150–52
Shake trick, 188
Shih Tzus, 205
Showing teeth, 9. *See also* Growling
   and baring teeth
Sit
   common problems, 154–55, 249
   how to control jumping with,
     155
   as missed obedience, 47
   opening the door and, 250
   Placement Sit, 54, 88–91
   Placement Sit, common problems,
     90–91
   Simple Sit, 54, 153–55
   Simple Sit, common problems,
     154–55
   Sit for Your Supper, 266–68
   Sit Is It, 91
   when to practice, 220
Six to nine month-old puppy: adoles-
   cence, 40–46
   behavioral trial balloons, 41–42

find and use a good praise level,
   45–46
helpful habits to build, 43–46
minor moments matter, 44
preventing and redirecting trouble, 44
questioning authority, 40
raise the bar for training, 43–44
unhelpful human habits, 40–41
Sleeping spot, 257, 258
Sleep needs, 5–6
   crate naps, 293
   "floppy" puppies and, 290
   overtired pup, 293
   overtired pup, symptoms, 5–6
Sneak attack from rear, 318
   lead kept on, 318
   make noise, 318
   prevention, 318
   Space Games, 318
   stay back, 318
   water sprayer, 318
Socialization, 173–213
   avoid overwhelming, 197
   biting, preventing, 210, 211
   calming a squiggly puppy, 184
   car rides, 176–77
   carrying your pup, 176
   Check It Out used for, 197
   children, yours, and, 210
   children and, 181, 211–12
   Come with, 192
   dog-friendly businesses, 176
   doggy day care, 202–3
   dog park warning, 200–202
   exercise and the growing puppy,
     203–7
   expose, don't overwhelm, 184–85
   field trips (where to go/where to
     avoid), 174–75, 185
   four-step timetable, 177–79
   frightening things to your pup,
     182–83
   goal of, 174
   greeting other dogs, 208–9
   greeting strangers, 176
   guests, 183
   guests, barking at, 260
   guests, fearful of, 260–61
   guests, piddling and, 237

Guided Downs with, 192, 193, 212

handling/touching your pup, 185–86

at home, 181–87

Leave It with, 212

Left Circles with, 212

Look At Me with, 181, 192, 212

Mine with, 181, 192, 212

mix up routines, 181–82

modeling desired behavior, 209

Near Is Dear with, 186, 192, 212

out and about: the rest of the world, 196–202

productive play, 187–91

puppy class, 208

pup scared of the city, 198–99

safety issues, 175–77

safe with other pets, 186–87

signs of puppy stress, 180–81, 210

Simple Sits with, 192

Sit Is It with, 181

socializing with other people, 209–10

support confidence, 196–97

treats used with, 176, 197

visiting: going to a friend's house, 192–95

walking around suburbia, 207–9

Walking the Walk, 198

where to walk, 207–8

in your yard, 192

Space Games, 55

Go, 54, 148–50, 257

Left Circles, 54, 119–21

Mine, 54, 82–85, 274

Move, 257, 275

Off, 54, 86–88, 257, 274

puppy slams into you, responding, 274–75

Wait, 54, 116–18

Wait There, 54, 150–52

Space invaders, 41

Spaying or neutering

housebreaking mistakes and, 229

lifting his leg indoors and, 233

Squeeze/pulse, 96

for barking, 262

Stair Safety, 131

START Games, 55–59

Attention Games, 57–58

chart, 54

Requirement Games, 58

Space Games, 55, 82–88

Touch, 55–57

Trust Games, 58–59

START Level I, 79–111

Attention: Catch My Drift, 99–101

Attention: Look at Me, 95–98

being too quiet, 81

expecting too much, 80

frustration, yours, dealing with, 80

getting to good, 79–80

going too fast, 81

how to squeeze/pulse, 96

mutual awareness, 79

play perspective, 80

Requirement: Come: Basics, 102–5

Requirement: Stay: Basics, 105–9

skipping practice, 81

Space: Mine, 82–85

Space: Off, 86–88

Touch: Guided Down, 92–95

Touch: Placement Sit, 88–91

Trust: Near Is Dear, 110–11

working too hard too long, 81

START Level II, 113–43

Attention: Door Chores, 129–31

Attention: Leave It, 132–33

bracing, 113

common problems, 114–16

consistency, 114

hesitation, 114

leadership, 113

magic thinking, 114–15

relentless understanding, 115–16

Requirement: Come: Making It Work, 134–36

Requirement: Out, 136–39

Space: Left Circles, 119–21

Space: Wait, 116–18

thinking that dog training is about the dog, 115

Touch: Calm=Release, 122–24

Touch: Guided Down, 124–29

Trust: Check It Out, 139–43

START Level III, 145–71
    Attention: Beat the Clock, 161–63
    Attention: Follow the Leader, 159–61
    common problems, 146–48
    creative coaching, 145
    energy drops, 146–47
    food dependency, 147–48
    intention, clear, 145
    Place, 166–67
    raising the bar, 147
    Requirement: No Eye Can, 167–68
    Requirement: Stay II: Working the 4 D's, 164–67
    reward and assist, 146
    routine training, 146
    Space: Go, 148–50
    Space: Wait There, 150–52
    Touch: Face It, 155–58
    Touch: Simple Sit, 153–55
    Trust: Say Hello, 169–71
Stay: Basics, 54, 105–9
    common problems, 107, 109
    as stressful, 108
Stay II: Working the 4 D's, 54, 164–67
    common problems, 165–66
Sticks, 206
Stress in your puppy
    chewing and, 280
    coping with, 181
    fainting, 317
    five ways dogs handle stress, 317
    heat, warning signs, 205
    modeling desired behavior, 317
    practice, 317
    sensitive/shy dogs, 316–17
    signs of, 180–81
    socializing with other people and, 210
    Trust Games, 316
    urination and, 237–38, 239
    urination on bed and, 235

T

T.E.E.T.H. (Tension, Ears, Eyes, Tail, Head), 8
Teething, 33
    chew toys and other aids, 305
    mouthing and, 305
    toy breed/mix owners, 33
Ten keys to understanding your puppy, 2–6
Tethering, 83, 84, 85
    to stop jumping up, 294
Three to six month-old puppy: the juvenile period, 32–39
    end of social attraction, 38–39
    five-month-old regrets, 39
    frustration for you during, 32, 33–35
    growth, questions about, 36–38
    teething, 33
Thyroid problems, 270
Touch, 55–57
    Calm=Release, 54, 122–24
    Face It, 54, 155–58
    Guided Down, 54, 92–95, 124–29
    Guided Down II, 54
    Placement Sit, 54, 88–91
    Simple Sit, 54, 153–55
Toys
    ball, 207
    ball playing danger, 201
    carrying during walks, 269
    cat toys, danger for dogs, 207
    chewy or food-filled toy taken on visits, 194
    as diversion from digging, 283
    food inside type, 189, 287, 314
    growling or baring teeth and, 299, 310–11
    Moo Tube, 308
    not recommended, 189
    possessiveness, 307–9
    possessiveness, guarding behavior, 310–11
    pup's attention span at five to six months, 194
    rawhide chews, water intake and, 286
    rocks, 207
    rotating, 280
    safety issues, 206–7
    sticks, 206
    for teething, 305
Training basics, 52–77. *See also* START Level I

alternate approaches, 251
anthropomorphizing, 73–74
beware of the 4 s's: sneaky, stubborn, spiteful, stupid, 248–49
choosing the right approach, 65, 70
collar, introducing pup's first, 74–75
commands, five types, 64
consequence is a gift, 252
consistency, 251–52
corrections, 62–63
demoting demanding or difficult dogs, 254–58
equipment, 65–70
every interaction and, 219–20, 251
getting to good, 79–80, 249–50
lead, introducing, 75–76
lead, walking on, 76–77
length of sessions, 60
modeling desired behavior, 26–27, 196
naked dog training, 163
play perspective, 80
pretraining, 248, 270, 280, 292
puppy's are congruent, 152
restraint creates resistance, 100
rewards, 71–73
rewards, understanding, 60–61
self-control, 226, 252
smart puppy person vs. problem owner, 227
START Games, 55–59
START Games (chart), 54
support confidence, 196–97
ten keys to perfect puppy problem solving, 248–53
think Fun, Fair, Firm, 252–53
train early, 180
train the puppy you have at this moment, 285
when to start, 59–60
words we train by, 321
Traveling. *See also* Car rides; Socialization; Visiting: going to a friend's house
supplies to bring, 195
Trust Games
Check It Out, 54, 139–43

Near Is Dear, 54, 110–11
Say Hello, 54, 169–71
Tug, how to play, 49–50
Two Fist Game, 133
Two-Treat Game, 105

U

Ultrasonic device, 266
Urinary tract infection, 232, 235, 238, 239
Urination. *See also* Housebreaking/paper training
anxiety or excitement and, 237–38
can't hold it during the day, 230–31, 234
on down comforter, 235
female dog leg lifts, 234
female licks herself after peeing, 235
housebreaking/paper training problems and, 230–32
interrupting, 221
large amounts, suddenly, 238–39
lifting his leg indoors, 233, 245
lifting his leg outside, endlessly, 233–34
Lyme disease and problems, 235, 239
mistakes while on medication, 239
out of your sight, causes, 236–37
paper training: problems and solutions, 243–45
paper training: the rules, 241–43
peeing when left alone, 239
scratching back feet afterward, 234
submissive behavior and, 183, 237
won't go outside (goes on paper), 239–41
on your bed, 235–36, 249

V

Visiting: going to a friend's house, 192–95
chewy or food-filled toy taken along, 194

(Visiting, continued)
foot on lead, 193–94
on lead, 193
praise, showering your puppy
with, 195
pup's attention span, 194
supplies to bring, 195
what not to do, 194–95

W

Wagging tail, meaning of, 9
Wait, 54, 116–18
common problems, 116–18
missed obedience, 47
"Throw Your Wait Around," 118
when to practice, 220
Wait There, 54, 150–52
common problems, 151–52
Walking the Walk, 198
Walking your puppy, 219. *See also*
Leads/leashes
frequency needed, 314
grabs at lead, 268–69
on leads/leashes, 76–77
leaps on door before walk, 250

lifting his leg outside, endlessly,
233–34
rules of walking, 222–23
tangles, 306–7
toy to carry, 269
walking around suburbia, 207–9
where to walk, 207–8
Watering
heat, need for clean supply and,
282
housebreaking/paper training
problems and, 230–32
puppy drinks too much, 286
rules, 223–24
Whining, 42, 319
Leave It, 319
Stay: Basics, 319
Wait There, 319
Won't come back inside, 319–20
Woodhouse, Barbara, 252
Words we train by, 321
Worm infestation
housebreaking/paper training
problems and, 231
poop, eating of, and, 286
quality dog food and, 289